10 THINGS

YOU MIGHT NOT KNOW

ABOUT NEARLY
EVERYTHING

10
THINGS
YOU MIGHT NOT KNOW
ABOUT NEARLY EVERYTHING

A Collection of Fascinating Historical,
Scientific and Cultural Trivia about
≡ PEOPLE, PLACES and THINGS ≡

MARK JACOB & STEPHAN BENZKOFER
𝕮𝖍𝖎𝖈𝖆𝖌𝖔 𝕿𝖗𝖎𝖇𝖚𝖓𝖊

MIDWAY
AN AGATE IMPRINT
CHICAGO

This is a revised and expanded edition of *10 Things You Might Not Know About Nearly Everything*, which was first printed in paperback in 2013. It was created from the Chicago Tribune's popular column 10 Things You Might Not Know by Mark Jacob and Stephan Benzkofer.

Printed in China

Illustrations by Serge Bloch

Chicago Tribune: R. Bruce Dold, Publisher & Editor-in-Chief; Peter Kendall, Managing Editor; Colin McMahon, Associate Editor; Amy Carr, Associate Managing Editor/Features.

Library of Congress Cataloging-in-Publication Data

Names: Jacob, Mark, author. | Benzkofer, Stephan, author.
Title: 10 things you might not know about nearly everything : a collection of fascinating historical, scientific and cultural facts about people, places and things / Mark Jacob & Stephan Benzkofer.
Other titles: Ten things you might not know about nearly everything
Description: Revised and expanded edition. | Chicago : Chicago Tribune : Midway, an Agate imprint, 2017. | Includes bibliographical references.

Identifiers: LCCN 2017023806 (print) | LCCN 2017025690 (ebook) | ISBN 9781572847996 (e-book) | ISBN 1572847999 (e-book) | ISBN 9781572842083 (hardback) | ISBN 1572842083 (hardcover)
Subjects: LCSH: Handbooks, vade-mecums, etc. | Curiosities and wonders. | BISAC: HISTORY / World. | REFERENCE / Trivia. | REFERENCE / Questions & Answers.
Classification: LCC AG105 (ebook) | LCC AG105 .J175 2017 (print) | DDC 030--dc23
LC record available at https://lccn.loc.gov/2017023806

10 9 8 7 6 5 4 3   19 20 21 22

Midway Books is an imprint of Agate Publishing. Agate books are available in bulk at discount prices. For more information, visit agatepublishing.com.

*The authors dedicate
this book to facts.*

CONTENTS

CHAPTER 9: Military & War

CHAPTER 10: Science & Technology

CHAPTER 11: Kids & Education

CHAPTER 12: Money & Finance

CHAPTER 13: Arts & Culture

CHAPTER 14: Sports

CHAPTER 1
Oddities & Oddballs

10 THINGS YOU MIGHT NOT KNOW ABOUT
CONSPIRACY THEORIES

1 Some Pakistanis doubt the story of Malala Yousafzai, the teenager who received world-wide support after she was shot and wounded in 2012 by the Taliban for promoting the education of girls. Suspicion that she is a CIA plant or a greedy hoaxer is so common in Pakistan that a journalist there ridiculed doubters with a satirical piece revealing that Yousafzai's "real name was Jane" and that the DNA in her earwax showed that she was "probably from Poland." But other media outlets missed the joke, citing the report as yet more evidence of the plot.

2 Psychologists say the best predictor for someone believing a conspiracy theory is belief in other theories, even if they're contradictory. Researchers at the University of Kent in England found that survey respondents who believed that Osama bin Laden died long before the U.S. Navy SEAL attack in May 2011 were actually more likely to also agree with the theory that he was still alive.

3 The Illuminati was a Bavarian secret society founded by Adam Weishaupt in the late 18th century that was extinguished within a few years. Or was it? Conspiracy theorists believe the Illuminati remains alive and is bent on world conquest. It's certainly bent on domination of book lists, with Dan Brown's novels as best-sellers, and other authors offering such titles as "Hip-Hop Illuminati: How and Why the Illuminati Took Over Hip-Hop" and "Mary Todd Lincoln and the Illuminati." Then there's the video "Die America Die!: The Illuminati Plan to Murder America, Confiscate Its Wealth, and Make Red China Leader of the New World Order."

4 The struggling New York Knicks desperately needed the NBA's No. 1 draft pick in 1985, certain to be Georgetown's Patrick Ewing. But seven teams were in the running, with the draft order determined by Commissioner David Stern picking envelopes out of a bowl. When the Knicks won the top pick, the "Frozen Envelope Theory" was born. Some suspect that the Knicks' envelope was chilled so Stern could identify it by touch. Others think a corner of the envelope was bent for the same purpose. But no one has ever proved anything.

5 Conspiracy theories are big business. Alex Jones is an Austin, Texas-based talk radio host with millions of listeners over the airwaves and on the internet who peddles apocalyptic tales of doom. He believes the U.S. government was behind the Oklahoma City bombing, the 9/11 attacks and the Boston Marathon bombings. As Jones spouts his dire warnings, a key advertising sponsor is a gold company called Midas Resources, which benefits from such hysteria as people seek out the traditional financial safety of precious metals. Midas Resources is owned by Ted Anderson, who also owns Genesis Communications—the network that carries Jones.

6 Did Marisa Tomei get the 1992 Academy Award for supporting actress by mistake when it was meant for Vanessa Redgrave? Some suspect so, despite no more evidence than the fact that Tomei was an underdog and that the award's presenter, Jack Palance, had behaved strangely at the show the year before. As Roger Ebert noted, accountants are poised in the wings to correct any error immediately, and there was only one name on the card that Palance read, so a mistake was unlikely. Chief purveyor of the theory is critic Rex Reed, whose credibility is not gold standard. (Reed was criticized for calling actress Melissa McCarthy "tractor-sized" and for panning the film "V/H/S/2" when he had watched about 20 minutes of it, among other transgressions.)

7 A "false flag" operation occurs when a group or country conducts an attack that is then blamed on another group or country. The burning of Germany's parliament building in 1933 was blamed on communists, providing justification for a Nazi crackdown. Historians are split on whether the Nazis actually torched the building or just took advantage afterward. But there's no doubt about a Nazi false flag operation six years later: A German radio station was attacked by Nazis dressed in Polish uniforms, a raid cited by Adolf Hitler as one reason for the invasion of Poland, which set off World War II.

8 Denver International Airport, which opened in 1995, is an epicenter for conspiracy theories. Depending on whom you believe, DIA houses a base for UFOs, vast bunkers to protect the elite during the apocalypse, an alien-run concentration camp or a temple to Freemasons and the New World Order. Theorists cite alleged clues, such as murals that depict environmental disaster and other world tumult, plus a reference to the New World Airport Commission. (A co-chair of the now-defunct commission thinks the name may have come from Dvorak's "New World Symphony.")

9 And what about the assassination of John F. Kennedy? Belief that multiple people conspired to kill the president in Dallas remains persistently high. In March 2001, a Gallup poll found 81 percent backed a conspiracy theory. In 2003, that number dropped to 75 percent, and in November 2013 it dropped to 61 percent. When was belief in this conspiracy theory at its lowest? Interestingly, that came in the period right after the actual event, when just about half of respondents believed Lee Harvey Oswald didn't act alone.

10 "Occam's razor" is a principle attributed to 14th-century friar William of Ockham. It states that when there are a variety of explanations, the simplest one is often the correct one. But a conspiracy theorist might respond: That's what they want you to think.

10 THINGS YOU MIGHT NOT KNOW ABOUT
CHEATERS

1 It's hard to imagine anyone having the gall to cheat in the Paralympics. But a Spanish basketball team did just that in 2000, winning the gold medal by fielding a supposedly mentally handicapped team in which only two of 12 players actually were. And they weren't bashful: Spain outscored its opponents by an average of 36 points per game.

2 Young people are conflicted about cheating. According to a 2012 survey by the Josephson Institute of Ethics, 99 percent of the more than 23,000 student respondents agreed it was important "to be a person with good character" and 93 percent were satisfied with their own "ethics and character." But more than half admitted to cheating on a test at school and nearly three-fourths admitted copying homework. Bizarrely, nearly one-third of the students also said they weren't completely honest responding to the anonymous ethics survey.

3 In the 1980s and '90s, Tommy Glenn Carmichael feasted on slot machines. His ingenious inventions—the "kickstand," "monkey paw" and "light wand"—cheated one-armed bandits with ease. At his peak, he played every day, crisscrossing the country and raking in thousands of dollars daily. He "dutifully paid his taxes," according to a 2003 Associated Press story, which may be why, after he was caught and sentenced in 2001, he got time served and probation.

4 To "crossbite" is an old British slang term for cheating, especially pulling a fast one on someone who is trying to pull a fast one on you.

5 A legendary figure in Chicago's long history of political high jinks is Sidney "Short Pencil" Lewis, who was accused of erasing votes for Mayor Martin Kennelly and marking them for Richard J. Daley during the 1955 Democratic primary. The Tribune printed photos of the alleged misdeeds, but Lewis denied wrongdoing. According to author James Merriner, "short pencil" also referred to other unfair tactics—providing voters with a stubby pencil that made it difficult for them to mark the ballot, and putting the pencil on such a short string that they couldn't mark the whole ballot and instead were encouraged to vote straight-ticket.

6 When the New York Giants' Bobby Thomson hit his famous "shot heard 'round the world" homer off Brooklyn Dodgers pitcher Ralph Branca in 1951, it might not have been the answer to 1,000 prayers so much as the result of careful planning. The Giants used a telescope for much of that season to steal opposing teams' pitching signs, a fact confirmed 50 years later by reporter Joshua Prager. The elaborate scheme required the team running an electrical line to the dugout to quickly relay the info. Thomson went to his grave denying that he knew a fastball was coming his way.

7 About a century ago, many of the American companies that made legitimate playing cards and poker chips also sold a variety of "advantage tools"—devices to help cheaters. Those included "card pricks," "poker rings," "punches" or "peggers" to mark a card by creating a subtle indentation, as well as "holdout machines" that allowed cheaters to pull cards out of the deck and hold them until needed—either up their sleeves or under the table.

8 Robert Kennedy, who would later become a senator and U.S. attorney general admired for his support of civil rights and his crackdown on the mob, left his Rhode Island boarding school abruptly at age 16 after becoming involved in a cheating scandal. Biographer Evan Thomas talked with multiple witnesses, including RFK's roommate at the time, who attested that Kennedy passed around a stolen English exam. Unclear is whether Kennedy left school on his own or was expelled.

9 According to a 2012 Pew Research Center survey, 70 percent of respondents said they would be very upset at people who had cheated the government out of benefits they weren't entitled to, but just 45 percent said the same about people who had not paid all the income taxes they owed.

10 Marathons seem to attract cheaters, and that includes 2014 Chicago Marathon women's winner, Kenya's Rita Jeptoo, for use of a banned performance-enhancing substance. But the champion marathon cheater of all time was Rosie Ruiz, whose apparent victory in Boston in 1980 was overturned when it became clear she had run hardly any of the race. Asked why she didn't seem particularly tired at the finish, she remarked, "I got up with a lot of energy this morning." Ruiz remained in denial 18 years later when the Palm Beach Post interviewed her. Insisting that she had achieved a legitimate "victory" in Boston, she claimed that the title was taken away because of "politics."

10 THINGS YOU MIGHT NOT KNOW ABOUT
LOSERS

1 One of the biggest losers in the history of Las Vegas was Terrance Watanabe, who blew at least $127 million during a gambling binge in 2007. Watanabe, an Omaha, Neb., businessman whose family made its fortune in the party-trinket business, reportedly liked to play three $50,000-limit hands of blackjack at the same time.

2 In sports, losers are supposed to play their hearts out until the game is over, regardless of how far behind they are. But in chess, it is considered poor form to keep playing if the position is hopelessly lost.

3 Losers in the vintage version of the Milton Bradley's The Game of Life end up in the Poor Farm; winners retire to Millionaire Acres.

4 When Alf Landon lost to Franklin D. Roosevelt in the 1936 presidential race, he managed to win just eight electoral votes, one of the worst showings in U.S. history. The governor of Kansas even failed to carry his own state. Still, Landon was gracious in losing, sending a telegram to FDR that read, "The nation has spoken. Every American will accept the verdict, and work for the common cause and the good of our country."

5 One of the biggest winners in Hollywood is a good loser. When the Razzie Awards dishonored Halle Berry in 2005 as the year's worst actress for "Catwoman," she actually showed up to accept the prize. Her sense of good humor might have been helped by the fact that she had won an Academy Award three years earlier for "Monster's Ball." At the Razzies, Berry said: "When I was a kid, my mother told me that if you can't be a good loser, you can't be a good winner. If you can't take the criticism, then you don't deserve the praise."

6 The Olympic stage doesn't always bring out the best in people. At the Seoul Olympics in 1988, South Korean boxer Byun Jong Il was penalized for head-butting and subsequently lost the match. Outraged South Korean coaches and officials jumped into the ring to yell at the referee. Somebody kidney-punched the New Zealander ref before he was rescued and escorted out of the arena. The poor sportsmanship didn't end there. Byun sat in the middle of the ring and refused to leave for more than an hour. Eventually, organizers just turned the lights out and let him sulk in the dark.

7 When it comes to U.S. presidential elections, winning can feel like losing. Five people have earned the most votes on Election Day only to win nothing but the honor of becoming the answer to a trivia question. Andrew Jackson, Samuel Tilden, Grover Cleveland, Al Gore and Hillary Clinton won the popular vote but fell short in the Electoral College and thus lost the White House. No need to feel sorry for Jackson or Cleveland; each got revenge by defeating their opponents four years later.

8 You've heard of a player losing his head and then the game? Well, the Mayans played a ballgame that was a mix of soccer, volleyball and basketball where sometimes players lost the game and then their heads. Priests sacrificed them to the gods.

> *"If at first you don't succeed, find out if the loser gets anything."* —WILLIAM LYON PHELPS

9 A defeat in which the losers fail to score is called a shutout, a goose egg, a whitewash or a bagel job. Other slang terms for being shut out are skunked, blanked and Chicago'd.

10 The late professor and author William Lyon Phelps offered one of the best quotations about failure: "If at first you don't succeed, find out if the loser gets anything."

10 THINGS YOU MIGHT NOT KNOW ABOUT
STUNTS

1 When Daniel Goodwin tried to scale the John Hancock Center in Chicago on Nov. 11, 1981, authorities didn't like it one bit. To try to stop "Spider Dan"—even as he climbed hundreds of feet off the ground—firefighters doused him with high-pressure water hoses and tried to block his path with a window-washing scaffold and pike poles. They even broke out windows and tried to pull him inside. Mayor Jane Byrne interceded, and Goodwin was allowed to finish the climb to the top—where he was promptly arrested.

2 Lincoln Beachey, one of the first great stunt pilots, was known for his "death dips," his loop-the-loop and his flights around the U.S. Capitol, under a bridge at Niagara Falls and inside a building in San Francisco. At a 1912 air show in Chicago, Beachey dressed as a woman and pretended to be an amateur pilot, flying wildly and buzzing cars on Michigan Avenue. He came to his end in 1915 when he tried an extreme maneuver and his plane's wings fell off, plunging him into San Francisco Bay. Beachey was found drowned, still strapped into the pilot's seat.

3 It was 25 feet tall, 5 feet wide, weighed 17 tons—and was melting fast. Snapple's attempt to clinch the world record for largest ice pop on the first day of summer 2005 in New York's Union Square rapidly turned into a sticky mess. The ice pop liquefied so quickly in the 80-degree heat that it sent bicyclists skidding, upended pedestrians and mucked up traffic. Firefighters had to be called in to rinse off the area. Said the Guinness Book of World Records official on the scene: "What was unsettling was that the fluid just kept coming. It was quite a lot of fluid."

4 According to a common myth, a stuntman died during the filming of the chariot-race scene of the 1959 movie "Ben Hur." But that never happened. Ironically, the director of that scene, Andrew Marton, may have fueled the rumors by denying them. Frustrated by reporters' questions, he said sarcastically that 20 people and 100 horses had died and added, "That's what you want to hear, isn't it?" In fact, there were no serious injuries, and a primary duty at the moviemaker's infirmary was dealing with actors' sunburns.

5 Edward Bernays, a New York publicity agent who was the nephew of Sigmund Freud, marketed cigarettes to women as a way to claim equal rights and stay slim at the same time. One slogan was: "Reach for a cigarette instead of dessert." For the 1929 Easter parade along New York's Fifth Avenue, he orchestrated a stunt in which classy-looking women at designated locations joined the promenade and lit up. The press ate it up. Bernays, who made sure these liberated women were supplied with his product, Lucky Strike, described the cigarettes as "torches of freedom."

6 The Tour de France bicycle race was started in 1903 as a publicity stunt to help save a struggling sports newspaper called L'Auto.

7 Alvin "Shipwreck" Kelly is most often credited—or blamed?—for popularizing the flagpole sitting craze in the late 1920s. In June 1927, he sat atop a pole on a Newark, N.J., hotel for 12½ days. He returned to the ground to wild acclaim and much fame, and it clearly went to his head. Seven years later, his wife had him forcibly removed from another pole and charged with abandoning her and their seven children.

8 Brett Hulsey, who ran for governor of Wisconsin in 2014, declared he would hand out Ku Klux Klan hoods outside the state's Republican convention to protest racism. But when he showed up, he had no hoods, and he told reporters he had left them in his car. He did not go stunt-free, however, wearing a makeshift Confederate soldier uniform he had assembled from thrift store purchases. Hulsey, denounced by officials of both parties, lost in the Democratic primary with 17 percent of the vote.

9 At the turn of the last century, people loved watching trains crash. It all started in 1896 when William Crush, an enterprising employee for the Missouri, Kansas and Texas Railway looking to make a name for himself and the railway, hatched a scheme to crash two locomotives into each other. Given the green light, he set up a pop-up town named—you guessed it, Crush—in a remote area of Texas. The event was free, but the train ticket to Crush was $2. As many as 50,000 reportedly made the trip. It looked to be a runaway success. But despite assurances the locomotives' steam boilers wouldn't blow up, they did, spraying the crowd with shrapnel. Three people were killed and dozens injured. That didn't stop the survivors from posing for photographs with the wreckage.

10 One of the Seven Wonders of the Ancient World was destroyed by a stunt. A man named Herostratus torched the ancient Greeks' Temple of Artemis merely because he thought it would make him famous. Authorities reacted by decreeing that no one could mention his name, but a Greek historian did, and Herostratus got his wish, appearing in the pages of the Chicago Tribune more than two millennia later.

10 THINGS YOU MIGHT NOT KNOW ABOUT
SELFIES

1 If you think the selfie craze proves 21st century Americans are a narcissistic bunch, consider that the earliest extant American portrait photograph, dating from 1839, was itself a selfie. Thanks to the technology of the day, Robert Cornelius had time to open the shutter, run to the front of the camera, stand there for a few minutes while the image was made, then run back to close the shutter.

2 New York Gov. Andrew Cuomo signed a bill in August 2014 cracking down on "tiger selfies." That's when people (well, men mostly) get close to big cats in traveling animal shows and fairs and take snapshots of themselves posing with wildlife. Such photos are sometimes posted on online dating sites.

3 According to a 2013 British survey, 36 percent of 18- to 24-year-olds admitted they altered their selfies before posting. Most of them opted to retouch skin tone (39 percent) or eye color/brightness (24 percent). It was a slippery slope apparently: 44 percent of those who edited their image said after changing one photo, they then edited every or most of the selfies they posted.

4 Alabama teen Breanna Mitchell came in for harsh criticism in 2014 when she tweeted a smiling selfie at a Nazi death camp. Her message: "Selfie in the Auschwitz Concentration Camp :)." In Mitchell's defense, she said she and her father liked to discuss World War II and Holocaust history, but he died before they could make the trip together. Undercutting that sympathetic explanation was another tweet by Mitchell when the backlash flared. "I'm famous yall," she wrote.

5 Artists have often created self-portraits that express their torment. Mexican painter Frida Kahlo, for example, depicted herself in various weird ways: standing beside her own extracted heart, wearing a necklace of thorns and sitting next to a second version of herself who had undergone surgery. Performance art also can be a way to share a strange self-image: In the 1970s, Chris Burden was nailed to the roof of a Volkswagen Beetle in a mock crucifixion, and Vito Acconci bit himself, then smeared the bite marks with ink and printed them. You might call them self-icks.

6 The "selfie stick" is a device on which a smartphone can be mounted to take self-portraits from farther away than an arm can reach. Particularly popular in Asia, it has proved unwelcome in some places. Laurence Allard, a French professor who studies mobile technology, told time.com that true selfies do not use a stick: "The selfie isn't just a portrait. It has its own codes and rules, and the main one is that a selfie has to have been taken by hand. An authentic selfie should show it was taken with your arm extended—that's a sort of signature."

> "The **SELFIE** isn't just a **PORTRAIT**. It has its own codes and rules."
> —LAURENCE ALLARD

7 As society becomes increasingly fascinated by selfies and video (witness the impact of videos of the Islamic State beheadings and the Ray Rice domestic violence episode), some people wonder whether the visual has gained too much influence. But that worry isn't new. In 1925, writer D.H. Lawrence was bemoaning how the snapshot culture gave people a fixed, absolute self-image: "Primitive man simply didn't know what he was; he was always half in the dark. But we have learned to see, and each of us has a complete Kodak idea of himself."

8 After Vincent van Gogh cut off part of his ear in 1888, he painted self-portraits showing it bandaged. Ever since, some people have mistakenly said he mutilated his right ear. In fact, it was his left—it only appeared to be his right because he painted his image in the mirror.

People register emotions more powerfully on the left side of the face.

9 Speaking of left and right, portrait artists have a well-known left-cheek bias (think the "Mona Lisa"). Scientists tell us it's an unconscious preference because people register emotions more powerfully on that side of the face. They argue that the right-cheek bias on artists' self-portraits confirms the issue because most of those are painted using a mirror. Skeptics argue that the artist's dominant hand, training and the arrangement of the studio offer a better explanation. In an attempt to settle the matter, an Italian study in 2013 found that people taking selfies with an iPhone—regardless of handedness—revealed the same unconscious left-cheek bias.

10 Why do some people hate seeing their own photo? According to one theory, it's the mirror factor again. Accustomed to seeing themselves in the mirror, a nonreversed image in a photo may seem odd. A 1977 study found that people preferred their mirror image to their real image, while their friends preferred the opposite. This has been chalked up to people's tendency to prefer things that they've been exposed to more often. As selfies become more common, will more people like seeing their photos but hate themselves in the mirror?

PREDICTIONS

1 Sociologist David Riesman made this statement in 1967, anticipating the rest of the 20th century: "If anything remains more or less unchanged, it will be the role of women."

2 In 1993, the Chicago Tribune's KidNews section asked young readers in a survey to predict life 20 years from then. Three-quarters (77 percent) were wrong in saying a woman would be elected president by 2013, but a majority (53 percent) correctly predicted that an African-American would win the White House. At the time, Barack Obama was two years away from his first political race, for the Illinois Senate.

3 Beware of know-it-alls about war. "You will be home before the leaves have fallen from the trees," Kaiser Wilhelm II assured his troops in August 1914 before four years of fighting killed 1.8 million Germans. Two months before the start of a civil war in which a half-million American soldiers died, North Carolina secessionist A.W. Venable dismissed the danger, saying: "I will wipe up every drop of blood shed in the war with this handkerchief of mine."

4 When the 1964 World's Fair arrived, Isaac Asimov wrote a New York Times essay looking forward to a fair a half-century later. Asimov envisioned that "the appliances of 2014 will have no electric cords." He also wrote: "Communications will become sight-sound and you will see as well as hear the person you telephone. The screen can be used not only to see the people you call but also for studying documents and photographs and reading passages from books." He was wrong about a key detail, though: There was no 2014 World's Fair.

5 Decca Records exec Dick Rowe told a rock 'n' roll band manager in 1962 that "we don't like your boys' sound. Groups are out. Four-piece groups with guitars, particularly, are finished." Rowe was referring to the Beatles. Six years earlier, the Chicago Tribune's Herb Lyon earned his own immortality by writing: "What mass madness brings on a rock 'n' roll craze and catapults an Elvis Presley to six months of immortality? (Watch, it won't be any longer.)"

6 The earliest Chinese writings ever found were predictions inscribed on tortoise shells and deer shoulder bones in the 14th century B.C. Before people went on trips or harvested crops, they would consult shamans, who would heat the shells and bones until they cracked and then interpret the cracks as messages from the spirit world. The shamans would inscribe the forecasts on these "oracle bones."

7 Psychologist Philip Tetlock's seminal research on predictions of world events found that experts in general were "roughly as accurate as a dart-throwing chimpanzee." Some experts are better than others, of course, and another animal metaphor explains why. Borrowing from a Greek poetic concept that "the hedgehog knows one big thing whereas the fox knows many," Tetlock found that experts who were "foxes"—open to a wide range of information— were better prognosticators than "hedgehogs" who embraced a single overarching concept and fit the facts into it.

8 William Preece, chief engineer of the British post office in the late 19th century, was no visionary. "Edison's electric lamp is a completely idiotic idea," declared Preece, who is also remembered for saying: "The Americans have need of the telephone, but we do not. We have plenty of messenger boys."

9 The Japanese attack on Pearl Harbor and the U.S. victory at Midway proved that aircraft carriers were a game-changer in naval combat. But a few decades before those World War II battles, U.S. Adm. Charles Benson dismissed the future of naval air power and tried to kill the program. "The Navy doesn't need airplanes," Benson said. "Aviation is just a lot of noise."

10 Did 16th-century French seer Nostradamus accurately predict Adolf Hitler and the 9/11 attacks? Nope, despite what some say. Nor did Nostradamus say that the end of the world would be signaled by South Korean singer Psy's song "Gangnam Style." That was an online hoax in December 2012 featuring a fake Nostradamus quote: "From the calm morning, the end will come when of the dancing horse the number of circles will be nine." South Korea is "the land of the morning calm," and Psy's dance style resembles a horse's trot. The "nine circles" referred to 1,000,000,000, and when Psy's video got 1 billion hits on YouTube that same month, we were supposedly doomed. But it did, and we weren't.

MASCOTS

1 Mascots sometimes are an unfortunate distraction, as demonstrated by wrangling over the Washington Redskins. But ideally, they're supposed to be lucky charms. In the comedic French opera "La Mascotte" by Edmond Audran, which opened in December 1880, the plot revolves around the conceit that a certain character—Bettina the turkey-keeper—brings good luck but only so long as she remains a virgin. A passing nobleman takes her to his court, and Shakespeare-like shenanigans ensue. Derived from a Provencal word meaning "witchcraft, charm or amulet," mascot had already jumped to English by 1881.

2 The teams from Coachella Valley High School were long known as the Arabs and were represented at sporting events by a snarling, hook-nosed mascot and belly dancers, iconography meant to reflect the school's location 120 miles east of Los Angeles in an area known for its dry climate, date crops and places named Mecca and Oasis. After years of complaints from Arab-Americans, the school finally agreed in November 2014 to redesign the offensive logo and change the team name to the Mighty Arabs.

3 Professional baseball's early mascots were often batboys—and more than one was a hunchback. It was not uncommon for the players to rub the boys' humps at critical times during the game. Possibly the most lucky batboy, at least in his ability to sign up with a winner, was Eddie Bennett. Working for the White Sox in 1919, the Brooklyn Robins (soon to become the Dodgers) in 1920 and the New York Yankees from 1921 to 1932, he went six seasons before his team failed to win a pennant. In the end, he was lucky enough to see nine league pennants and four World Series victories.

4 Students at East Knox County Elementary School call themselves the Cougars, which wouldn't be worth mentioning except that East Knox is in Mascot, Tenn.

5 Many mascots are beloved, but not a certain Microsoft Office "helper" known as Clippit or Clippy. Starting in the late '90s, the animated paper clip would pop up on computer screens and say, "It looks like you're writing a letter. Would you like help?" The overwhelming answer was NOOOOO, and the feature was phased out. In 2010, Time magazine listed it as one of the 50 worst inventions of all time. Microsoft offered other office assistants that attracted less notoriety, including an Einstein look-alike called The Genius and a cat named Scribble.

"Would you like help?"
—CLIPPY

"NOOOOO!"
—EVERYONE

6 Alfred E. Neuman, the cover boy and mascot for Mad magazine, has a girlfriend named Moxie Cowznofski who has made rare cover appearances (a few in the 1950s, then a featured spot on the front of Mad Color Classics in 2004).

7 The Hamburger Helper "helping hand," used in TV commercials and on packaging, has only a thumb and three fingers. A General Mills spokeswoman once explained that the omission of the fourth finger was "artistic license."

8 Does the Chicago Symphony need a mascot? We ask because the Utah Symphony once featured Seymour the Symphony Seagull, who got kids interested in classical music. The mascot was launched in 1997 but later phased out.

9 The Census Bureau uses a ferret mascot to promote a data-crunching tool called DataFerrett. "Ferrett" is an acronym for Federated Electronic Research Review Extraction and Tabulation Tool.

10 Stanford University's marching band has a mascot called the Tree, which may be inspired by the trees on the seals of the school and its home city, Palo Alto, Calif. At a 2006 basketball game, police said they saw the student portraying the Tree drinking from a flask and measured her blood-alcohol level at 0.157. She was evicted from courtside and later fired. You might say the Tree got trunk and was asked to leaf.

DOOMSDAY

1 One in 5 Americans believed the world would end in his or her lifetime, according to a 2012 Ipsos survey. In the poll of more than 16,000 adults in 21 countries, only people from Turkey and South Africa were similarly pessimistic about the future. In the same poll, 12 percent of Americans said they believed the doomsday craze based on the misconception that the Mayan calendar ended on Dec. 21, 2012, and so would the world. Interestingly, just 9 percent report being anxious about that.

One in 5 Americans believe the world will end in his or her lifetime.

2 A phenomenon known as "New England's Dark Day" occurred May 19, 1780. Blackened skies prevailed, with no sign of normal daylight, causing people to fear the world was ending. Some historians attribute the phenomenon to forest fires combined with fog. Connecticut legislator Abraham Davenport famously insisted lawmakers meet by candlelight. If it was not Judgment Day, he said, there was work to be done. But "if it is, I choose to be found doing my duty."

3 The Large Hadron Collider near Geneva, Switzerland, went into operation in 2008, accelerating atomic particles and agitating people who were worried it could create a black hole that would swallow the Earth. Scientists downplayed such concerns, but as Amherst College physicist Kannan Jagannathan explained, they are opposed to saying there's zero chance. Jagannathan did say the odds of the collider ending life on this planet were no better than the odds of his college president opening a kitchen faucet and a dragon popping out.

4 Possibly the oldest doomsday prediction is found on an Assyrian clay tablet dated to 2800 B.C. While it's nearly 5,000 years old, it sounds amazingly current: "Our Earth is degenerate in these latter days. There are signs that the world is speedily coming to an end. Bribery and corruption are common. Children no longer obey their parents. Every man wants to write a book, and the end of the world is evidently approaching."

5 The apocalyptic lyrics of the R.E.M. song "It's the End of the World as We Know It (and I Feel Fine)" cite composer Leonard Bernstein, Soviet leader Leonid Brezhnev, comedian Lenny Bruce and rock critic Lester Bangs. Singer Michael Stipe says people with the initials L.B. were included after he had a dream in which he was the only guest at a party without those initials. (Bonus trivia: The song was once played for 24 hours by the Cleveland radio station WENZ when it changed format to alt-rock and called itself "107.9 The End.")

6 German astrologer Johannes Stoeffler predicted in 1499 that the world would be engulfed in a great flood on Feb. 20, 1524. Many people believed him. One of those was German Count von Iggleheim, who made like Noah and built a three-story ark. On the big day, crowds gathered at the riverbank to mock the good count. Then it started to rain. People panicked and stormed the ark. The count protested, so he was stoned to death. Afterward, Stoeffler said he miscalculated and meant 1528. The correction came too late for the count.

7 Some Christians anticipate a series of cataclysmic events that will lead to the Second Coming of Christ and the end of the world as we know it. A website called raptureready .com attempts to show how close we are to "end times" by maintaining a Rapture Index, which puts numerical ratings on the weather, immorality and geopolitics. The index, described as a "prophetic speedometer," has been above 170 since 2010. The site warns that any score above 160 means "fasten your seat belts."

8 Kurt Vonnegut Jr.'s novel "Cat's Cradle" features a substance called ice-nine that can turn water into ice at room temperature, thereby threatening all life on Earth. Vonnegut said General Electric researcher Irving Langmuir suggested the concept to science fiction writer H.G. Wells in the 1930s. But Wells was uninterested, and Vonnegut later heard about the idea when he worked as a GE publicist. "I thought to myself, 'Finders, keepers—the idea is mine,'" Vonnegut said. (Other finders were the Grateful Dead, who named their music publishing company Ice Nine in reference to the Vonnegut novel.)

9 It is easy to mock the hysteria caused centuries past by doomsday prophecies, but consider that Hal Lindsey, the grandfather of modern prophecy and author of the 1970 best-selling book "The Late Great Planet Earth," was invited to speak at the Pentagon and Air War College.

10 Will the Earth suffer a death by comet or asteroid? NASA is concerned enough that it tracks "near Earth objects" and launched a spacecraft in September 2016 to investigate asteroid Bennu, which poses a remote threat around 2170. A century ago, Halley's Comet caused a public uproar, especially after The New York Times reported a scientist's view that toxic gas in the comet's tail could "possibly snuff out all life on the planet." Sales of bottled air and "comet pills" climbed, but Halley passed harmlessly in 1910. A Chicago Tribune headline announced "We're still here," with a subhead reading "World is just the same."

10 THINGS YOU MIGHT NOT KNOW ABOUT
SWEATERS

1 Many people don sweaters to fend off the cold. Turns out, they're powerful protection during Cold Wars too. In 1978, an assassination attempt on Bulgarian defector Vladimir Kostov, a former state radio editor who lived in Paris, was thwarted because a poisoned dart failed to penetrate his thick woolen sweater.

2 James Thomas Brudenell was the British officer who led the Charge of the Light Brigade during the Crimean War. He is also remembered as the man whose subordinates wore a distinctive type of knitted clothing to ward off Crimea's chilly weather. That garment was ultimately named for Brudenell, the 7th Earl of Cardigan.

3 Some people describe "Peanuts" character Charlie Brown's zigzag garment as a sweater, and others call it a shirt. In any case, that's not what he was wearing when the comic strip started in 1950. "For the first two weeks of the strip, he wore a plain white T-shirt," cartoonist Charles Schulz recalled. "But then I realized the strip needed more color, so I drew the sweater."

4 A cardigan worn by a man is sometimes called a mandigan.

5 That inexpensive cashmere sweater you got for a steal cost more than you think. The world's insatiable appetite for the famously soft garments led to overgrazing on the Alashan grasslands in China, which in turn was a major factor in the increase of dust storms so vast that they crossed the Pacific Ocean and polluted air in the United States.

6 Hockey players don't wear jerseys; they wear sweaters. Or at least they're called sweaters, harking back to the days when games were often played outdoors.

7 English playwright Noel Coward popularized the turtleneck sweater in the 1920s, giving men the courage to come out of their shells and flout the shirt-and-tie status quo. But it was 1967 that was declared the "Year of the Turtle" by a fashion magazine. Popular with beatniks and artists, the fad was powered by the likes of Johnny Carson, Sammy Davis Jr., Sen. Robert F. Kennedy and Steve McQueen.

8 For a short time in late 1968, Francine Gottfried was famous. Dubbed "Wall Street's Sweater Girl," the 21-year-old bank data processing worker took the same route to work every day at the same time, and large crowds of men began gathering near the New York Stock Exchange to ogle her tight sweaters. Before the furor subsided, 10,000 gawkers showed up one day. "These people in Wall Street have the responsibility of handling millions of dollars and they act like they're out of their minds," said Gottfried, who moved on to work elsewhere. Her treatment inspired feminists to stage an "Ogle-In" on June 9, 1970, leering at male passers-by and commenting loudly about their body parts.

9 In October 2013, Norway's NRK television network broadcast "National Knitting Evening," a show lasting about 12 hours—yes, 12 hours—that covered the complete sweater-making process, from lamb shearing to the knitting of the garment. More than 1.2 million people watched the show.

10 Ugly Christmas sweaters used to be what made your grandmother special. Now they're a thing, a meme, a point of (ironic) hipster pride—and big business. There are numerous pub crawls and a national 5k race series for charity. The so-called National Ugly Christmas Sweater Day is the second Friday of December. People hold ugly sweater-themed parties, and if you can't figure out how to do that by yourself, there's a book. Major retailers claim to have the ugliest ugly sweater. And there's a robust market for used ugly sweaters . . . so go raid your grandma's closet.

10 THINGS YOU MIGHT NOT KNOW ABOUT
DESPERADOES

1 A Wyoming ne'er-do-well known as "Big Nose George" Parrot tried to derail a payroll train by removing rail spikes. When a posse went after him, he and an accomplice killed two pursuers. Finally captured, Parrot was lynched in 1881. Dr. John Osborne, a local physician, skinned Parrot's body and arranged for the hide to be tanned and made into a pair of shoes.

2 In many books, a photo shows William Bonney, aka Billy the Kid, with a Winchester carbine in his right hand and a Colt single-action pistol holstered on his left hip. That has led people to assume that the gunslinger was left-handed. A 1958 film in which Paul Newman played Billy the Kid was titled "The Left-Handed Gun." But the photo of Billy the Kid was a tintype, which means the image was reversed. In fact, the Kid fired his pistol with his right hand.

3 A desperado is defined as a "bold, reckless criminal or outlaw." But it's also slang for a chess piece that behaves in a kamikaze fashion, destined to be captured but doing as much damage to the opponent as possible. And it was a member of Dallas' team in the Arena Football League. And it's a beverage featuring beer, limeade and tequila.

4 "The Lady in Red" didn't wear red. Anna Sage, who helped FBI agents ambush John Dillinger outside Chicago's Biograph Theater, was wearing an orange skirt that appeared red under the theater's marquee lights.

5 The movie "Butch Cassidy and the Sundance Kid" embraced the story that the two desperadoes died in a 1908 shootout in Bolivia. But it's not a certainty that Cassidy met his end there. Cassidy's sister, Lula Parker Betenson, said he visited her in Utah in 1925. Others suspect Cassidy was a man known as William Phillips who died in Spokane, Wash., in the 1930s.

6 Convicted of killing a police officer, "Terrible" Tommy O'Connor awaited the hangman in Chicago's Criminal Court Building in 1921. But he got hold of a gun—some said it was smuggled in a pork chop sandwich—and he managed to escape. After a series of carjackings, he disappeared for good, or for bad. In 1977, Cook County finally sold off the wooden gallows it intended to use on O'Connor if he had ever been caught.

7 The modern equivalent of Robin Hood was India's "bandit queen," Phoolan Devi. Forced into an arranged marriage at age 11 to a man three times her age, she repudiated the marriage and took up a life of crime. She joined a band of dacoits (bandits), and led them in raids, including a notorious massacre of about 20 high-caste men in 1981. After spending more than a decade in prison, she was elected to parliament in 1996. Five years later, she was assassinated by masked gunmen.

8 Nat Turner was a desperado, but he also was a freedom fighter. Guided by messianic visions, Turner led a Virginia slave rebellion that massacred 55 whites before he was captured and hanged in 1831. A decade earlier, Turner had escaped from slavery, but voluntarily came back after 30 days, explaining that a spirit had told him to return to bondage.

9 Desperadoes routinely come to a bad end. Sixteenth century Japanese outlaw Ishikawa Goemon was captured and boiled in oil. Virgulino Ferreira da Silva, the bespectacled Brazilian bandit leader known as Lampiao, was killed with 10 members of his gang in 1938, and their heads were cut off and displayed in public.

10 Dillinger was behind bars when Bonnie Parker and Clyde Barrow were grabbing headlines. Annoyed that they were knocking off only small-time banks, Dillinger complained that they were "giving bank-robbing a bad name."

John Dillinger complained that Bonnie and Clyde were "giving bank-robbing a bad name."

10 THINGS YOU MIGHT NOT KNOW ABOUT
STANLEYS

1 In honor of the Chicago Blackhawks' Stanley Cup successes, we honor the name Stanley. Its popularity as a boy's name in the United States peaked in 1915-1917, when it was the 34th most popular name three years running, as tracked by the Social Security Administration. It has been downhill ever since. In 2015, it was No. 688.

2 President Barack Obama's grandfather was Stanley Dunham, and—far more unusually—Obama's mother was named Stanley too. A childhood friend recalled Stanley Ann Dunham explaining that "my dad wanted a boy and he got me. And the name Stanley made him feel better, I guess." After high school, Obama's mother stopped introducing herself as Stanley and switched to Ann.

3 "Stanley" is Chicago slang for a Pole or Polish-American.

4 Actor Marlon Brando beat out John Garfield and Burt Lancaster to play the brutish Stanley Kowalski in Tennessee Williams' play "A Streetcar Named Desire." Brando won the part by visiting Williams' home in Provincetown, Mass., in 1947 and performing three virtuoso acts: reading the script well, repairing Williams' overflowing toilet, and fixing a blown fuse that had forced the playwright to read by candlelight.

5 A young Welshman named John Rowlands immigrated to New Orleans, where he was befriended by merchant Henry Morton Stanley and adopted the man's name as his own. The new Stanley joined Confederate forces, was captured at Shiloh and was imprisoned in Chicago. At war's end, things got even more interesting. Stanley became a newspaper correspondent in Spain, Crete, Ethiopia and what is now Tanzania, where he found missing Scottish missionary David Livingstone and uttered the famous line, "Dr. Livingstone, I presume." Though they were in what Stanley called "darkest Africa," they drank champagne in silver goblets to celebrate the meeting.

6 Among the secret Stanleys in show business are Bobby Vinton (Stanley Robert Vinton Jr.) and M.C. Hammer (Stanley Kirk Burrell). But KISS co-founder Paul Stanley merely moved the "Stanley" in his name. At birth, he was Stanley Eisen.

7 The Stanley Steamer was the most famous of the steam-powered cars, which had their heyday in the early 1900s. As crazy as it sounds, driving around on top of a boiler was surprisingly safe. That said, the internal-combustion engine eventually won the day. But some Stanley enthusiasts wouldn't let it go. So in 1951, the Museum of Science and Industry and Popular Mechanics magazine staged a race from Chicago to New York between a 1913 Stanley Steamer and a 1911 gas-powered Stoddard-Dayton to settle which car was better. The Stanley won.

8 For decades, Flat Stanley was just a 2D character from Jeff Brown's 1964 book and series. But in 1995, Canadian third-grade teacher Dale Hubert gave him a whole new dimension when he used him as part of a letter-writing project. It went viral, to say the least. Today, the Flat Stanley Project is worldwide. Its website features photos of Flat Stanley with, among others, former Presidents Barack Obama and George W. Bush and actor Clint Eastwood.

9 Stanleys have had some success playing hockey. Allan Stanley played on a powerhouse Toronto Maple Leafs team that won four of Lord Stanley's cups in the 1960s. But for Chicagoans, you need look no further than Stan Mikita, who helped the Blackhawks win it all in 1961, for the most famous hockey-playing Stan.

In 1924, the Stanley Cup was misplaced—left on the side of the road on a **SNOWBANK**— while en route to a victory party.

10 A low point for the Stanley Cup came in 1924. The triumphant Montreal Canadiens put the trophy in their car trunk to drive to the victory party. But their car got a flat, and they took the trophy out and perched it on a snowbank so they could take out the spare tire. After changing the tire, they arrived at the party, only to realize they had misplaced the Stanley Cup. They found it where they had left it: on the snowbank.

10 THINGS YOU MIGHT NOT KNOW ABOUT
UNDERWEAR

1 People have been wearing things under there for a long time. The Otzi Man, found in 1991 in the Italian Alps, lived 5,300 years ago and was wearing a loincloth. In 1352 B.C., Pharaoh Tutankhamun was buried with myriad priceless objects—including 145 loincloths.

2 There's no Otto Titzling, and he did not invent the bra. The fictional character in Wallace Reyburn's 1971 novel "Bust-Up: The Uplifting Tale of Otto Titzling and the Development of the Bra" has been taken for real in various places, including Trivial Pursuit.

3 Minnesota Gov. Jesse Ventura announced in a 1999 autobiography that he was a commando in more ways than one. The former Navy SEAL and professional wrestler wrote that he didn't wear underwear. Fruit of the Loom promptly sent 12,000 pairs.

4 Madonna wasn't the first to cause a scandal by wearing underwear for outerwear. Marie Antoinette reportedly shocked France by wearing a chemise to court. Prior to that, it was considered an undergarment.

5 There's a huge market for used underwear—of the famous. John Kennedy's GI boxers, Jackie Kennedy's slip, Queen Victoria's massive bloomers (50-inch waist!), as well as underwear once owned by Madonna, Michael Bolton, members of ZZ Top and Arnold Schwarzenegger have been sold for profit or to benefit charities. In 2000, Greek opera star Maria Callas' belongings, including underwear, were auctioned off. A buyer identified only as a former Greek diva bought all of the underwear and promised to burn it to "preserve the honor and dignity" of the legend.

6 While governor of Arkansas, Bill Clinton donated his used underwear to charity, valued it at $2 a piece and deducted it from his federal income taxes.

7 In 1856, some belles wore as many as 16 petticoats, a not inconsiderable weight. So the cage crinoline, an undergarment made of a series of lightweight steel or cane hoops that provided the same bell shape, was a boon. Though easier to wear, it wasn't without its own problems. On windy days it could blow inside out like an umbrella. And when a woman leaned forward, she had to be wary of how much her dress tipped up in back. And just moving around was tricky. Consider: The hoops could be nearly 6 feet in diameter.

8 What's with King Henry VIII's codpiece? The need for that piece of clothing came about because men's hose at the time was actually two separate stockings with no crotch. As the tunic hemline rose, the chance for embarrassing viewings rose with it, thus the introduction of the codpiece. But by the early 1500s, it was the fashion to wear grossly oversized and bejeweled codpieces to flaunt one's masculinity. They also doubled as pockets to carry valuables or even small weapons.

9 Just because a woman became pregnant didn't mean she gave up her corset. Special pregnancy and nursing corsets were available.

10 Maidenform had a long-running ad slogan in the 1950s and '60s that used the line, "I dreamed I (fill in the blank) in my Maidenform bra." Some examples: "I dreamed I stopped traffic . . . ," "I dreamed I grabbed a bull by the horns . . ." and "I dreamed I was a social butterfly . . ." One pictured a woman in a boxing ring, wearing gloves, shorts and bra with the line, "I dreamed I was a knockout in my Maidenform bra."

10 THINGS YOU MIGHT NOT KNOW ABOUT
ATHEISTS

1 Poet Percy Bysshe Shelley was expelled from Oxford University for co-writing a pamphlet called "The Necessity of Atheism" in 1811. When Shelley drowned in a boating accident at age 29, a British newspaper observed that "now he knows whether there is a God or not."

2 To 20th century philosopher Bertrand Russell, dogmatic belief in God was irrational. He said it would be like him demanding that people believe there was a china teapot orbiting the sun between Mars and Earth, too small to be detected by any telescope.

3 A contemporary version of Russell's teapot is the Flying Spaghetti Monster. In 2005, when the Kansas School Board considered allowing the theory of intelligent design to be taught alongside evolution, an Oregon State University physics graduate named Bobby Henderson wrote a letter to the board demanding equal time for the Church of the Flying Spaghetti Monster. Since then, the church has become an internet sensation, embraced by atheists and other skeptics who call themselves Pastafarians.

4 The cover of Time magazine on April 8, 1966, asked a question that many Americans had not considered: "Is God Dead?" The cover attracted considerable attention, and a scene in the child-of-Satan film "Rosemary's Baby" shows Rosemary reading that famous issue of Time.

5 Books rejecting the existence of God have had a major impact in recent decades. Christopher Hitchens' "God Is Not Great" was a finalist for the 2007 National Book Award. Richard Dawkins says his 2006 book "The God Delusion" has sold 3 million copies. Not everyone was impressed. Turkey banned Dawkins' website in 2008.

6 A USA Today/Gallup poll in 2015 found that Americans would sooner have a gay president than an atheist one. Gays were rejected by 24 percent, atheists by 40 percent.

7 Ron Reagan, son of the former president, says he can never win elective office because he is an atheist. But attitudes may be changing. In 2007, U.S. Rep. Fortney "Pete" Stark Jr. (D-Calif.) declared his disbelief in God. He was thought to be the first member of Congress ever to make that declaration.

8 Until a U.S. Supreme Court ruling in 1961, some states banned atheists from holding public office.

9 Katharine Hepburn, who portrayed a missionary in "The African Queen," was an atheist.

10 The expression "There are no atheists in foxholes" asserts that even disbelievers come to God in their most needful moments. But a group called the Military Association of Atheists and Freethinkers would disagree. Author James Morrow once wrote that the expression about no atheists in foxholes is "not an argument against atheism—it's an argument against foxholes."

Until 1961, some states **BANNED** atheists from holding public office.

APRIL FOOLS' DAY

1 The origin of April Fools' Day may be lost to history. One theory centers on people confused by the transition to the Gregorian calendar, but even before that time, there were April Fools'-like hoaxes. In 1983, Boston University professor Joseph Boskin said the practice began when court jesters and fools told the Roman emperor Constantine that they could do a better job than he did, and Constantine made one of them king for a day. Many newspapers picked up Boskin's story—which was an April Fools' Day joke.

2 Ranked by the Museum of Hoaxes as the best April Fools' prank ever was a 1957 BBC report about Switzerland experiencing an early spaghetti harvest. The television show included video of peasants pulling spaghetti from trees and explained that a uniform length for the spaghetti had been achieved through expert cultivation. The BBC got hundreds of phone calls, with most callers asking serious questions, such as where could they buy spaghetti trees.

3 Oh, those Brits. Astronomer Patrick Moore told BBC Radio 2 on April 1, 1976, that the alignment of the planets Pluto and Jupiter would cause a temporary decrease in Earth's gravity at 9:47 a.m. If people jumped in the air at that time, Moore said, they would float for a short while. Indeed, many listeners called the station to say they had floated.

4 Most people know they need to read the Web with a healthy skepticism, but that doesn't mean hoaxes about the internet don't catch the unwary. In 1994, PC Computing magazine wrote that Congress was considering a bill making it illegal to surf the internet while drunk. The outcry was great enough that Sen. Edward Kennedy was forced to deny being the sponsor of the nonexistent legislation. In 1996, an e-mail, purportedly from the Massachusetts Institute of Technology, informed people that the internet would be shut down for a day for spring cleaning. The day that users were told to disconnect computers? April 1.

5 In 1997, newspaper readers found chaos on the comics pages. Billy from "Family Circus" was joking with Dilbert. The "Family Circus" mom sported a Dilbert boss-like pointy hairdo. What was going on? The Great Comic Switcheroo. Urged on by "Baby Blues" creators Rick Kirkman and Jerry Scott, more than 40 cartoonists swapped strips for the day. Among the other switches: Blondie and Garfield, and Shoe and Beetle Bailey.

6 Chicago's WXRT-FM 93.1 has a history of April Fools' hoaxes going back to the 1970s. In 1980, the station promoted the Mayor Jane Byrne April Fool Fest on Navy Pier. On a warm spring day, hundreds of people showed up at what was then a rather derelict padlocked Navy Pier to hear live music, despite the fact that some of the promised artists were dead. In 1998, the station announced it had been purchased by Playboy, was changing the call letters to XXXRT and was touting itself as True Adult Radio. Outraged listeners bombarded not only the station with calls but also Playboy.

7 Chicago's downtown streets devolved into gantlets of tomfoolery in the 1880s and 1890s when armies of newsboys gathered to harass and taunt passers-by. In 1880, the Tribune reported that one ingenious youngster created a wooden apparatus that chalked the words "April Fool" when tapped lightly on a victim's back.

8 Australian businessman Dick Smith had long discussed his plans to tow an iceberg from Antarctica into Sydney Harbor so he could sell especially pure ice cubes to the public for 10 cents apiece. So, when a barge towed a huge white object into the harbor on April 1, 1978, Sydney residents got excited. But then it rained, which dissolved the faux berg—a giant mound of firefighting foam and shaving cream that had been piled on sheets of white plastic.

9 On April 1, 1998, Burger King took out a full-page ad in USA Today to announce a fast-food breakthrough: the Left-Handed Whopper. It featured the same ingredients as the regular Whopper, except the condiments were rotated 180 degrees. According to Burger King, thousands of customers requested the new burger, and others asked for a right-handed version.

10 Among the true things that have happened on April 1: The first speaker of the House was elected (1789); American forces landed on Okinawa (1945); the first U.S. weather satellite was launched (1960); and Steve Wozniak and Steve Jobs founded Apple (1976). Born on April 1, 1929, were Czech author Milan Kundera ("The Unbearable Lightness of Being") and University of Michigan football coach Bo Schembechler ("The Unbearable Heaviness of Losing to Ohio State").

CHAPTER 2
The Human Condition

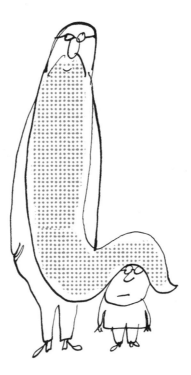

BLAME

1 Why did Greece's economy go into a free fall? Blame the Nazis! Then-Deputy Prime Minister Theodoros Pangalos did just that in 2010, explaining to BBC, "They took away the Greek gold that was at the Bank of Greece, they took away the Greek money, and they never gave it back."

2 When people hold a brainstorming session to decide who is at fault, it's called blamestorming.

3 According to ancient tradition, two goats were sacrificed during the Jewish Day of Atonement. One was slain in the community, while the other received all the sins of the people on its back and was driven out into the wilderness. That second animal got a special name in a biblical translation in the 16th century: It was called the scapegoat.

4 Musical titles often include the phrase "Blame It on . . ." Among those being blamed: the Bossa Nova, the Boom Boom, the Boogie, Bad Luck, Gravity, Waylon, Cain, Bush, Obama, Texas, the Fish, the Girls, the Love of Rock 'n' Roll, the Changes, the Trains, the Tetons, the Mistletoe, the Night, the Rain, the Sun, the Weatherman, My Youth, Your Heart and Me.

5 Researchers at Stanford and the University of Michigan, studying the annual reports of various publicly held companies from 1975 to 1995, found that self-blame came with a bonus: Firms that attributed their problems to their own actions rather than to external factors ultimately performed better on the stock market.

"It's all my fault."
—GEN. ROBERT E. LEE

6 Some of America's great military leaders were willing to accept blame. After Gen. Robert E. Lee's defeat at Gettysburg in 1863, he declared, "It's all my fault," even though he had reason to blame several subordinates. Before Gen. Dwight Eisenhower led the successful D-Day invasion in 1944, he wrote a statement just in case of failure and put it in his wallet. "If any blame or fault attaches to the attempt," he wrote, "it is mine alone."

7 In July 1840, some inhabitants of the remote North Atlantic island of St. Kilda were excited to catch a rare penguin-like bird that hadn't been seen there for many years. Unfortunately for the great auk, its capture coincided with a particularly violent storm. The hunters, cowering inside their rudimentary lodging with their new pet, got to thinking that this strange bird might be more than they first assumed. In the end, the superstitious lot blamed the storm on the bird, which was declared a witch and stoned to death. And that was the last time the now-extinct great auk was ever seen in the British Isles.

8 The expression "pass the buck" comes from the way poker players once kept track of who was supposed to deal: They passed around a knife with a handle made from the antler of a deer. If a player wanted to skip his turn to deal, he passed the buck. President Harry Truman made a related phrase famous when he put a sign on his desk saying, "The buck stops here," meaning that everything was ultimately his responsibility. (Bonus trivia: The other side of Truman's sign had the less memorable phrase "I'm From Missouri.")

9 Who's to blame for the Great Chicago Fire? For many decades, the "person of interest" wasn't a person at all—it was Catherine O'Leary's cow, which supposedly kicked over a lantern in her barn. But in recent decades, Ald. Edward Burke has championed the theory that O'Leary's neighbor, Daniel "Peg Leg" Sullivan, was the culprit. Various theorists have put forth other causes as well, including spontaneous combustion, sparks from a chimney and even a meteor shower. The meteor idea has its detractors, but it fits nicely with the fact that Chicago's fire coincided with devastating blazes elsewhere in the Midwest—in Peshtigo, Wis., and Manistee, Mich.

10 Steve Bartman—not to blame. Simple as that.

DISTRACTIONS

1 A "red herring"—something irrelevant that is raised as a distraction—may have its origin in British fox hunts of the 18th century. Anti-hunting activists supposedly used smoked herring—which has a brownish-red color and a pungent smell—to lure hounds away from the proper hunting route. By "drawing a red herring across the path," they sent the hounds chasing after the fish instead of the fox.

2 The reason cellphone use and driving don't mix is that the human brain doesn't truly multi-task. According to University of Michigan professor David Meyer, the brain has one channel for each type of information—auditory, visual, manual, etc.—which is why you can't read a text and a road sign at the same time. But some conflicts aren't so obvious. If the driver has a conversation with somebody describing in detail what his new office looks like, the information could occupy not only the driver's auditory channel but also the visual channel and could impair his driving.

3 If being distracted didn't worry you enough already, consider that the word was once a synonym for insane.

4 For decades, basketball fans have tried to distract visiting players at the free-throw line by screaming and waving their arms. Also popular are spinning signs and bare-chested, overweight male fans. But such techniques seemed to have little effect until Arizona State unveiled in 2013 its Curtain of Distraction, which is hung on PVC pipes and opened just before the free throw, revealing fans performing surreal scenes. Among them: men doing calisthenics in their underwear, unicorns kissing, Santa Claus bearhugging an elf and a man riding an inflatable duck. According to statistics, visitors to ASU made just 61 percent of free throws in the first two seasons of operation, compared with about 70 percent in the three seasons before.

5 Vail Reese, a San Francisco dermatologist and film buff, mimics the Oscars by awarding the Skinnies. He honored the 2003 film "Mystic River" by citing "the dark spot on Sean Penn's neck" as most distracting lesion.

6 Advances in technology threaten to overwhelm young minds to the point of distraction. Students' memories will atrophy because so much information is so readily and instantly available. Students will know a great many things but "have learned nothing." A diatribe against the internet? No, Socrates worried about the development of writing and the Greek alphabet about 2,500 years ago.

7 When someone uses chitchat, noises or mannerisms to distract or mislead an opponent during poker or another game, it's called "coffeehousing."

8 On Dec. 29, 1972, Eastern Air Lines Flight 401 crashed into a swamp near Miami, killing 101 people. Investigators said the three crew members and a jumpseat occupant were so distracted by a malfunctioning warning light that they didn't notice the autopilot was disengaged until it was too late.

9 When you make an effort to ignore one thing and focus on another, you are flexing your "executive function," which is something the brain must learn. A child's ability to do this explodes around age 4, and it appears to peak at about 30. Scientists aren't sure why some have a stronger function than others, but research suggests aerobic exercise, of all things, can help strengthen and sustain it.

10 The most mind-blowing fact about distractions that almost no one could possibly imagine is . . . oh, look, it's a cat video!

10 THINGS YOU MIGHT NOT KNOW ABOUT
LIES

1 Psychologist Robert Feldman found that, on average, two people just getting to know each other lied three times in 10 minutes.

2 Two years ago, Egyptian lawmaker Anwar al-Bulkimy said bandages on his face were the result of an attack by masked gunmen who robbed him of $16,000. But a doctor disputed the story, insisting that al-Bulkimy had undergone plastic surgery. The member of parliament—dubbed the "nose-job MP" in the press—then admitted the lie, but excused himself by saying it occurred while "I was under the influence of anesthesia."

3 Children as young as 2 can fib, but those terrible toddlers are terrible liars. First, they don't really know what they're doing; their brains aren't developed enough to understand that mommy or daddy might actually believe the untruth. And they can't maintain the falsehood: After denying doing something, like peeking inside a bag, they then willingly describe the toy inside.

4 Barack Obama's keep-your-health-care promise and George W. Bush's weapons-of-mass-destruction claim—were they intentional lies or simply misunderstandings? The debates may never be settled. But there's no doubt another president, Dwight Eisenhower, knew his administration was telling a whopper in 1960. The Soviets shot down a U-2 spy plane, and the U.S. said it was a weather research plane that went off course. Pilot Francis Gary Powers was equipped with a needle filled with poison, and the CIA figured he would use it. But after the U.S. told its lie, the Soviets sprang their trap, revealing that Powers had been captured alive and admitted spying.

5 People tend to lie about lying, or at least they tidy it up with euphemisms. The truth is "embroidered," or the dissembler has a "failure of memory." Language expert Ralph Keyes recalled a psychiatrist describing his client as "someone for whom truth is temporarily unavailable." British official Robert Armstrong popularized the phrase "economical with the truth" in the 1980s. In 2014, CIA Director James Clapper was accused of lying to Congress and insisted he had testified in the "least untruthful manner" possible.

6 Robert Hunt was a con man who claimed to be at various times a space shuttle astronaut, a gynecologist, a Marine, a U.S. senator, an inventor, a contractor and a major league ballplayer. According to a 1992 Boston Herald story, his father said his son's shenanigans started early. When Hunt was 14, he sold a neighbor a bunch of canaries. A few days later, the man was screaming and pounding on the Hunts' door, demanding his money back. Turns out, when the birds took a bath, the yellow chalk washed off to reveal sparrows.

7 George Washington's "I cannot tell a lie" story about a hatchet and a cherry tree is itself total blarney. Without a hint of irony, the lie was perpetrated by Mason Weems—an

Anglican pastor no less—who clearly had no problem laying it on thick in deifying the first president. The "story" ends with George's father so proud of his son's honesty that he allegedly said, "Such an act of heroism in my son is worth more than a thousand trees, though blossomed with silver and their fruits of purest gold."

8 "No one has any intention of building a wall," said East German leader Walter Ulbricht in June 1961, less than two months before construction of the Berlin Wall began.

9 Whom do you lie to the most? Possibly yourself. The apparent contradiction of self-deception—how can you believe an untruth you tell yourself?—has roiled the academic world since Sigmund Freud turned our inner worlds inside out. But consider: In a survey of 1 million high school seniors, every student thought they were above average in getting along with others.

10 Slang terms for a lie include: blarney, bulldust, humbug, bark, ben, bleeder, blazer, bounce, caulker, clanger, clanker, clincher, cobber, crammer, double-thumper, fib, fudge, hum, porky, old moody, whopper, tall tale . . . and Bernie Madoff. (OK, that last one isn't true—yet. You could say we embroidered.)

10 THINGS YOU MIGHT NOT KNOW ABOUT
GAFFES

1 He's not a giant of the 20th century, but he played one in a movie. A billboard in India intending to honor Nelson Mandela after his death in December 2013 mistakenly used actor Morgan Freeman's photograph instead of the former South African president's.

2 It would be hard to make this worse: On Oct. 31, 2000, German Chancellor Gerhard Schroeder, paying his respects at Yad Vashem Holocaust memorial in Israel with Prime

Minister Ehud Barak, unfortunately turned a handle the wrong way and accidentally extinguished the eternal flame, which stands in the Hall of Remembrance for the 6 million Jews killed by the Nazis. Barak tried to relight it but failed. A memorial employee finally reignited it with a cigarette lighter.

3 During the 2012 presidential campaign, Mitt Romney committed numerous gaffes that put his wealth in an unfavorable light, including his comment that 47 percent of Americans are "dependent upon government" and his offer of a $10,000 bet with a debate opponent. Less publicized was a 2011 statement in which he actually misstated his own name. At the start of a 2011 debate, CNN's Wolf Blitzer said: "I'm Wolf Blitzer, and yes, that's my real name." Romney said: "I'm Mitt Romney—and yes, Wolf, that's also my first name." But Romney's first name isn't Mitt—that's his middle name. His first name is Willard.

4 The man who beat Romney delivered his own share of erroneous statements, such as saying he had visited "57 states" and suggesting that Charleston, S.C., Savannah, Ga., and Jacksonville, Fla., are on the Gulf Coast. But perhaps former President Barack Obama's most painful gaffe came in a 2011 speech to the troops when he referred to a Medal of Honor recipient killed in Afghanistan as if he were still alive. He later called the family to apologize.

5 Movie promotion seems to invite misjudgment. Gandhi Jayanti is a holiday celebrated in India every Oct. 2 to mark the birth of Mohandas Gandhi, a champion of nonviolence. But that didn't stop promoters of the new Indian film "Bang Bang!" from picking that day for the premiere, and even promoting it that way: "On the most peaceful day of the year . . . bullets will fly." In 2014, Paramount Pictures Australia advertised the new "Teenage Mutant Ninja Turtles" film by tweeting a poster of the turtles flying out of an exploding skyscraper, with the release date: Sept. 11.

6 The gaffe-prone have often been tripped up by references to the Sept. 11 attacks. Esquire.com accidentally ran a headline reading, "Making Your Morning Commute More Stylish," next to a photo of a man falling out of one of the Twin Towers. The Tumbledown Trails Golf Course in Wisconsin apologized for its tasteless $9.11 golf rate to "commemorate" Sept. 11. But perhaps the most cynical move occurred within hours of the attacks, when British bureaucrat Jo Moore realized that the events in America were so distracting that any bad news at home might be overlooked. "It is now a very good day to get out anything we want to bury," she wrote in an email. After it was leaked, she said she was sorry.

7 Former IRS honcho Lois Lerner, under fire over accusations that her agency had targeted conservative groups, made a strange statement for a tax official: "I'm not good at math." But she knew enough about arithmetic to take the Fifth before Congress.

8 One of the most infamous mistakes in American politics was apparent only in hindsight. The infamous "Mission Accomplished" banner—displayed on the USS Abraham Lincoln for President George W. Bush's May 1, 2003, speech declaring the end of major military operations in Iraq—is now considered a blatant gaffe, but it was not immediately recognized as such. The banner wasn't cited at all in The New York Times' Page 1 stories in the next day's edition. The Chicago Tribune's stories barely mentioned it. The Iraq insurgency, which would extend the fighting for years and cost thousands of lives, hadn't yet begun in earnest.

9 Minnesota Vikings defensive end Jim Marshall picked up a loose ball during a game in October 1964 and ran 66 yards to the end zone. Unfortunately, he ran the wrong way and scored a safety for the San Francisco 49ers. The Vikings managed to win anyway. The University of California's Roy Riegels, a center, didn't have the same luck. Playing in the 1929 Rose Bowl, he ran a fumble nearly 70 yards in the wrong direction before a teammate slowed him down enough for opposing Georgia Tech players to tackle him on the 1-yard line. Tech scored a safety the next play—and won the game 8-7. Though in tears after the game, Riegels learned to laugh about it later. In 1964, Marshall got a letter from Riegels that opened, "Welcome to the club!"

10 Al Gore committed a major gaffe by claiming that he invented the internet, right? Well, no, not really. In a 1999 interview, Gore said: "During my service in the United States Congress, I took the initiative in creating the internet." While that statement was self-promotional, it was not a claim of invention—it was a claim of taking the initiative, which Gore clearly did. Two pioneers of the internet, Robert Kahn and Vinton Cerf, once wrote: "Al Gore was the first political leader to recognize the importance of the internet and to promote and support its development."

10 THINGS YOU MIGHT NOT KNOW ABOUT
FEAR

1 Scientists say we get goose bumps when we're afraid partly to make us look bigger and more imposing. Unfortunately, we are no longer covered with hair, so the effect is not that impressive.

2 Two visionary writers about space exploration were afraid to fly. Isaac Asimov says his aviophobia was instilled by his parents, who feared for his safety after a childhood illness. Ray Bradbury feared both flying and driving. He blamed his driving phobia on a fatal accident he witnessed as a teen. Ultimately, Bradbury overcame his fear of flying. The reason? "A car breaking down in so many small Southern towns and the chauffeur taking three miserable days just to get through Florida," he said. "After the second tire blew, I got the word. In a loud and clear voice from the heavens above, I heard the message: 'Fly, dummy, fly!'"

3 The amygdalae, a pair of almond-size parts of the brain, are often called the fear centers, but it is more accurate to consider them akin to guardhouses. They prompt us to pay attention, help us identify what to look for and kick-start other areas of the brain to assess and analyze the threat, according to Dartmouth neuroscientist Paul Whalen. People with impaired amygdalae aren't truly fearless; they just don't know where to look to find danger. For example, when asked to view photos of scared people, they won't register that fear. But when directed to concentrate on the eyes—something healthy amygdalae know to do—they register fear like anybody else.

4 Hippopotomonstrosesquippedaliophobia is the fear of long words. (Now that's just cruel.)

5 A dozen years before Orson Welles' radio play "The War of the Worlds" elicited widespread panic in the U.S., a similar public hysteria occurred with a BBC play called "Broadcasting from the Barricades." Both used the format of a radio broadcast interrupted by breaking news, and both warned explicitly that they were only make-believe. In the U.S., the fictional threat was a Martian invasion; in Britain, it was a protest by "The National Movement for Abolishing Theatre Queues" that got out of hand, with the Houses of Parliament blown up and Big Ben in ruins. British police stations were swamped with calls by gullible, upset listeners. The BBC, admonished by a critic to "take no risks with its public's average standard of intelligence," issued an apology, according to historian Joanna Bourke.

6 "I'm the most fearful and cowardly man you'll ever meet . . . I'm frightened of my own movies. I never go seem them. I don't know how people can bear to watch my movies." So said legendary filmmaker and master of suspense Alfred Hitchcock.

> *"I'm frightened of my own movies."*
> —ALFRED HITCHCOCK

7 The fear of being mistakenly buried alive led to New Jersey inventor Franz Vester's patent in 1868 for a coffin featuring a tube and a ladder allowing the occupant to escape to the surface. The coffin also provided food, wine and a rope with a bell. Some later versions even featured telephones.

8 Genuphobia is the fear of knees.

9 The original version of Franklin D. Roosevelt's first inaugural address did not include the line for which it is now famous: "The only thing we have to fear is fear itself." The 1933 speech was drafted by Raymond Moley and then edited by FDR, but the famous line—a variation of Henry David Thoreau's "Nothing is so much to be feared as fear"—likely was added by Louis Howe, another close adviser and a Moley rival. Moley got the last laugh, though, writing decades later that Howe surely hadn't read any Thoreau and must have picked up the line in a newspaper advertisement.

10 In the late 1990s, model Christie Brinkley sued the National Enquirer for reporting that she had an irrational fear of cows and had ordered police to shoot one because it mooed at her while she played tennis. A New York judge threw out the $42 million libel suit, finding the Enquirer's reporting "truly obnoxious" but not defamatory.

10 THINGS YOU MIGHT NOT KNOW ABOUT
SWEAT

1 Human sweat is odorless. The eccrine and apocrine glands' emissions do, however, provide the perfect home for bacteria to grow and thrive—and that's where the smell comes from.

2 Antiperspirants work because the active ingredient (usually aluminum) forms a plug in the sweat duct. So it's most useful if applied before going to bed and when the armpit is completely dry. And it becomes even more effective if applied twice daily for a week or more.

3 If you were standing under hot lights and millions of people were watching, would you sweat? Of course. But ever since Richard Nixon got shiny during his debate with John Kennedy in 1960, perspiration has been viewed as a sign of candidate weakness. In 2012, Mitt Romney was ridiculed for sweating during a debate. Comedian Albert Brooks, recalling his own "flop sweat" scene in the 1987 film "Broadcast News," tweeted: "If Romney sweats anymore I get a royalty." Another tweeter, Lisa McIntire, countered: "Guys, Romney didn't have flop sweat. He had victory shine."

4 Wrestlers in ancient Greece competed in the nude, covered in oil, and did not wash with soap afterward. Instead, they cleaned with a strigil, a squeegeelike instrument used to scrape off the oil, dirt and sweat.

5 It's often recalled that Winston Churchill used the phrase "blood, sweat and tears" in his famous speech to Britain's House of Commons in May 1940. But what he actually said was "blood, toil, tears and sweat." Churchill had previously written "blood, sweat and tears" in an article about the Spanish Civil War, and even that was not original, according to quotation expert Ralph Keyes. More than three centuries earlier, poet John Donne had penned "thy teares, or sweat, or blood." And in the 1880s, playwright John Davidson wrote of "blood-sweats and tears."

6 Even without exercising, the human body loses about 2.5 liters of water each day, more than half of that from urination. Get that body moving, though, and it can sweat more than 2 liters per hour and as much as 12 liters per day.

7 Romanian gymnastics coach Bela Karolyi believed rigorous training and a diet that included raw garlic would produce Olympic champions. His athletes knew it produced something else: stinky sweat. "We hated garlic because when we worked out and sweat, we smelled like hell," recalled Karolyi protege Nadia Comaneci, who earned a perfect 10 at the 1976 Olympic Games. She recalled that other coaches copied Karolyi's dietary regimen. "I remember saying to myself, 'It's not the garlic, people, it's the training!'"

8 James Brown, a founding father of funk, knew how to work up a sweat, and even had a hit song called "Cold Sweat." A Brown biographer, James Sullivan, cites Yale professor Robert Farris Thompson's theory that African-American use of the word "funky" comes from the Ki-Kongo word lu-fuki, which refers to body odor in a positive way—as the smell of someone who has worked up a sweat through hard work.

9 The next breakthrough in skin care may come from magic hippo sweat. Researchers say its pinkish-red excretion not only helps regulate heat but also acts as a sunblock, antiseptic and insect repellent.

10 When LeBron James, then playing for the Miami Heat, tossed off his signature headband near the end of Game 6 of the NBA Finals in 2013, a Twitter account called @Lebronzheadband tweeted: "Lebron im on the sideline next to the bald camera guy help he wont stop looking at me."

HIPPO SWEAT acts as a sunblock, antiseptic and insect repellent.

APOLOGIES

1 The U.S. government has officially apologized for slavery, mistreatment of Native Americans, the overthrow of Hawaii's native leaders in 1893, the Tuskegee syphilis study, the Japanese internment in World War II, the protection of Gestapo officer Klaus Barbie after the war and other mistakes and misdeeds. But the U.S. has said explicitly it will not apologize for dropping atomic bombs on Japan to end World War II. And after the downing of an Iranian jetliner in 1988, the U.S. said it regretted the loss of innocent life and paid compensation, but it never formally apologized.

"The Lord told me it's flat none of your business."

—JIMMY SWAGGART

2 One of the most famous apologies of recent decades was preacher Jimmy Swaggart's tearful, televised "I Have Sinned" sermon in 1988 in Baton Rouge, La. Caught with a prostitute, Swaggart apologized to his wife, his son, his church, his fellow evangelists and his God. Three years later he was found with a hooker again, but this time he told his congregation: "The Lord told me it's flat none of your business."

3 A candidate for the most-belated mea culpa came from the Roman Catholic Church, which admitted in 1992 that it shouldn't have punished Galileo Galilei 360 years earlier for suggesting the planets revolved around the sun.

4 In 1934, Japanese Emperor Hirohito was visiting the city of Kiryu when his entourage was directed on the wrong route. The mistake meant people along the road weren't properly dressed, and he arrived at his destination before the reception committee was ready for him. About a week later, all of Kiryu's 65,000 residents faced southeast to the palace at Tokyo and observed a minute of silent prayer to express their apologies.

"I don't give a damn about your yellow buzzards. Why should I care?" —JOHNNY CASH

5 The art of public apologies includes the "if" apology ("I'm sorry if you were offended") and the autopilot apology ("mistakes were made"). There's also the surgical apology, as shown by George W. Bush after a 2000 campaign gaffe in Naperville. An open mic caught Bush telling running mate Dick Cheney that New York Times reporter Adam Clymer was "a major league (expletive)." Bush later said: "I regret that a private comment I made to the vice presidential candidate made it through the public airways." But he didn't express regret for saying it, and he didn't apologize to Clymer.

6 After The Associated Press' Edward Kennedy and other reporters witnessed the Nazis' formal surrender on May 7, 1945, Allied censors ordered them to keep it secret for 36 hours so the Soviets could stage another ceremony. But Kennedy heard the news on German radio and decided to go with the story right away, in one of the biggest scoops in history. His reward? The AP fired him. Sixty-seven years later, the news agency apologized. "It was a terrible day for the AP," president Tom Curley said. "It was handled in the worst possible way." The apology was too late for Kennedy; he died in a traffic accident in 1963.

7 After an amphetamine-pumped Johnny Cash started a wildfire in Los Padres National Forest in California in 1965, the blaze devastated the endangered condor population: 49 of the region's 53 birds were killed. At a deposition later, he was asked if he started the fire. He responded, "No. My truck did, and it's dead, so you can't question it." (He admitted in his autobiography that he was also high during the questioning.) He was then asked if he felt bad about what happened to the birds. He unapologetically said, "I don't give a damn about your yellow buzzards. Why should I care?"

8 Holy Roman Emperor Henry IV, who was excommunicated after calling for Pope Gregory VII's resignation and appointing his own bishops, stood barefoot in the snow for three days in January 1077 to apologize in the hope that the Holy Father would lift the excommunication. Gregory did so, but Henry was back at it in a few years and was excommunicated again.

9 After Madonna received a bouquet of hydrangeas from a fan in 2011, she sniffed, "I absolutely loathe hydrangeas." The negative reaction to Madonna's remark inspired her to produce a short video in which she pretended to apologize to hydrangeas but then stomped on them and said she liked roses better.

10 Apologies are generally seen as gracious gestures, but George Steinbrenner was an exception to the rule. The New York Yankees owner issued a written apology to Yankees fans after his team lost the 1981 World Series. That not only annoyed his own players but seemed to disparage the team that had won, the Los Angeles Dodgers.

10 THINGS YOU MIGHT NOT KNOW ABOUT
TATTOOS

1 It's too bad that tattoo machines don't come with spell check, as there are few errors so bad as the ones inked on a person's skin. Pro basketball player Kevin Durant experienced that firsthand last year after unveiling an ornate illustration and Bible verse on his back that misspelled "mature." Durant has lots of company. Soccer superstar David Beckham's wife's name is misspelled (in Hindi) on his arm, actress Hayden Panettiere's ink misspelled the Italian phrase "live without regrets"—we can't make this up—and singer Britney Spears' attempt to ink the Japanese characters for mysterious on her lower back ended up just "strange." In 2012, Jerri Peterson's attempt to memorialize her moment in the sun became "Oylmpic torch bearer."

2 The word "tattoo" comes from the Polynesian word tatu or tatau, but the practice of permanently inking human skin is not unique to the South Pacific and appears to have developed independently in cultures around the world.

3 The fear of nuclear attack during the Cold War inspired officials to call for every American to be tattooed with his or her blood type. Chicago civil defense leaders said they favored tattooing on the left underarm rather than on legs or arms, which might be blown off in an atomic blast. When the Tribune's "Inquiring Camera Girl" asked people about the idea in 1950, the paper printed five responses, and not one opposed the notion. Law student Francis O'Byrne said: "I think the tattoo should be put in a less conspicuous spot than under the arm because many women will object because of strapless evening gowns." The blood type tattoo idea never really took off.

4 According to a 2015 Harris Poll, a third of all Americans have at least one tattoo, up from 21 percent in 2012, but 47 percent of Millennials say they have a tat. More women reported having a tattoo than men, 31 percent to 27 percent. The U.S. tattoo industry—21,000 parlors strong—brings in $2 billion annually.

5 One of the first tattooed ladies in the United States, Nora Hildebrandt, sported 365 tats as a Barnum & Bailey Circus attraction during the 1890s and claimed she was forcibly inked while a captive of Native Americans. The truth was that her father, a German immigrant who also was one of the nation's first tattoo artists, had no qualms about perfecting his craft on his own daughter.

6 Traumatic tattoos can occur if you fall on a rough surface, such as an asphalt parking lot, and debris is embedded under your skin. If it isn't removed, it can permanently color your skin. A similar effect can be caused by firecrackers or other such explosions. Such unintentional "natural tattoos" were common among coal miners, whose frequent cuts were dirtied by coal dust and rarely cleaned properly.

7 In 2012, the mayor of Osaka, Japan, banned all city employees, including teachers, from having tattoos, which were considered by authorities to be a sign of the organized crime syndicate Yakuza. In January 2014, a 23-year-old school clerk became the first person punished under the ban. Her salary was docked for a month.

8 Tattooing was prohibited in New York City from 1961 to 1997, supposedly to prevent the spread of hepatitis B. But cultural objections appeared to be at work as well. One judge who upheld the ban wrote that "the decoration, so-called, of the human body by tattoo designs is, in our culture, a barbaric survival, often associated with a morbid or abnormal personality."

9 The Maori of the South Pacific are famous for their intricate facial tattoos, called ta moko, and for the custom of preserving human heads, called mokomokai. In the late 18th and early 19th centuries, when Europeans started trading guns for mokomokai, it got so bad that slaves, who wouldn't traditionally be honored with a moko, would be tattooed and decapitated and their heads cashed in for guns. H.G. Robley, an early ethnographer, wrote in 1896 about a European man declining to buy a head because the artistry wasn't good enough. Acknowledging the point, the local chief gestured to his followers, asked the European if any of their tattoos sufficed and promised to prepare and dry the head quickly.

10 Among the news coming out of the Reagan administration in 1987 was the fact that Secretary of State George Shultz had a tiger tattooed on his rear end. Confirmation came from Shultz's wife, Helena, as she chatted with reporters on a plane bound for China. "He got it at Princeton," she explained, adding: "When the children were young, they used to run up and touch it and he would growl and they would run away."

10 THINGS YOU MIGHT NOT KNOW ABOUT
BLONDS

1 People have gone to great lengths to achieve blondness. In ancient Rome, people used pigeon poop; in Renaissance Venice, horse urine. Throughout history, nonblonds have also tried white wine, olive oil, ivy bark, soap and saffron.

2 Alfred Hitchcock cast so many blondes in his movies that film critics now write of "Hitchcock blondes:" beautiful, aloof, smart leading ladies. Think Grace Kelly, Tippi Hedren and Kim Novak. Hitchcock offered myriad reasons for his preference for light-haired actresses,

> *"Blondes make the best victims. They're like virgin snow that shows up the bloody footprints."* —ALFRED HITCHCOCK

including that they film better in black and white, but one quote seems to sum it up: "Blondes make the best victims," Hitchcock said. "They're like virgin snow that shows up the bloody footprints."

3 According to Victoria Sherrow's "Encyclopedia of Hair," there was an original "dumb blonde." An 18th century French actress and prostitute named Rosalie Duthe was known for being very beautiful but incapable of intelligent conversation. She was satirized in a play called "Les Curiosites de la Foire" in 1775. But dumb is relative: Duthe was extremely wealthy as a mistress of royalty.

4 If the director yells "Kill the blonde!" on a movie set, he's probably ordering the crew to shut off an open-face, 2,000-watt spotlight.

5 Actress Marilyn Monroe colored her hair using a shade of blond called dirty pillow slip.

6 In junior high, Kurt Cobain was profiled in his school newspaper, the Puppy Press: "Kurt is a seventh-grader at our school. He has blond hair and blue eyes. He thinks school is alright. . . . His favorite saying is 'Excuse you.'"

7 Actress Veronica Lake's peekaboo hairdo, with long blond hair over one eye, was a 1940s sensation. According to Life magazine, she had about 150,000 hairs on her head, with her tresses 17 inches long in front and 24 inches long in back. The downsides: "Her hair catches fire fairly often when she is smoking" and "it has a bad habit of snagging on men's buttons." About the buttons, Life wrote: "If Miss Lake were in fact the kind of girl she portrays on the screen, this might lead to all kinds of fascinating complications. . . ."

8 Only one in 20 white American adults is naturally blond.

9 In the early '80s, Brad Pitt dropped out of the University of Missouri two credits short of graduating and went to Hollywood. But before his light-haired good looks became famous, Pitt worked a variety of odd jobs in California—delivering refrigerators, serving as a chauffeur for strippers and dressing as a chicken to promote El Pollo Loco "flame-grilled" chicken.

10 Former members of the '70s rock group Stilettos were searching for a name for their new group and settled on Blondie. Lead singer Debbie Harry said the name came from truck drivers who would pass her and shout, "Hey, Blondie!" In 1997, the band performed on an Iggy Pop tribute album using the pseudonym Adolph's Dog. It's probably not a coincidence that Adolf Hitler had a pet dog named Blondi.

10 THINGS YOU MIGHT NOT KNOW ABOUT
HEIGHT

1 There's a discrepancy about President Donald Trump's height. His New York driver's license lists him at 6 foot 2, but his doctor said he is 6-3. Photos seem to indicate the former is closer to the truth. Such an inconsistency is par for the course with presidential heights, but it appears that Abraham Lincoln was tallest at 6 foot 4, with Lyndon Johnson between 6-3 and 6-4. Thomas Jefferson, Franklin Roosevelt, George H.W. Bush, Bill Clinton, George Washington and Chester Arthur would all have seen eye to eye with the current president. The shortest? James Madison at 5-4.

2 According to studies, tall people have higher incomes, higher IQs and longer life spans than short people.

3 Among the famous people afraid of heights: Steven Spielberg, Wayne Gretzky, Sarah Palin, Billie Jean King, Ray Bradbury, Adolf Hitler, Bridget Fonda, Frank Sinatra and Whoopi Goldberg. Even Spiderman—Tobey Maguire—has admitted to acrophobia.

4 A healthy fear of high places may be innate. In 1960, Cornell University psychologists Eleanor Gibson and Richard Walk conducted a "visual cliff" experiment. In the study, babies of various species (humans, rats, chickens, cats, goats and sheep) refused to venture onto a glass panel that covered what looked like a sharp drop-off. Most of the 6- to 14-month-old human babies recognized the apparent danger of the drop-off and wouldn't cross it, despite coaxing by their mothers. Only three of the 36 infants ventured onto the glass, though some backed onto it without realizing it. None of the chicks, kittens, kids and lambs—some less than a day old—made the same mistake and mistakenly walked off the "cliff."

5 Because of spine compression, people lose height during the day, becoming 1 to 2 percent shorter than when they woke up. The same trend occurs long-term: In adulthood, the average person loses a half-inch every 20 years.

6 An American B-25 bomber collided with the 79th floor of the Empire State Building on a foggy Manhattan morning at the end of World War II. Three crew members died, along with 11 people in the building. A worker in the building survived a bizarre double accident: Badly burned by the fireball, she was taken to an elevator to be lowered to safety. But the impact had damaged the elevator cable, and it snapped, sending the woman and her helper hurtling toward the ground. An automatic braking system saved them.

7 How tall can grass grow? Up to 120 feet, if it's bamboo.

8 Mount Everest is not the highest point on the Earth. A dormant volcano in Ecuador beats out the 29,035-foot Himalayan peak. Mount Chimborazo, at just over 20,500 feet, gets a step-stool boost from Earth's equatorial bulge, which pushes the mountain an extra few miles into space and farther from the center of the planet. For the record, Mount Everest is the highest point above sea level.

9 According to a 1998 study, North America's Plains Indians were the tallest people in the world during the mid-19th century.

10 Language purists may get annoyed that the smallest coffee on the Starbucks menu is labeled "tall." But it wasn't always that way. The 12-ounce "tall" used to be a medium, in between the 8-ounce "short" and the 16-ounce "grande." Later, a 20-ounce "venti" was added and the "short" was taken off the menu (though some stores still sell it).

SKIN COLOR

1 Melanin, the pigment that gives color to skin (and eyes) is produced in cells called melanocytes. Every person has about the same number of these cells, regardless of race, but those with darker skin have larger cells that produce more pigment. Melanin not only colors the skin but also protects it from the sun's harmful ultraviolet rays.

2 Crayola once had a color called "flesh," which was the color of Caucasian flesh. After complaints from civil rights activists, "flesh" became "peach" in 1962. A similar controversy involved "Indian red." Crayola said the color was based on a pigment found near India, but some thought it was a slur against native Americans, so the company solicited consumer suggestions for a new name. Among the ideas: "baseball-mitt brown" and "crab claw red." But "chestnut" was chosen in 1999.

3 A jaundiced baby has yellowish skin. A traveler suffering from seasickness takes on a greenish hue. And a silver miner suffering from argyria turns blue or bluish-gray.

4 The Incredible Hulk was born gray. It wasn't until issue No. 2 that Bruce Banner's alter ego turned green, and that was because the printer couldn't hold a consistent gray. The Hulk's skin shifted from light gray to almost black through the comic book.

The **INCREDIBLE HULK** was originally drawn with **GRAY** skin.

5 It's difficult to understand how a painting of a woman in an evening dress could have scandalized 1884 Paris. But "Madame X," John Singer Sargent's portrait of Virginie Gautreau, caused a stir, and part of the reason was her skin color. In contrast to the black dress, her lavender-powdered skin was jarringly pale, except for her ears, which were adorned by rosy makeup. The result was an image of womanhood that was both corpselike and sexually dangerous, causing discomfort to upper-crust Parisians.

6 "The Simpsons" have jarringly yellow skin because, as animator Gabor Csupo told writer John Ortved, the characters were "primitively designed, so we thought we could counterbalance that design with shocking colors. That's why we came up with the yellow skin and the blue hair for Marge." John Alberti, in his intellectual treatise "Leaving Springfield," describes the Simpsons as "people of color" and notes that Bart has called himself "yellow trash."

7 African-American author Zora Neale Hurston offered this color scale for blacks: "high yaller, yaller, high brown, vaseline brown, seal brown, low brown, dark brown." The use of the word "yellow" (or "yaller") for light-skinned African-Americans is reflected in the song "Yellow Rose of Texas," referring to a mixed-race servant girl who, according to legend, distracted Mexican Gen. Santa Ana with her charms, contributing to his defeat at the battle of San Jacinto in 1836.

8 Former Soviet President Mikhail Gorbachev and supermodel Cindy Crawford have something in common: prominent birthmarks. Crawford's mole and Gorbachev's port-wine stain are just two forms of the skin discoloration that affects about 1 in 3 infants. Birthmarks come in two types: pigment (light-brown cafe au lait spots, dark-brown moles and gray or blue Mongolian spots) or vascular (port-wine stains, stork bites and hemangioma). Scientists don't know what causes birthmarks.

9 The first European references to Asians as "yellow" have been traced to the late 1600s and probably had nothing to do with skin color. They appear linked to the fact that the Chinese embraced yellow as a symbol of grandeur. By 1904, the color had a far scarier tinge when American adventure writer Jack London wrote an essay called "The Yellow Peril." But even London didn't think all Asians were yellow. He warned that the Western world would be threatened if "millions of yellow men" from China came under the control of "the little brown man" from Japan.

10 Actor George Hamilton said he had an "epiphany" as a young man: "Suntanning was going to be to me what the phone booth, funny blue suit and cape were to Superman. Without a tan, I was just another paleface in the crowd. With one, I could do some pretty amazing things."

10 THINGS YOU MIGHT NOT KNOW ABOUT

BEARDS

1 Peter the Great, enamored of Western ways, encouraged cleanshavenness among Russians by imposing a tax on beards. Noblemen paid 100 rubles a year for a medallion that served as a beard license and carried the inscription: "The beard is a useless burden."

2 Talk about being "in the cross hairs." In the early '60s, the CIA plotted to ruin Cuban dictator Fidel Castro's image by making his beard fall out. One idea was to grab his shoes when they were put out to be shined, and to insert thallium salts, used by women as a depilatory. But the plot was never carried out.

3 Members of the rock trio ZZ Top are known for their facial hair, but only two of the three main band members sport beards. The third, who is mustachioed, is Frank Beard.

4 Pogonotomy is a $10 word for shaving. (The other side of that razor is: pogonotrophy, the growing of a beard.)

5 The ancient Egyptians wore fake metallic beards in front of their faces to mark special occasions, such as solar eclipses. These hairpieces, called postiches, adorned the faces of men and women.

6 Brigham Young University's dress code states: "Men are expected to be cleanshaven; beards are not acceptable." But BYU will make "a beard exception for medical reasons." If you're wondering whether the school's namesake, Mormon leader Brigham Young, ever wore a beard, the answer is: yes.

7 According to legend, the Christian daughter of the king of Portugal was commanded to marry the pagan king of Sicily. Instead, she prayed to God to disfigure her so the plans would be scuttled and she could remain a virgin. Those prayers were answered—she grew a

> *"You would look a great deal better [with a beard], for your face is so thin."* —11-YEAR-OLD GRACE BEDELL TO ABRAHAM LINCOLN

beard and lost a fiance. Her angry father had her crucified. The bearded virgin became known as Wilgefortis, the patron saint of unhappily married women.

8 Two well-known beards were Linda Lee Thomas and Phyllis Gates. They were married, respectively, to gay celebrities Cole Porter and Rock Hudson. The term "beard" describes someone who poses as the lover of a closeted homosexual. But it's also slang for someone who places a bet for a horse trainer. Among other beard-related slang: a "crimea" is a small beard; a "doorknocker" is a beard running just below the jawline. And if people say you have "a crumb in your beard," it might mean they think you're drunk.

9 Before Sir Thomas More was beheaded in 1535, he moved his lengthy beard aside, saying it "had never committed any treason."

10 Abraham Lincoln grew a beard in late 1860 after getting advice from an 11-year-old New York girl named Grace Bedell, who wrote, "You would look a great deal better, for your face is so thin." After Lincoln became the first bearded U.S. president, the Illustrated News of New York made a bogus claim that the president had used a hair-growing product called Bellingham's Stimulating Onguent, and "with this extraordinary paste he soon started the manly adornment." Bellingham's just happened to be an Illustrated News advertiser.

CHAPTER 3
Controversies & Ideas

GUNS

1 Around Christmas 1928, Ernest Hemingway came home to Oak Park, Ill., to attend his father's funeral and asked his mother if he could have the .32-caliber Smith & Wesson revolver that his father had used to kill himself. A few months later, Hemingway's mother sent him the handgun, along with a chocolate cake.

2 In October 2016, a Gallup survey found that about four in 10 Americans say a gun is kept in their home. That statistic has wavered up or down only about 10 percentage points since Gallup first asked the question in 1959. Gallup reported in 2011 that demographic groups that topped 50 percent included men, Republicans, Southerners, Midwesterners and people who had not gone to college.

3 In the infamous Valentine's Day Massacre, Al Capone's henchmen wielded Tommy guns, but the weapon's use by 1920s gangsters likely wasn't as extensive as popular culture and movies would lead us to believe. The gun was quite difficult to use and was dangerous to the shooter if he or she wasn't properly trained. A hooligan with a heavy trigger finger could empty one of those infamous 100-round drums in just four seconds.

4 Clement Vallandigham, a former Ohio congressman, served as an attorney in 1871 defending a suspect accused of a barroom murder. Vallandigham theorized that the victim had in fact shot himself by accident while trying to pull a handgun out of his pants pocket. Conferring with colleagues in a hotel room, Vallandigham acted out his theory. He believed he was using an unloaded gun in his demonstration; he was wrong. But he was right about a gun going off accidentally; it did, and it killed him.

5 The Minie ball, developed by French officer Claude-Etienne Minie about a decade before the American Civil War, greatly increased the effective range of rifles. But some veterans failed to understand how warfare had changed. Just before Union Gen. John Sedgwick was fatally shot by a faraway sniper near the Spotsylvania Courthouse, he uttered his last words: "They couldn't hit an elephant at this distance."

6 John F. Kennedy was a member of the National Rifle Association.

7 It should be no surprise that the biggest gun ever built was created for the Nazi war machine. Krupp A.G.'s Gustav was truly a monster, weighing in at 1,344 tons, including its railway carriage. At four stories tall and 140 feet long, it required a 500-man crew. It could throw a 5-ton explosive shell 29 miles or an 8-ton concrete-piercing shell 23 miles. It was built to demolish France's famed Maginot line, but the German blitzkrieg rendered the Gustav irrelevant for that task. It was eventually used against the Soviets to wicked effect before it was captured by the Americans and cut up for scrap.

8 John Moses Browning designed a staggering number of famous guns, including the lever-action Winchester repeating rifle, the Browning automatic rifle (BAR), used by the U.S. military in every major conflict from World War I to Vietnam, and the Colt .45. The son of a gunsmith, Browning was 14 when he built his first firearm, a rifle he gave to his brother.

9 Two Australian swimmers were barred in June 2012 by that country's Olympic officials from using social media during the London Games after the pair posted photos of themselves posing with pistols and rifles at a gun shop. Not only that, but Nick D'Arcy and Kenrick Monk were forced to leave the Games early after they finished their events. It's unclear if athletes competing in the 15 medal events involving shooting would face the same punishment.

10 Some gun inventors, such as Richard Gatling and Mikhail Kalashnikov, have expressed regrets about their legacies. Gatling felt that his machine gun took attention away from his work on more peaceful innovations, such as seed drills and steam-driven plows. Kalashnikov, the AK-47 creator who died in 2013, was proud that his invention helped Russia defend itself but said "when I see (Osama) bin Laden on television with his Kalashnikov, I'm disgusted." And he admitted: "I wish I had invented a lawn mower."

"I wish I had invented a lawn mower."
—MIKHAIL KALASHNIKOV

IMMIGRATION

1 A staggering 630 million people worldwide would move to another country if given the chance, according to a 2013 Gallup poll. And nearly a quarter of them would choose to come to the United States. So if the U.S. opened its borders, who would show up? About 19 million Chinese, 13 million Nigerians and 10 million Indians. (Not everybody wants to live here. Count among them as many as 6.8 million Americans who live abroad, according to the State Department.)

2 On the first Monday of March, Illinois' schoolchildren stay home to honor Casimir Pulaski, a Polish nobleman and Revolutionary War hero who is considered the father of American cavalry. But the more appropriate Polish horseman to honor might be Peter Kiolbassa. After fighting in the Civil War, he settled in Chicago, where he helped found St. Stanislaus Kostka Church. The Catholic parish, which at one time reportedly was the largest in the United States with about 45,000 members, was the heart of a large and influential Polish community that re-shaped Chicago in many ways. In fact, the Kennedy Expressway jogs east at Division Street to steer clear of the impressive structure.

3 Illegal immigration from Mexico dominates the news, but Mexicans also are far and away the largest group of legal immigrants to the U.S. In 2010-2015, more than 850,000 Mexicans became legal permanent residents. That dwarfs the next largest group: mainland Chinese, with about 462,000

4 U.S.-born children of immigrants are more likely to graduate from college than Americans as a whole, according to a Pew Research Center analysis.

5 It is an enduring but erroneous view that immigrants to the U.S. have almost always stayed. During a five-year period in the Great Depression, 120,000 immigrants arrived and 260,000 left. One study of pre-1930 immigration showed that Jews and Irish were most likely to stay (a remigration rate of less than 1 in 8), while 87 percent of those in the "Bulgarian/Montenegrin/Serbian" category went back.

6 Film director/writer Billy Wilder fled Nazi Germany and got a temporary U.S. visa to work on a movie, but it expired and he left—for Mexicali, Mexico, where he tried to persuade the U.S. consul to let him back into the country even though he lacked the proper documents. He recalled the consul asking, "What do you do?" and him answering, "I write movies." The consul stamped his passport and said, "Write some good ones." When Wilder accepted the Irving Thalberg award, in 1988, he thanked that unnamed U.S. official in Mexicali.

7 One of the most infamous mass deportations in American history occurred during the Great Depression. In response to economic hardship, U.S. officials rounded up hundreds of thousands of Hispanics and shipped them to Mexico. Thousands were U.S. citizens who were denied a chance to appeal their deportation.

8 "If as a nation we have the right to keep out infectious diseases . . . we surely have the right to exclude that immigration which reeks of impurity and which cannot come to us without plenteously sowing the seeds of moral and physical disease, destitution and death," said Sen. James Blaine, R-Maine, in making an astoundingly offensive case for the Fifteen Passenger Bill of 1879, which would have turned away ships with more than 15 Chinese on board. That bill was vetoed, but three years later the Chinese Exclusion Act was passed and signed, leading to severe limits on Chinese immigration for 60 years—until the U.S. eased up to placate World War II ally China.

9 One of Chicago's most famous immigrants was also the nation's first saint: Mother Frances Xavier Cabrini. After coming to the U.S. from Italy in 1889, she opened scores of hospitals, schools, nurseries and other institutions to help the poor and sick. Mother Cabrini died in Chicago on Dec. 22, 1917, and was canonized in 1946. In 1950, she was proclaimed the patron saint of immigrants.

10 Could Bill Clinton immigrate to France and quickly become its leader? The American ex-president raised the purely theoretical possibility in an interview, asserting that he could be fast-tracked into French politics because he was born in a place that was once part of the French Empire—Arkansas. But even if the relevant provision of French law applied to the lands of the Louisiana Purchase (and some doubt it), the French closed the loophole in 2006.

MARIJUANA

1 In 19th century Nepal, the marijuana harvest was performed by men who ran naked through fields of flowering plants and then had the sticky resin scraped off their bodies and formed into bricks of hashish.

2 Marijuana is known for its mellowing effect, but it has fueled many warriors in history. The word "assassin" is believed to come from the hashish used a millennium ago by Middle Eastern killers (called "hashshashin" or "hashish eaters"), though some historians doubt they were under the influence while on their missions. Mexican bandit Pancho Villa's henchmen were pot smokers. And some believe Zulu fighters in southern Africa were high on dagga—aka marijuana—when they attacked the Boers at Blood River in 1838. The Zulus lost 3,000 fighters, while only four Boers were wounded. Talk about a buzzkill.

3 Louisa May Alcott, author of "Little Women," wrote a short story called "Perilous Play" about marijuana. In it, a character declares, "If someone does not propose a new and interesting amusement, I shall die of ennui!" Another character produces a box of hashish-laced bonbons, and hedonism ensues.

4 Around 1900, the U.S. government briefly grew marijuana along a stretch of the Potomac River to study the plant's medicinal value. A more potent plant has since risen on that site: the Pentagon.

5 A white Chicago jazz musician named Milton "Mezz" Mezzrow moved to Harlem in 1929, declared himself a "voluntary Negro," and began selling marijuana. Known as "The Man Who Hipped the World" and "The Link Between the Races," Mezzrow sold fat joints called mezzrolls. Soon a new piece of Harlem slang emerged: Something genuine was described as "mezz."

6 Marijuana interferes with short-term memory so that users forget what they just said or did. Not only that, marijuana interferes with short-term memory so that users forget what they just said or did.

7 Billy Carter, the late brother of former President Jimmy Carter, believed the illegality of marijuana was part of its attraction. "Marijuana is like Coors beer," he said. "If you could buy the damn stuff at a Georgia filling station, you'd decide you wouldn't want it."

8 Before Congress voted to ban marijuana in 1937, the birdseed industry got the bill amended to exempt marijuana seeds (known as hemp seeds) as long as they were sterilized and could not be used to grow plants. An industry spokesman denied that the seeds made birds high, but an ardent marijuana foe, Dr. Victor Robinson, had previously written that the seeds had caused birds to "dream of a happy birdland where there are no gilded cages, and where the men are gunless and the women hatless."

9 One of the least typical supporters of the decriminalization of marijuana was conservative icon William F. Buckley, who died in 2008. Buckley once sailed his yacht into international waters so that he could smoke pot without breaking U.S. laws.

10 Former President Bill Clinton said famously that he smoked marijuana but "didn't inhale." Former President George W. Bush never admitted taking the drug, but his drug use was strongly suggested in recorded conversations between him and a friend—the interestingly named Doug Wead. Two of the top 2008 presidential contenders, Hillary Clinton and John McCain, denied that they had ever smoked pot. Barack Obama, on the other hand, said, "When I was a kid, I inhaled frequently. That was the point."

"When I was a kid, I inhaled frequently. That was the point." —BARACK OBAMA

C*NS*RSH*P

1 Some call it the "Great Firewall of China"—the Beijing government's attempts to quash dissent on the internet. In June 2012, on the 23rd anniversary of the Tiananmen Square massacre, the Shanghai stock market index dropped 64.89—reminiscent of the massacre's date: 6/4/89. Chinese censors already had banned "6/4" and even "5/35," which is dissidents' attempt to evade the censors by referring to the massacre date as the 35th of May. After the suspicious stock drop, Chinese authorities added "Shanghai stock exchange" to their list of banned phrases.

2 Tweety Bird, the animated Looney Tunes character, was originally pink. But censors complained that Tweety looked naked, so animators gave the bird yellow feathers.

3 The original Roman censor not only counted heads, but also upheld the public morality. The censor assessed property and decided what standing his fellow citizens would have in the state. In addition, a man had to conduct himself as befitted a Roman. If he didn't—as decided by the censor—the man's rights as a citizen could be curtailed. The censor quickly became a very powerful and feared figure.

4 The city of Chicago has censored thousands of movies. Beginning in 1907, a government censor, usually a police officer but in many years a member of a civilian board, could order new wording for subtitles (in the silent era) or the removal of specific scenes before a film could be shown to the public. In 1913, "The Miracle" was banned because it depicted "murder, drunkenness and immorality, and is insulting to religion." In 1934, it was revealed that Mayor Edward Kelly ordered that scenes showing mob violence be stricken from movies—and newsreels—because it is "not educational" and has a "bad effect on immature minds." Chicago didn't kill the Police Department's Film Review Section until 1984.

5 For financial reasons, artists sometimes censor themselves. Such was the case with Richard Wright and "Native Son" in 1940. The influential Book of the Month Club told Wright it would select the Chicago novelist's work as its first by an African-American—if he would downplay the lust of the white female victim and tone down other sexual aspects of the story. Wright agreed and bought a house with his earnings.

6 The Marx Brothers' 1931 film "Monkey Business" was banned in Ireland, whose censors feared the film would provoke the Irish to anarchy. For reasons that are unclear, Latvian censors took their scissors to the Marx Brothers' 1935 movie "A Night at the Opera," removing a scene where Harpo makes a sandwich out of Groucho's cigar.

7 Anthony Comstock, founder of the New York Society for the Suppression of Vice, was the namesake for the 1873 Comstock Act, which empowered U.S. postal authorities to ban obscene materials—including information on birth control. Comstock once took credit for the conviction of 3,600 people and the destruction of 160 tons of obscene material.

8 A prominent modern example of attempted censorship through violence was the radical-Muslim campaign to threaten Danish journalists who published cartoons of the Prophet Muhammad. But intolerance of Muslims inspired one of history's most famous quotes about censorship: "Wherever they burn books they will also, in the end, burn human beings." That's from German-Jewish writer Heinrich Heine's 1821 play "Almansor," in reference to the Spanish Inquisition's burning of the Quran. (Heine's books, of course, were burned by the Nazis.)

> "Wherever they **BURN BOOKS** they will also, in the end, burn **HUMAN BEINGS**."
> —HEINRICH HEINE, "ALMANSOR"

9 One of the most extensive and long-lasting efforts to censor books was undertaken by the Catholic Church, which from the mid-16th century until 1966 forbade books it deemed heretical or immoral. As you would expect, some people turned to the index, as it was called, to see what to read.

10 Did you know that --- --- --- --- flying pigs --- --- --- --- kumquats --- --- --- --- ---?

JURIES

1 One of the longest jury deliberations in a U.S. civil trial occurred in Guam in 2001—and 2002. It took 14 months for jurors to sort out the liability for a hotel collapse during an earthquake. Their deliberations seemed so open-ended that at one point they requested a refrigerator.

2 Before Chicago lawyer Clarence Darrow reached the zenith of his fame with the Leopold-Loeb case and the Scopes monkey trial, his career was nearly destroyed because of two charges of juror bribery in a California case. Luckily for Darrow, he had a good attorney—himself. On the first charge, he gave such an emotional closing argument that many of the jurors wept, and they acquitted him in about half an hour. In the second case, a mistrial was declared, and the charge ultimately was dropped. Even so, many historians believe Darrow indeed tried to bribe jurors in that case.

3 Sometimes a jury summons is an invitation to party. In a 1981 mail fraud and conspiracy trial, jurors regularly drank beer and downed carafes of wine at lunch. Two others took cocaine. During the trial, some slept. When lawyers complained, the judge responded, "If the jurors are sleeping, that's your problem." The Supreme Court upheld the conviction. In Tanner v. United States, the justices ruled 5-4 that the drugs and alcohol were not an improper "outside influence" and didn't constitute jury misconduct.

4 President Barack Obama was called for Cook County jury duty in early 2010 but got out of it. He had another important duty scheduled that week—the State of the Union address.

5 The first woman to receive a jury summons was a schoolteacher named Eliza Stewart in 1870 in the Wyoming Territory, which had just granted women the right to vote. According to the March 22, 1919, edition of The Woman Citizen magazine, Laramie at the time was beset by a "mass of depraved humanity and desperate characters," and the town's menfolk asked the women to serve on juries to help "put down the anarchy."

6 Imagine facing the judgment of 500 of your peers. That's how many jurors were estimated to have assessed the guilt of Socrates, who was accused of impiety and corrupting the youths of Athens. The jury favored conviction on a split vote, 280-220, but that was enough to order up a cup of hemlock for the great philosopher.

7 Teamsters union leader Jimmy Hoffa was convicted of jury tampering in 1964, but apparently that didn't teach him a lesson. On appeal, his defense team produced affidavits from three prostitutes who claimed they had sex with the judge and some jurors during the trial. That didn't go over so well. Hoffa went to jail, and the women were convicted of perjury.

8 One of Jim Crow's most powerful weapons was the all-white jury. In the Scottsboro Boys case, nine young African-Americans were charged in 1931 with raping two white women, a capital offense in Alabama. Through multiple trials and despite one of the women admitting she made it all up, juries found the defendants guilty. Even after the Supreme Court, in Norris v. Alabama, overturned Clarence Norris' conviction on the grounds that all-white juries were unconstitutional, Norris was found guilty at another jury trial riddled with suspect testimony. He ended up serving 15 years in prison for a crime that never happened. He won a pardon in 1976.

9 Despite what you might read or see in some movies, Judge James Wilkerson didn't dramatically order the bailiff to swap juries before Al Capone's tax evasion trial. If he did, the reporters from the Chicago Tribune, Chicago Daily News and Chicago Herald-Examiner missed it or decided it wasn't worth mentioning. Instead, Wilkerson quietly had the jury pools swapped. The source of the confusion probably is Frank Wilson, an Internal Revenue agent who did most of the investigative work that sealed Capone's fate and who went on to lead the Secret Service. Some 28 years after the trial, his "as-told-to" account propagated the more theatrical tale. A 1936 Tribune story headlined "I was a Capone juror" explains how the jury pools were switched before the trial started.

10 For about 50 cents, a Chicagoan in the '30s could legally buy his way onto a "jury." A section of the Wrigley Field bleachers jutting into left center field was nicknamed "the jury box" because it looked like one. But it would take eight more decades for the Cubs to fully acquit themselves with a World Series victory in 2016.

1968

1 When the Mexico City Olympics is mentioned, many Americans think first of the black power salute given by Tommie Smith and John Carlos on the victory stand. Fewer may remember the massacre of unarmed student protesters in Mexico City's Tlatelolco area just 10 days before the Games. The Olympics went on as the government downplayed the incident, saying protesters in a plaza shot first and police and troops fired back, killing four. Documents released long afterward indicate that government snipers were first to fire, triggering gunshots by the police and troops. At least 40 deaths were documented; some activists believe the toll was much higher.

2 Firsts this year included: the 911 emergency telephone system, the Big Mac, Hot Wheels toy cars, "60 Minutes," "Mister Rogers' Neighborhood," the first heart transplant in the U.S.—and the computer mouse.

3 Many beloved cultural symbols were besieged, including the barber pole. In November 1968, an Evanston, Ill., building inspector ordered the poles removed, saying they violated city rules requiring that business signs not revolve or hang less than 10 feet from the ground. Barbers lodged a protest, and a City Council committee later backed a waiver.

4 The Chicago Tribune was obsessed with miniskirts in 1968, mentioning them in more than 200 articles. Headlines included "Library Artist, 23, is Fired; Puts Blame on Her Mini-skirt"; "Nurse Rips Off Skirt, Saves 2 Boys in Fire"; and "What They Wear Under Mini-Skirts," an article that was primarily about pantyhose.

5 How crazy was 1968? The U.S. lost a nuclear bomb, and it might not crack the top 25 biggest stories of the year. In January, a B-52 loaded with four 1.1-megaton hydrogen bombs, conventional armaments and a full load of fuel crashed onto the sea ice off the Greenland coast, setting off a massive fireball. The safety triggers prevented a thermonuclear blast, but H-bomb parts and the radioactive elements were widely scattered. Despite a huge cleanup effort in the

How crazy was 1968? The U.S. **lost a nuclear bomb,** *and it might not crack the top 25 biggest stories of the year.*

ice and snow that work crews dubbed "Dr. Freezelove," classified documents released in the 1990s revealed that one of the H-bomb assemblies and as much as half of the plutonium was probably never recovered.

6 G, M, R or X became part of the movie-going public's vocabulary with the introduction of the voluntary movie rating system. Parents were confused by M for mature versus R for restricted, so M pretty quickly morphed into PG. One of the movies to challenge the previous rules and bring about the now-famous letters was the 1966 Elizabeth Taylor-Richard Burton classic "Who's Afraid of Virginia Woolf?" What language was deemed scandalous in the late 1960s? "Friggin'," "screw you" and "hump the hostess."

7 The America of 1968 was more violent than the America of the early 21st century, with a significantly higher homicide rate. In the June week when Sen. Robert Kennedy was assassinated, a Dallas man was fatally shot while golfing; a New Orleans cop went berserk and wounded two officers before shooting himself to death; and Chicago police Officer Edward Simanek was shot and partly paralyzed. The second most famous gunshot victim of that week was Andy Warhol, who was wounded by a disturbed writer in New York two days before the RFK tragedy.

8 Alexander Dubcek, the Czechoslovakian leader whose reform movement triggered a Soviet military crackdown in August 1968, was the son of Chicagoans and nearly a Chicagoan himself. Dubcek's parents were Slovak immigrants who met, married and conceived Alexander in Chicago before returning to Europe, where he was born.

9 In November 1968, U.S. television went where no man had gone before when Capt. James T. Kirk, played by William Shatner, kissed Lt. Uhura, African-American actress Nichelle Nichols, on "Star Trek." That first scripted interracial kiss between a white man and black woman was supposed to be with Leonard Nimoy as Spock, according to Nichols, but she said Shatner declared, "If anybody is going to kiss Uhura, it is going to be the captain."

10 On Dec. 10, 1968, four Japanese bank workers were riding in a car with 300 million yen in cash (the equivalent of $800,000 at the time) to be paid as bonuses to factory workers. A man in a police uniform stopped the car and told them their branch manager's house had been blown up and a bomb might be planted in their car. The four stepped out, and when smoke started pouring from underneath the car, they fled, leaving the money in the car. The uniformed man drove away in the car, leaving the remnants of a smoke bomb in the road. The crime has never been solved.

10 THINGS YOU MIGHT NOT KNOW ABOUT

FLAGS

1 Two of the most famous World War II photos depict flag-raisings, and both involve dishonesty for propaganda purposes. Joe Rosenthal's picture from Iwo Jima was not posed—despite rumors to the contrary—but it also was not the first flag raised on Mount Suribachi; it was the second. After Rosenthal's photo created a sensation, a general suppressed photos of the first flag-raising, preferring to leave a public misimpression. In the second case, the controversial image shows the Soviets' flag-raising over Germany's Reichstag. Photographer Yevgeny Khaldei traveled from Moscow with the flag in his luggage and set up the shot two days after the fall of Berlin. Later, the photo was retouched to darken the smoke and remove a watch from a soldier's wrist. Why would Soviet censors care about a watch? Because the soldier originally had one on each wrist, an indication he had been looting.

2 The study of flags is vexillology.

3 The Chicago flag's four stars represent Fort Dearborn, the Great Chicago Fire, the World's Columbian Exposition and the Century of Progress Exposition. There have been campaigns to add a fifth star to recognize the city's role in the nuclear age or to honor Mayor Richard J. Daley. A South Chicago family business, WGN Flag & Decorating, even sells five-star city flags. "My great-great-grandfather overheard some bigwigs talking about adding a star for Daley," and WGN quickly stocked a five-star flag, said company CEO Carl "Gus" Porter III. The Daley honor fell through, but those flags came in handy when there was talk of a fifth star if Chicago hosted the 2016 Olympics. WGN provided five-star flags as gifts for visiting Olympics officials, Porter said. But Chicago lost the Olympics anyway and remains a four-star city.

4 Fiji's flag features a dove, but several other flags sport symbols of war. An old West African flag shows one man beheading another. The flags of Kenya and Swaziland feature spears, while Angola's has a machete. Mozambique's banner includes a more modern weapon—an AK-47.

5 The U.S. Supreme Court ruled in 1989 that protester Gregory Lee Johnson was exercising his First Amendment rights when he burned an American flag. Weeks after the ruling, about a dozen congressmen heard a rumor that Johnson planned to burn a flag on the court steps, and they showed up with fire extinguishers and a bucket of water. Johnson stayed away, so the politicians sprayed and drenched an effigy of him. A reporter said it was "the first time someone was doused in effigy."

6 Every modern national flag is rectangular—except Nepal's. It boasts a double-decker triangle, called a double pavon.

7 The American Civil War was a very real, very bloody game of capture the flag. A regiment's colors were a point of pride; when the "boys rallied 'round the flag," it was more likely the regimental flag than the Stars and Stripes (or the Stars and Bars). The flag was heavily guarded because its capture or even a fall to the ground was unthinkable. Few incidents better illustrated its importance than the fight for the Sunken Road during the Battle of Antietam in Maryland in 1862, when no fewer than eight men in the Irish Brigade died carrying the New York regiment's distinctive green banner.

8 The half of the flag farthest from the pole is called the fly, and the outer edge is the fly edge.

9 The North American Vexillological Association offers guidelines for good flag design: Keep it simple, limit the colors, define the borders, don't use lettering or seals—and use smart, distinct symbols. Most U.S. state flags are notoriously bad. Illinois' complex flag violates most, if not all, of these tenets with its lettered, multicolored seal featuring a bald eagle and a rock—all anchorless on a white background.

10 In designating how long Old Glory should fly at half-staff to honor a deceased official, the U.S. Flag Code makes it perfectly clear how government officers stack up: 30 days for a president, but just 10 days for a vice president, a chief justice of the United States or a U.S. House speaker. A Cabinet secretary, high court justice or state governor should be honored from death until interment, according to the code. A member of Congress? Two days.

10 THINGS YOU MIGHT NOT KNOW ABOUT
UNIONS

1 Why is a labor stoppage called a "strike"? Because in 1768, English sailors unhappy about a wage cut expressed their anger by taking down, or striking, the sails on ships in the port of London.

2 The Air Line Pilots Association reached an agreement with National Airlines in the late 1940s after airline executive Ted Baker attended a religious retreat, came to a realization and called pilots to ask forgiveness, attributing the discord to the "power of Satan."

3 The "Yes, we can" slogan from Barack Obama's 2008 presidential campaign was far from original. Even Obama had used the phrase before—in his 2004 U.S. Senate race. Three decades earlier, the United Farm Workers union embraced the Spanish version, "Si se puede," as coined by UFW co-founder Dolores Huerta during Cesar Chavez's hunger strike in Arizona in 1972. In an apparent coincidence, "Yes, we can" also was a rallying cry for the Philadelphia Phillies in 1974.

4 Few Americans are aware of the Battle of Blair Mountain, one of the largest civil uprisings in U.S. history. In 1921, a coal-mining strike in West Virginia led to the 10-day clash pitting at least 7,000 armed miners against about 3,000 deputies, hired guns and volunteers. Federal troops stopped the fighting after a death toll estimated at 30 to 100 miners and 10 to 30 on the other side. The situation was so serious that bomber planes under Gen. Billy Mitchell were deployed. Asked how he would subdue the miners, he said: "Gas. You understand, we wouldn't try to kill people at first." In the end, Mitchell's planes performed only reconnaissance, but private aircraft did drop homemade bombs.

5 About 14.6 million or 10.7 percent of all U.S. workers were members of a union in 2016, but the percentage of public-sector employees carrying a union card was 34.4 percent. Overall union membership peaked in the mid-1950s but never topped 35 percent.

6 A Chicago union official named Angelo Inciso was interviewed by a U.S. Senate subcommittee in the mid-1950s about why he spent $1,200 in union funds for a men's diamond ring. The labor boss said the ring was a reward to a union ally, and he didn't get rank-and-file approval because that would have taken too long and the jewelry would have gone "out of style." Inciso also took a union-paid overseas trip that he called a "goodwill tour," prompting a question from the subcommittee: "To whom were you spreading goodwill?" His answer: "Myself."

7 Famed African-American labor leader A. Philip Randolph almost became an actor. In his early 20s, Randolph played parts in Shakespeare's "Othello," "Hamlet" and "The Merchant of Venice," but when he wrote his parents that he'd gotten a break in Harlem theater, his African Methodist Episcopal preacher father told him to forget it. And he did. Instead, Randolph went into politics and labor activism, becoming head of the Pullman Porters union.

8 The Nordic countries of Iceland, Finland, Sweden, Denmark and Norway are five of the six most unionized nations in the world, according to 2012 data. A whopping 82.6 percent of Iceland's workers are members of a union.

9 Chicago has hosted huge Labor Day parades. On Sept. 1, 1902, more than 46,000 laborers in more than 200 unions marched in a procession that took five hours to pass the reviewing stand. The Chicago Tribune listed 86 trades, including gravel roofers, elevator constructors, steamfitters, boxmakers, hat finishers, soda water bottlers, chandelier makers, bakers, granite carvers, cracker packers, barbers, mosaic tile layers, longshoremen, sign painters, egg inspectors and bootblacks.

10 The skilled artisans at Deir el-Medina working for Pharaoh Ramesses III didn't receive their wages as expected one month in 1158 B.C., so they walked off the job and into history with what is commonly considered the first recorded labor action. The pharaoh, a militaristic ruler who enjoyed cutting off the penises of enemy captives, scrambled to appease the workers. Why? The artisans were building his tomb. As it turns out, ensuring that your boss can safely pass into eternal life puts you in a strong bargaining position.

10 THINGS YOU MIGHT NOT KNOW ABOUT
DEFECTIVE PRODUCTS

1 The folks who brought us Reddi-wip whipped cream had another brainstorm in the 1960s: Reddi-Bacon. Precooked and put in foil packaging, Reddi-Bacon was supposed to be dropped into the toaster and heated. But consumers complained that the packages leaked, posing a fire hazard. Reddi-Bacon was pulled after test marketing.

2 A Scottish shop assistant named May Donoghue went to a cafe in 1928, and a friend bought her an ice cream float with ginger beer. She drank some, and when the rest of the bottle was poured into her glass, she complained that it included a decomposed snail. Treated by a doctor for shock and stomach pain, Donoghue sued the bottler. The controversial case went all the way to the House of Lords, which ruled that the bottler had a duty of care, establishing a key legal point about negligence. The case was ultimately settled out of court, with no legal proof that the snail ever existed, and some doubt that it did.

3 The Consumer Product Safety Commission has the authority to issue a mandatory recall, but that entails a lengthy legal battle—time when the product remains on the market. Officials have another arrow in their quiver: the "unilateral announcement." Though just a news release, it alerts consumers, puts merchants on notice and shames the obstinate company.

That's what happened in August 2008 with certain Simplicity bassinets after the company "refused to cooperate and recall the products." The announcement prompted major retailers to pull the product.

4 The word "shoddy" was a term for woolen fluff thrown off in the textile manufacturing process that was gathered and recycled. But cloth made with shoddy was "short-stapled" and less durable. The use of "shoddy" as a more general negative description became popular during the Civil War when profiteers used too much shoddy in Yankee uniforms, causing them to wear out quickly.

5 In the era of patent medicines at the turn of the last century, remedies sold as nostrums, elixirs, salves and bitters were offered as cures to nearly every known ailment—including cancer, cholera, arthritis and syphilis. Most were just alcohol—or worse. Copp's Babies' Friend, marketed to parents to ease colic and teething, was sugar water and morphine.

6 Babylon's King Hammurabi commanded: If a homeowner's son is killed because of faulty construction, the homebuilder's son shall be put to death.

7 A stuck valve can mean that your basement gets flooded, or it can mean that Pennsylvania is threatened with nuclear catastrophe. The Three Mile Island nuclear plant accident near Harrisburg, Pa., occurred in 1979 after a relief valve stuck open, causing cooling water to drain away so that nuclear fuel overheated. On top of that, a design flaw in monitoring equipment misled control room staff into thinking the valve was closed. Radiation was released before the situation was brought under control. Research has found no major health impact from the accident, though long-term effects of radiation are not fully understood. One casualty was obvious: the nuclear energy industry.

8 According to a 2014 report by the Chicago-based advocacy group Kids in Danger, only 10 percent of children's products recalled in 2012 were corrected, replaced or returned.

9 During the 2013 trial over faulty breast implants manufactured by the French firm Poly Implant Prothese that affected as many as 500,000 women worldwide, a company engineer was asked how he figured out what mix of substances to use instead of medically approved silicone. He answered: "You use your best guess."

10 Sometimes what's defective about a product is its name or description. Target came under fire in 2013—and quickly apologized—for selling plus-size dresses in a color it called "manatee gray." The manatee is also known as the sea cow.

SECURITY MEASURES

1 Before the Sept. 11 attacks in 2001, hardly any American used the word "homeland." Yet President George W. Bush created the Department of Homeland Security, upsetting writers such as Peggy Noonan, who thought it sounded too Teutonic: "It summons images of men in spiked helmets lobbing pitchers of beer at outsiders during Oktoberfest." She and others unsuccessfully suggested Heartland Security, Homefront Security and Mainland Defense.

2 The moat is one of the earliest security measures and one of the smelliest, as it often became an open sewer for the castle residents.

3 Perhaps the biggest White House security breakdown of modern times occurred at President Barack Obama's first state dinner in November 2009. A gate-crashing couple, Michaele and Tareq Salahi, got through two checkpoints and greeted the president. Later the White House discovered there was a third gate-crasher, society blogger Carlos Allen, who walked in with guests from the Indian delegation who had been prescreened at a hotel.

4 Libyan leader Moammar Gadhafi was protected by an all-female group of bodyguards known by some as the Amazonian Guard and by others as the Revolutionary Nuns. The despot required the women to pledge virginity, dress in camouflage and wear nail polish and mascara. Why women as guards? Some think Gadhafi simply liked female companionship, but others believe he thought a would-be assassin would be less likely to shoot at him if he was surrounded by women.

5 The areas around new buildings often feature large sculptures and heavy benches. Such architecture blocks bomb-laden vehicles. The knee-level posts sticking up near building entrances serve the same purpose. They're called bollards. That word, also used for mooring posts at wharves, is believed to come from a Middle English word for tree trunk.

6 Romanian dictator Nicolae Ceausescu once upset Britain's Queen Elizabeth by bringing a food tester to dinner at Buckingham Palace. He regularly used a mobile chemical lab to check his meals for bacteria, poison or radioactivity, and preferred to travel with his own things to eat, keeping them in a locked cart, which had a code that changed every day.

7 The need to feel safe starts at an early age. Peanuts creator Charles Schulz coined the term "security blanket," in reference to Linus' blue flannel cloth. The blanket, which almost became a character of its own in the strip, wasn't just emotional support. On at least one occasion, Linus used it like a whip to show he wasn't helpless.

8 Indian Prime Minister Indira Gandhi's bloody crackdown on Sikh separatists at the Golden Temple in Amritsar caused so much enmity that she started wearing a bulletproof vest. But on an October morning in 1984, she skipped the vest because she wanted to look good for a television interview with British actor Peter Ustinov. Walking to meet Ustinov, she was shot by two of her bodyguards who were exacting revenge for the temple attack.

9 An inventive Canadian marijuana grower turned to a plentiful local resource to discourage anybody from snooping around his illegal crops. When police raided his British Columbia farm in August 2010, they were confronted by at least 10 black bears. Fortunately, they were quite mellow because they had been fed dog food to keep them around.

10 Homeland Security officials have started field-testing a screening process in which they use eye movements, breathing patterns and other physical indicators to identify people who have "mal-intent," or plans to do harm to others. Once known as Project Hostile Intent, it's now called Future Attribute Screening Technology Project. Such technology, if perfected, would be vital in identifying terrorists, and might have applications in regular crime prevention.

PRISON

1 In the late 1800s, Chicago businessmen purchased a former Confederate prison in Richmond, Va., dismantled it, shipped it to Chicago on 132 railroad cars and rebuilt it on Wabash Avenue from 14th to 16th streets. It became the Libby Prison War Museum but included non-Civil War items, such as the alleged "skin of the serpent that tempted Eve in the Garden of Eden." After about a decade, the old prison was torn down again, except for a castellated wall that became part of the new Chicago Coliseum. That arena, which hosted political conventions, the Blackhawks and even Jimi Hendrix, closed in the early 1970s.

2 The U.S. population has increased about 200 percent since 1920. The U.S. prison population has risen more than 1,900 percent.

3 In Bolivia's infamous San Pedro prison in La Paz, the 1,500 inmates have the run of the place. The guards generally stay outside the gates. The prisoners, who have to pay for their rooms, make money by selling groceries, working in food stalls, cutting hair, repairing TVs or radios and peddling drugs. The inmates also handle their own disputes, which leads to about four deaths a month, officials say. More disturbing: About 100 children—boys and girls—live in the prison with their fathers, a common practice in Bolivia.

4 Some prisons are nicer than others. Case in point: the Justice and Detention Centre in Leoben, Austria. Inmates of the facility, completed in 2005, enjoy amenities many law-abiding individuals would envy, such as floor-to-ceiling windows, private restrooms, balconies and a common room with a kitchenette. During the 2008 U.S. presidential campaign, photographs of the deluxe prison made the rounds on the internet posing as a new Cook County jail under the headline, "Wow! Your Tax Dollars at Work"—and were blamed on then-Sen. Barack Obama.

5 Johnny Cash, famed for writing "Folsom Prison Blues" and performing for inmates, had some scrapes with the law but never served time in prison, contrary to popular myth.

"In fact, I've never served any time at all in any correctional institution anywhere," he wrote. "During my amphetamine years I spent a few nights in jail, but strictly on an overnight basis: seven incidents in all, different dates in different places where the local law decided we'd all be better off if I were under lock and key."

6 In 2012, former Illinois Gov. Rod Blagojevich began his 14-year sentence in a federal prison in Colorado, a state that may have more famous inmates than any other. While Blago is at the low-security Englewood facility, the Florence supermax about 100 miles south holds Sept. 11 plotter Zacarias Moussaoui, Ted "The Unabomber" Kaczynski, FBI turncoat spy Robert Hanssen, Oklahoma City bomb plotter Terry Nichols, Olympics bomber Eric Rudolph and Richard "Shoe Bomber" Reid.

7 When Mohandas Gandhi was held at Yeravda prison for threatening the British occupation of India, he gave "prison food" a whole new meaning. He promised his mother he would always drink goat's milk instead of cow's milk, so authorities arranged for a goat to be brought into his cell and milked in his presence.

8 "The land of the free" has a bigger share of its population behind bars than any other country except the tiny Indian Ocean nation of Seychelles. According to the International Centre for Prison Studies, more than 660 U.S. residents per 100,000 are imprisoned, compared to 436 per 100,000 in Russia, 510 in Cuba, 192 in Mexico and 114 in Canada. India's incarceration rate (33) is less than one-20th the U.S. rate.

9 People in prison have run for president (Socialist Eugene Debs, winning 913,664 votes in 1920), found the inspiration to write a classic (Miguel de Cervantes' "Don Quixote") and assembled a collection of more than 70,000 four-leaf clovers (Pennsylvania kidnapper George Kaminski).

10 Popular history has it that the Bastille was stormed on July 14, 1789, to free prisoners being held by the tyrannical Louis XVI. Not quite. The Parisian mob actually needed gunpowder for the muskets it had commandeered earlier that day. While it may be true that liberating the inhabitants was a secondary goal, just seven people were confined there, and two were quickly recaptured and moved to an insane asylum.

10 THINGS YOU MIGHT NOT KNOW ABOUT
FOX NEWS

1 When former Fox News host Greta Van Susteren's parents got married, their best man was Sen. Joseph McCarthy, the Wisconsin politician whose demagoguery in the 1950s inspired the term "McCarthyism."

2 Megyn Kelly, who rose to prominence on Fox before moving to NBC in 2017, was rejected by Syracuse University's communications program, so she majored in political science instead. Now she reportedly makes as much as $20 million a year in the communications business.

3 While many people on Fox News denounce immigrants who become criminals, the network itself is named after an immigrant who became a criminal. Wilhelm Fuchs was born in Hungary to German parents and arrived in the U.S. as a baby. With the Americanized name of William Fox, he went into the movie business in 1904 but ran into financial difficulties, lost control of Fox Films, tried to bribe his bankruptcy judge and served six months in prison. His former company became part of the 20th Century Fox empire that ultimately included Fox News.

4 Fox News personalities have some interesting marital connections. Chris Wallace is married to the ex-wife of comedian Dick Smothers. Kimberly Guilfoyle was first lady of San Francisco when Gavin Newsom was mayor, but they have since divorced. Geraldo Rivera has been married five times. Wife No. 2 was novelist Kurt Vonnegut's daughter, and the author once wrote a letter describing Rivera as a "closet Marxist."

5 Among the Fox luminaries from Illinois are John Stossel, born in Chicago Heights, and Chicago natives Eric Bolling and Chris Wallace. Bolling attended Loyola Academy in Wilmette, where he was known for his baseball prowess. Critics of Fox News may remember Bolling best as the host who joked about a woman in the military as "boobs on the ground." (He apologized.)

6 A Pew Research Center analysis found that during the later stages of the 2012 presidential race between Barack Obama and Mitt Romney, 46 percent of Fox News stories about

Obama were negative and only 6 percent were positive. But liberal competitor MSNBC was even more lopsided toward Romney—71 percent negative and 3 percent positive. CNN was in the middle but also tougher on Romney, whose CNN coverage was 36 percent negative compared to Obama's 21 percent.

7 Former Fox host Bill O'Reilly, an Irish-American from Long Island, N.Y., and Juan Williams, an African-American journalist born in Panama, were on the radio in 2007 when their discussion caused a racial uproar. O'Reilly was talking about his visit to the Harlem restaurant Sylvia's with black activist Al Sharpton, saying he was pleasantly surprised that the restaurant's patrons behaved like white patrons. "There wasn't one person in Sylvia's who was screaming, 'MF-er, I want more iced tea,'" said O'Reilly. That drew outrage, but Williams came to O'Reilly's defense, saying O'Reilly's critics didn't want "an honest discussion about race."

8 Conversations about ethnicity have sometimes landed Fox News in trouble. Host Brian Kilmeade celebrated National Taco Day in 2013 by asking his Nicaraguan-born co-host Maria Molina, "You grew up on tacos, correct?" To which she answered that no, she didn't, because tacos aren't a native food in Nicaragua. In 2015, Fox guest Steven Emerson declared erroneously that Birmingham, England, was "totally Muslim, where non-Muslims just simply don't go in." British Prime Minister David Cameron said: "When I heard this, frankly, I choked on my porridge and I thought it must be April Fool's Day. This guy is clearly a complete idiot."

9 Fox host Tucker Carlson grew up in a prominent family. His father, Richard, was director of Voice of America and president of the Corporation for Public Broadcasting. Family dinner guests in La Jolla, Calif., included future Gov. Pete Wilson and Ted Geisel, aka Dr. Seuss. But what seemed to crystallize liberal annoyance with Carlson was not his background but his neckwear. Carlson wore a bow tie on the air until the ridicule became too much a decade ago and he switched to a standard necktie. "It took me 20 years to realize that wearing a bow tie is like wearing a middle finger around your neck," he told The New York Times.

10 In 2010, Sean Hannity's Fox News show played a video clip of Obama saying, "Taxes are scheduled to go up substantially next year, for everybody." Hannity credited Obama for his "rare moment of honesty," but critics didn't praise the honesty of Hannity's video editors. In fact, what Obama said was: "*Under the tax plan passed by the last administration,* taxes are scheduled to go up substantially next year, for everybody."

CHAPTER 4
Food & Drink

EXTREME EATING

1 For the daring gourmand, ordering fugu may be just the ticket. Popular in Japan, blowfish is considered a delicacy, despite the fact that its liver, blood and sex organs are packed with a poison many times deadlier than cyanide. So how will the connoisseur know if his latest meal is really his last supper? According to one veteran Japanese fugu chef: "If you're eating fugu and your lips turn numb, you're well on your way to being dead."

> If you're eating fugu and your lips turn numb, you're well on your way to being **DEAD**.

2 Alberto Santos-Dumont, a wealthy Brazilian aviation pioneer, hosted "aerial dinner parties" at his high-ceilinged Paris apartment around 1900. The meals took place at a 7-foot-high dinner table with matching chairs that were reached by using a ladder.

3 Few dishes exemplify America's Thanksgiving excess quite like six-legged turkeys. In 1990, announcers John Madden and Pat Summerall awarded a turkey leg to two stars of the traditional holiday football game and lamented they didn't have more legs to award. In stepped Joe Pat Fieseler, an Irving, Texas, restaurateur. In 1992, he affixed four extra legs to a turkey with wooden skewers, though he joked the birds were raised near a nuclear power plant. Some people didn't get the joke. "It is amazing the amount of mail we've gotten," said Summerall in 1998. "They think we're being cruel to animals by growing six-legged turkeys."

4 A particular population of killer whales in the northeastern Pacific loves to feast on shark liver—but only the liver. In one example, a pod of five orcas killed 11 sleeper sharks in one day, wasting most of the carcasses. Researchers suspect that these orcas eat so many shark livers, which naturally are encased in tough abrasive shark skin, that their teeth are ground down to the gum line.

5 Laffit Pincay, a horse-racing jockey watching his weight, took a plane trip from California to New York in 1982 and declined the in-flight dinner, opting instead for a single peanut. He ate half of it, waited for hours, then ate the other half.

6 According to the teachings of Pope Gregory I, the sin of gluttony is not simply eating too much. Gregory cited five ways in which gluttony is committed: eating too much, snacking between meals, eating with excessive eagerness, demanding a high quality of food and dining too elaborately, which is described in religious teachings as "seeking after sauces and seasonings for the sensual enjoyment of the palate."

7 Man Ray, an artist known for his avant-garde photographs, drank vast quantities of mineral water and orange juice in the 1930s as part of a fad diet in which he shunned potatoes and meat if he had eaten fruit on the same day.

8 Fletcherism was the practice developed by diet guru Horace Fletcher (1849-1919) of prolonged chewing of food to improve digestion and avoid overeating. According to conflicting reports, Fletcher advocated giving every bite 32 chews (one for each tooth) or 100 chews or simply chewing until the food was completely liquefied. Followers included writer Upton Sinclair and John Harvey Kellogg, the famed Battle Creek, Mich., health advocate. "Nature will castigate those who don't masticate," Fletcher famously said.

9 Plasmodium, the malaria parasite, can manipulate its host mosquito's eating behavior so that it limits its blood intake—thereby minimizing its risk of death—while the parasite matures. Then Plasmodium makes the mosquito really hungry, so much in fact that it risks certain death at the hand of an irate human, which is just fine for Plasmodium. It has already moved on to its human host.

10 The Rev. Thomas Baker, a Christian missionary, was killed and eaten by Fijian villagers in 1867. For more than a century afterward, villagers felt cursed by bad luck. In a 2003 ceremony, they gave woven mats, whales' teeth and a slaughtered cow to Baker's Australian relatives as reparations. No word on when the Fijians will make amends to the relatives of the whales and the cow.

HAMBURGERS

1 Americans eat an astounding 48 billion burgers a year, or about three per week per person. While burgers are pretty cheap, getting them to our table isn't. According to the Center for Investigative Reporting, 6.5 pounds of greenhouse gases are produced to make one tasty quarter-pounder. Over a year, that's equal to 34 coal-fired power plants. If you were willing to give up one burger a week, it would be like not driving your car 350 miles.

2 When amateur pilots say they're going for "a $100 hamburger," they mean they're taking a short jaunt for pleasure, often winding up at an airport restaurant. The $100 refers to the cost of fuel to get there, not the cost of the burger.

3 People frustrated with their careers might take comfort in the fact that McDonald's mogul Ray Kroc was a late bloomer who didn't get into the hamburger business until he was past age 50. Before that, the Oak Park, Ill., native was a soda fountain worker, ambulance driver, bordello piano player, stock-market board operator, cashier, paper cup salesman, radio DJ and milk-shake-mixer salesman.

4 The privately owned In-N-Out Burger chain is famous for discreetly printing Bible citations on its cups and burger wrappers. The company's image could have gone another way. The company chairman's older brother, Guy Snyder, had just received an order of T-shirts featuring an illustration of a girl sitting on top of the chain's famous Double-Double burger when the Bible idea was unveiled. The T-shirts never made it out of their boxes.

5 Investment guru Warren Buffett has an unusual health food regimen: "It's amazing what Cherry Coke and hamburgers will do for a fellow," he once wrote. The billionaire thinks broccoli, asparagus and Brussels sprouts look "like Chinese food crawling around on a plate," and adds: "I don't even want to be close to a rhubarb, it makes me want to retch." He especially hates it when one of those despised vegetables brushes up against his hamburger on a plate.

"It's amazing what Cherry Coke and hamburgers will do for a fellow." —WARREN BUFFETT

6 When British Prime Minister Gordon Brown visited the White House in 2008, President George W. Bush cited the hamburger as proof that they were getting along. "Look," Bush said, "if there wasn't a personal relationship, I wouldn't be inviting the man to (have) a nice hamburger. Well done, I might add."

7 Marty's Hamburger Stand in west Los Angeles is "home of the combo"—that's a hamburger and sliced hot dog on the same bun.

8 One of the most memorable battles of the Vietnam War was the U.S. assault on Ap Bia Mountain, aka Hill 937, aka "Hamburger Hill." Gen. William Westmoreland refused to use the slang name, which was coined by his troops. The common explanation is that the hill got that name because the attack was a "meat-grinder," with heavy casualties. Others note the similarity to the Korean War's Battle of Pork Chop Hill, another vicious battle with little strategic significance.

9 The White Castle hamburger franchise, which claims to be the oldest, originated in Wichita, Kan., but it has a Chicago connection—its buildings were loosely modeled after the Water Tower on North Michigan Avenue.

10 In the quirky slang of short-order cooks, a hamburger was known as "choked beef" and "a grease spot." To cook one was to "brand a steer," and to add a slice of onion was to "pin a rose" on it. A less cheery term came from U.S. prisons, where a hamburger was known as a "Gainesburger," named after Gaines-burgers dog food.

WINE

1 Wine was first produced about 8,000 years ago in the South Caucasus, according to scientists who tested residue from an ancient pottery shard dated to about 6,000 B.C. Which means history waited about 2,500 years before it saw its first drunken driver. The wheel wasn't invented until about 3,500 B.C.

2 Even in his wine drinking, President Richard Nixon was sneaky. He would offer run-of-the-mill wine to his guests while servers poured Chateau Margaux into his glass from a bottle wrapped with a towel or napkins to hide the label.

3 Wine grapes are a finicky bunch. A superb vintage requires a perfect mix of sun, soil and rain, which is why scientists say you'll be saying bye-bye to Bordeaux and Napa wines by as early as 2050 because global warming will push prime growing conditions elsewhere—to such wine hot spots as Britain, the Netherlands and the Yellowstone National Park area of the American West.

4 What do you call a leprechaunlike creature that likes to drink? It's a clurichaun. According to an Irish folk legend, clurichauns are fairies that hang out around the wine cellar, either guarding the stock or raiding it or both.

5 In the mid-1980s, about 36 million bottles of wine went undrunk, with their contents used instead to cool the ovens of a cement factory. Why? Because Austrian producers had adulterated their wines with a toxic substance, diethylene glycol, to sweeten it so it was more valuable. They got caught, and the wine was banned. No one died in the scandal, but the Austrian wine industry was badly injured.

6 Benjamin Franklin famously wrote in a lighthearted letter to a friend that wine is "a constant proof that God loves us." Later in the same letter, to further his point, he raises a

"[Wine is] a constant proof that God loves us."

—BENJAMIN FRANKLIN

toast to the elbow, so ingeniously designed as to allow the arm to bring a goblet of wine "exactly to the mouth," a sure sign of God's "benevolent wisdom."

7 Many people have likely seen or heard of a magnum of wine, equal to two regular bottles. But how about a Jeroboam (six), Salmanazar (12), a Balthazar (16) or the Nebuchadnezzar, the equivalent of 20 bottles? The larger bottles are prized for their rarity and also because the wine ages more slowly.

8 It wasn't William Sokolin's night. At a gathering of wine enthusiasts at the Four Seasons in Manhattan in April 1989, he was showing off a bottle of Chateau Margaux 1787. That vintage is worth a mint, but this bottle, etched with the initials "Th J," was believed to have come from Thomas Jefferson's own wine cellar. Sokolin said it was worth more than $519,000. Unfortunately, he accidentally hit the bottle against a table, breaking two holes into the back of the bottle. Wine gushed out. Horrified, he bolted from the restaurant with the broken bottle and went straight home. But his bad night wasn't over. He had attended the event with his wife, who was left behind. She had to borrow taxi fare to get home. (It was later discovered the Jefferson link was most likely faked.)

9 Before early Champagne bottlers perfected the use of the cork, the drink was called the "devil's wine" because the bottles were prone to shatter if jostled—or even explode without warning if gas built up in a defective bottle.

10 Ludwig van Beethoven, on his deathbed, accepted a parade of well-wishers bearing pastries and drink. But the arrival of a case of Rudesheimer Berg inspired his last words: "Pity, pity—too late!"

BEER

1 Why did the Pilgrims land at Plymouth Rock instead of pushing on to Virginia? Well, for one thing, they were nearly out of beer. A Mayflower passenger's diary reads: "We could not now take time for further search or consideration; our victuals being much spent, especially our beere."

2 In the 1600s and 1700s, midwives in Europe and Colonial America gave delivering mothers "groaning ale," which was fermented for seven or eight months and tapped when contractions began. After the birth, the child might even be bathed in the ale, since it was likely to be more sanitary than the water then available.

James Madison proposed creation of a **NATIONAL BREWERY** and appointment of a "secretary of beer."

3 As president, James Madison proposed creation of a national brewery and appointment of a "secretary of beer." But Congress wouldn't go along. If such a Cabinet position existed today, who might fit it? Actor George Wendt of "Cheers," perhaps? Or Windell Middlebrooks, who portrayed the Miller High Life truck driver who confiscates beer from overpriced establishments?

4 Beer can kill, but it usually doesn't do it nine at a time. The exception occurred in London in 1814 when the rupture of a brewery tank sent a giant wave of 3,500 barrels of beer cascading upon nearby residents. Two houses were demolished, and nine people died.

5 The North Side's Diversey Parkway and Lill Avenue were named after two early Chicago brewers, Michael Diversey and William Lill.

6 The Great Chicago Fire of 1871 devastated the local beer industry, allowing Milwaukee brewers to swoop in and seize market share. After grabbing a strong foothold in Chicago, Schlitz and other Milwaukee companies took advantage of Chicago's railroad hub to purvey their products across the country.

7 "The Guinness Book of World Records" was begun in 1955 at the suggestion of Guinness Brewery's top executive to settle gentlemanly disputes, such as those that would arise over mugs of beer.

8 Joe Charboneau, a Belvidere, Ill., native who played outfield for the Cleveland Indians in the early '80s, used to open beer bottles with his eye socket and drink beer through a straw in his nose.

9 You've heard of "beer goggles"—the idea that someone who has had a few quaffs finds members of the opposite sex more attractive. A study at Glasgow University in 2002 confirmed the effect. Tipsy students were 25 percent more likely to rate a person as sexually attractive than students who were sober.

10 During Prohibition, only "near beer" (less than 0.5 percent alcohol) could be sold. Such beer was sometimes illegally turned into high-octane "needle beer" when alcohol was injected into the barrel. The opposite of near beer might be called severe beer, such as Samuel Adams' Utopias. At 25 percent alcohol, its kick is five times as strong as Budweiser's. Reportedly, it tastes like cognac. It is so alcoholic that it violates the laws of 14 states, not including Illinois.

10 THINGS YOU MIGHT NOT KNOW ABOUT
DRUNKENNESS

1 St. Cummian of Fota, a 7th century Irish priest, distributed rules for the drinking clergy such as: "If a monk drinks till he vomits, he must do 30 days' penance; if a priest or deacon, 40 days. But if this happens from weakness of stomach, or from long abstinence, and he was not in the habit of excessive drinking or eating, or if he did it in excess of joy on Christmas or on Easter Days, or the commemoration of some saint, and if then he did not take more than has been regulated by our predecessors, he is not to be punished."

2 Among the slang terms for being drunk: Ossified, boiled as an owl, squiffy, sozzled, torn off the frame, pie-eyed, seeing two moons, Boris Yeltsinned, locked out of your mind, three sheets to the wind and holding up the lamppost. "Plotzed" is another term, based on the Yiddish word "platsn," meaning to crack, split or burst. Also, "gaysted" is slang for being so wasted that you flirt with men even though you are a heterosexual man.

3 In the 1820s, Michigan Territory Gov. Lewis Cass complained that the Midwest's Indians "give themselves up to the most brutal intoxication whenever this mad water can be procured." But sometimes it was procured from the U.S. government. Cass ordered 932 gallons of whiskey for the Ottawa, Chippewa and Potawatomi when they held treaty talks in Chicago in 1821.

4 W.C. Fields wasn't always a drunk. Quite the opposite. As a young man in vaudeville, his act demanded sobriety and precision: He was a juggler. Only later when he became a comedian did Fields also become a souse. "Always carry a flagon of whiskey in case of snakebite," he said. "And furthermore, always carry a small snake."

5 William Faulkner was stereotyped as a drunken novelist. But he rarely drank while writing and could abstain for long periods of time. He built his bad reputation through binges, such as the time at the Algonquin Hotel in New York when he drunkenly fell onto a radiator, badly burning himself. Faulkner's drinking was rivaled or surpassed by fellow Southern writers, such as Tennessee Williams and Carson McCullers. One summer in Nantucket, Williams and McCullers wrote in the same room while passing a whiskey bottle back and forth.

6 Drunkenness is a common excuse when people do stupid things. Rarer is it for a person to perform brilliantly and say he was "half drunk," as New York Yankees pitcher David Wells did after throwing a perfect game in 1998. More accurate would be to say that Wells was hung over and sleep deprived, having partied until 5 a.m. and slept 3½ hours before reporting for a day game.

7 Imagine the shame of being considered a drunk when you haven't consumed any alcohol. That's the burden of some people who suffered inner-ear damage from the antibiotic gentamicin. Their poor sense of balance makes some people think they're boozers. They prefer the term "wobblers" and have formed a support group called Wobblers Anonymous.

8 Three co-workers went out drinking one night in 1990. Two of them shared seven pitchers of beer, and a third had 15 rum-with-colas. A few hours later, they reported for work—as the pilots of a Northwest Airlines Boeing 727. Their 91 passengers arrived safely on the flight from Fargo, N.D., to Minneapolis. The pilots were fired and served at least a year in prison.

9 Drunken driving is a scourge that has cost many innocent lives. But some civil libertarians believe preventive measures have overreached. Exhibit A: Keith Emerich, who was never accused of drunken driving but told his doctor he drank six or more beers a day at home after work. Pennsylvania law required the doctor to report anything that might impair a patient's driving ability, and in 2004 the state revoked Emerich's driver's license.

10 Dean Martin fostered a boozy reputation, sporting a vanity license plate of DRUNKY and declaring, "You're not drunk if you can lie on the floor without holding on." The singer commonly appeared onstage holding a whiskey glass, but it was often filled with apple juice.

> *"You're not drunk if you can lie on the floor without holding on."* —DEAN MARTIN

10 THINGS YOU MIGHT NOT KNOW ABOUT
CANDY

1 The Arabs are often credited with inventing caramel. But an early use of the hot, sticky substance was not so sweet: Women in harems applied it as a hair remover.

2 Most Americans knew nothing about chocolate in 1893, when the World's Columbian Exposition in Chicago featured a display of chocolate-making equipment from Germany. Among the fairgoers was Milton Hershey, who bought every piece of equipment on display and went into the chocolate business.

3 Early American chocolate-makers often touted their products' nutritional value. During the Depression, candy bars had such names as Chicken Dinner, Idaho Spud and Big Eats. The Hershey's chocolate wrapper once carried the slogan "More sustaining than meat."

4 The Chicago area has been at the center of the U.S. candy industry, producing such treats as Tootsie Rolls, Atomic Fireballs, Lemonheads, Baby Ruths, Butterfingers, Milk Duds, Milky Ways, 3 Musketeers, Snickers, Oh Henry! bars, Frango Mints, Cracker Jacks, Turtles, Doves, Jelly Bellies and Pixies. Candy historian Tim Richardson credits Chicago candymakers with popularizing the tradition of giving sweets to Halloween trick-or-treaters, calling it "a simple marketing ploy that emanated from the city's confectioners."

5 The Baby Ruth candy bar debuted in 1921, and even today the origin of the name remains in dispute. The Chicago-based Curtiss Candy Co. insisted that it named the bar after President Grover Cleveland's daughter Ruth. But some historians find it odd that a company would name a new candy after a girl who had died 17 years earlier. They also find it mighty suspicious that the candy's name was similar to that of baseball star Babe Ruth, who never collected royalties and was prevented from selling his own Babe Ruth Home Run Bar because of a Curtiss lawsuit.

6 When the Mars candy company marketed Snickers in Britain, it changed the name to Marathon to avoid any jokes about Snickers rhyming with knickers. (Many years later, Mars renamed Marathon as Snickers.)

7 Producers of the film "E.T." wanted to use M&M's as the candy that lured the extraterrestrial from hiding. But when Mars said no, Hershey jumped at the chance to showcase Reese's Pieces instead. Sales soared.

8 Cotton candy is known as "candy floss" in Britain and "fairy floss" in Australia.

9 The rock band Van Halen had a contract clause requiring a bowl of M&M's backstage at its concerts—but all of the brown M&M's had to be removed. The clause is sometimes cited as an example of ridiculous rock-star demands, but it made practical sense, singer David Lee Roth has written. If a concert venue got the M&M's wrong, it was a red flag that promoters hadn't read the contract closely and were likely to mess up on other, more important details.

10 The National Confectioners Association says 90 percent of parents admit sneaking Halloween goodies out of their kids' trick-or-treat bags.

10 THINGS YOU MIGHT NOT KNOW ABOUT
ICE CREAM

1 Haagen-Dazs is not an exotic Scandinavian recipe. It's a brand name created by a Polish immigrant and his wife in the Bronx. Reuben Mattus' family sold ice cream for decades, but the product didn't really take off until the early 1960s, when Mattus and his wife, Rose, came up with the Haagen-Dazs name out of thin air and put a map of Denmark on the carton. They used an umlaut (two dots) over the first letter "a" in Haagen even though there's no such usage in Danish.

2 The Evinrude outboard motor was invented because of ice cream. A young man named Ole Evinrude was picnicking with his fiance on a Wisconsin lake island in 1906 when she expressed interest in a dish of ice cream. Evinrude rowed to shore to satisfy her desire, and en route realized that if he had a motor, the errand would be a lot easier—and the ice cream would be less likely to melt. So inspired, he designed an outboard motor that made him famous.

3 When comedian Jackie Gleason dined out, he sometimes ordered roast beef with a scoop of ice cream on it.

4 In the ice cream industry, "overrun" is a term for the amount of air that's inserted into ice cream as it's produced. Without some aeration, ice cream would be a solid mass, difficult to scoop and serve. So overrun is a good thing, within limits: Cheaper ice cream has more overrun. Long before Margaret Thatcher became Britain's prime minister, she was a chemist investigating the air in ice cream. As the Times of London put it, she studied "methods for preserving the foamy quality of ice cream by injecting it with air."

5 Ice cream vendors in the Mexican town of Dolores Hidalgo have featured such flavors as beer, cheese, cactus petal, avocado, tequila, corn, black and red mole, pigskin and shrimp.

Thomas Jefferson's recipe for vanilla ice cream is housed at the Library of Congress.

6 The Library of Congress houses many of Thomas Jefferson's writings, including a draft of the Declaration of Independence and his recipe for vanilla ice cream. Jefferson, an obsessive foodie, kept his ice house carefully stocked and corresponded with acquaintances in Paris to secure vanilla beans.

7 Who was the nation's first great ice cream entrepreneur? We nominate Augustus Jackson, an African-American. In the late 1820s—when nearly 2 million other black Americans were still in bondage—Jackson was a free man who left his job as a chef at the White House and moved to Philadelphia to establish a successful catering business that supplied ice cream to restaurants.

8 It's surprising that the Republicans didn't raise the ice cream issue against Barack Obama in 2008. Most Americans like ice cream; Obama apparently doesn't. In an "Access Hollywood" interview during the campaign, Obama's daughter Malia said: "Ice cream is my favorite food. I could eat ice cream forever." Then Obama's younger daughter, Sasha, said: "Everybody should like ice cream. Except Daddy. My dad doesn't like sweets." Perhaps Obama's distaste stems from his part-time job at Baskin-Robbins as a teenager in Hawaii. But one of the most romantic scenes in the Obama biography also involves ice cream. On his first date with Michelle Robinson, Obama took her to a Baskin-Robbins. He later described the scene: "I asked if I could kiss her. It tasted of chocolate."

9 When actor Clint Eastwood ran for mayor of Carmel, California, in 1986, a major issue was ice cream. Town leaders had banned the sale of ice cream cones, incensing Eastwood and his supporters. They won, and overturned the ordinance.

10 People for the Ethical Treatment of Animals wrote a letter to Ben & Jerry's in 2008 urging the company to start making its ice cream with the milk of nursing mothers rather than the milk of cows. A PETA spokeswoman acknowledged that the idea was "somewhat absurd" but said it was intended to publicize the alleged cruelty of the dairy industry. There was no comment from People for the Ethical Treatment of Nursing Mothers.

10 THINGS YOU MIGHT NOT KNOW ABOUT
SALT

1 Salt has seasoned English in many ways. Because Romans put salt or brine on their vegetables, the word "salad" developed. Because Roman soldiers were given money to buy salt, "salary" was coined.

2 "Glitter" is 1950s prison slang for salt.

3 In promoting the Louisiana Purchase, President Thomas Jefferson cited reports of a "salt mountain" in the territory. "This mountain is said to be 180 miles long and 45 in width, composed of solid rock salt, without any trees or even shrubs on it." The New York Evening Post mockingly asked whether there was "an immense lake of molasses, too." The salt mountain was never found; some think the reports referred to Oklahoma's Great Salt Plains.

4 The adult human body contains about 250 grams of salt—about half a pound.

5 According to a superstition, spilling salt can cause bad luck—an idea that may have originated with Leonardo da Vinci's painting "The Last Supper," which shows Judas Iscariot knocking over a salt container.

6 Dozens of advice books tell the story of a job applicant who went to lunch with his prospective boss, only to lose the job because he salted his food before tasting it—thus demonstrating a closed mind. But one of the most famous Americans, Elvis Presley, routinely showered his food with salt before taking a single bite.

7 Chicago is America's salty center, thanks to the Morton Salt Co. The company was owned by Joy Morton, a man who got his first name from the maiden name of his mother, Caroline Joy. Morton's father was agriculture secretary under President Grover Cleveland and is credited with starting Arbor Day. Reminders of the family's philanthropy include the Morton Arboretum in Lisle and the Morton Wing of the Art Institute of Chicago.

8 Though salt is necessary for human life, overconsumption contributes to heart disease and other problems. However, modern table salt addresses a separate health concern: iodine deficiency, which can cause low IQ and goiter, an enlargement of the thyroid gland. A century ago, goiter was so prevalent around the Great Lakes that the area was considered part of a "goiter belt." Doctors pushed for adoption of a Swiss tactic of adding iodine to table and cooking salt, and Morton Salt began selling its iodized salt in 1924.

9 Michael Jordan's mother, Deloris, and sister, Roslyn, wrote a children's book in 2000 called "Salt in His Shoes," about how young Michael was upset about being smaller than his basketball-playing friends and was comforted when his mom told him he would grow taller if he put salt in his shoes and prayed.

10 There is an enormous salt mine under the city of Detroit, about 1,200 feet below ground. According to Detroit Salt Co., the century-old mine spreads out more than 1,500 acres and has more than 100 miles of underground roads.

10 THINGS YOU MIGHT NOT KNOW ABOUT
TOMATOES

1 The tomato originated in South and Central America, and the earliest variety was probably a yellow cherry tomato. The Aztecs, who called them "tomatl," grew an amazing variety, including the bigger, red fruit we know today.

2 Originally, there was no tomato in ketchup. Early versions relied on such ingredients as fish, vinegar, shallots and wine. The origin of the word "ketchup" is debatable, but one popular theory traces it to the word "ke-tsiap" from China's Amoy dialect, meaning "the brine of pickled fish."

3 When Nelson Mandela was a political prisoner in South Africa, he grew tomatoes and other produce, carefully studying proper soils and fertilizers. Knowing that his letters were censored, he sometimes wrote in metaphor, including two letters to his wife, Winnie, about how he had nurtured a tomato plant only to see it wither and die. He later said the story reflected his worries about their marriage.

4 Seeds of the Galapagos tomato—unique to the islands lying 600 miles west of Ecuador— need to be softened for a few weeks in the digestive system of a giant tortoise to germinate. This also helps disperse the plant because even a giant tortoise gets around in a few weeks.

5 Latomatina.org, the official website of the famous tomato throwing festival in Bunol, Spain, offers a number of tips. They include: Bring a change of clothing (because you can't get on the bus out of town soaked in tomatoes), wear goggles (acidic tomato juice really stings) and squash the tomato before you throw it (the goal isn't to hurt anyone).

6 Ever heard of a tomato called Radiator Charlie's Mortgage Lifter? A West Virginia auto mechanic named M.C. Byles, aka Radiator Charlie, crossbred large tomatoes in the 1930s and came up with a whopper that he sold for $1 a plant, making enough money that it was appropriately called the Mortgage Lifter.

7 When Romanian dictator Nicolae Ceausescu visited New York City in 1978, protesters threw tomatoes and eggs at his motorcade. Ceausescu protested to Mayor Ed Koch, who downplayed the incident, asking, "A couple of tomatoes and a few eggs?" Responded Ceausescu: "They could have been hand grenades." The dictator joined a long history of tomato targets. Others include Margaret Thatcher, Sarah Palin, Frank Sinatra and Cubs slugger Hack Wilson. And the Paris debut of Igor Stravinsky's "Rite of Spring" was tainted by tomato tossers.

8 Europeans once thought the tomato was poisonous—and not without reason. The plant is related to deadly nightshade, and tomato leaves are toxic in quantity. German legend held that nightshade could be used to summon werewolves, so the earliest German name for tomato translated to "wolf peach." It took centuries for the tomato to repair its reputation.

The earliest German name for tomato translated to "wolf peach."

9 Tomatoes are far and away the most popular grow-it-yourself food. According to the National Gardening Association, 86 percent of the nation's backyard plots included tomatoes in 2009. The cucumber was a distant second at 47 percent.

10 If the fruit or vegetable debate confuses you, you're not alone. The U.S. Supreme Court muddied the issue way back in 1893 when it ruled—for tax purposes and contrary to scientific fact—that the tomato was a vegetable. The court's reasoning: People eat them at dinner and not for dessert. The federal government famously weighed in again in 1981 when the Reagan administration, in an attempt to save money, briefly suggested that tomato ketchup should satisfy the vegetable requirement for school lunches. Finally, Arkansas declared in 1987 that the tomato was both the state fruit and the state vegetable.

10 THINGS YOU MIGHT NOT KNOW ABOUT
TURKEY

1 Hunting a wild turkey is exceedingly difficult. The bird may appear dumb and slow, but looks can be deceiving. In fact, Tom Turkey has fantastic hearing, amazing eyesight, can flat-out run (15 mph and three-foot strides) and can fly even faster. And he is paranoid—because everyone is out to get him—so he'll flee at the slightest provocation.

2 Eccentric billionaire Howard Hughes liked Swanson's frozen TV dinners, especially the turkey entree. But Hughes was a picky eater. He didn't approve of Swanson's mixing of white and dark meat. And he wished the dinner came with a dessert of peach cobbler rather than apple cobbler. Through an aide, Hughes asked Swanson's to switch to peach cobbler in its turkey dinners. When Swanson's refused, Hughes tried to buy the company but was unsuccessful.

3 In the spring, a wild male turkey's head can turn a brilliant red, white or blue, often changing in just seconds. That fact was not one of Benjamin Franklin's arguments for why the turkey would be a better national symbol than the bald eagle.

4 Joe Engel, an executive with the minor league Chattanooga Lookouts baseball team, was famous for stunts, such as having his players ride into the ballpark on elephants. The topper came in 1931 when he traded his shortstop to Charlotte for a Thanksgiving turkey. The trade turned out badly, he said, because the turkey meat was tough.

5 Before the Turkey Trot became the go-to name for a 5K race in November, it was a controversial ragtime-style dance in the early 1900s. It was considered quite vulgar, and it was often banned, which, of course, just made it insanely popular.

6 Italian composer Gioachino Rossini claimed that he wept only three times in his life: when his opera "Tancredi" was booed on opening night, when he heard Nicolo Paganini play the violin and when his truffle-stuffed turkey fell out of a boat during a picnic.

7 Playwright Arthur Miller and his wife, photographer Inge Morath, were counterfeit carnivores during Thanksgiving. "Since we're vegetarians," Morath told The New York Times in 1981, "I usually make a pretend turkey out of vegetables—a piece montee. I put a loaf of bread underneath, and over the top I arrange carrots, leeks, beans, apples, all kinds of cold cooked and raw vegetables, Chinese vegetables bought at Korean markets, like a painting. With pieces of avocado I make beautiful wings. It looks more like a live turkey than a dead one."

8 If an adult male turkey is a tom, what's a young male turkey? A jake.

9 During family Christmas celebrations, Gen. George Patton turned the carving of the turkey into a circus act. He waved the knife like a saber, explained that the warrior Saladin wielded a sword so sharp it could cut a floating feather in half, then he shouted a rebel yell and plunged a carving fork into the turkey's breast. His daughter Ruth Ellen recalled: "Then he would carefully withdraw the fork, put his ear to the turkey's breast, nod in a sad, wise way, and say, 'She's gone alright,' and then start carving."

10 If you feel like taking a nap after your Thanksgiving feast, don't blame the turkey. The whole tryptophan-in-the-turkey-makes-you-sleepy idea is a myth. In fact, turkey doesn't contain any more tryptophan than many other meats. The real culprit is the sheer quantity of food you just inhaled.

CHAPTER 5
People & Places

MEXICAN-AMERICANS

1 Baseball legend Ted Williams, who started playing in the mid-1930s, was part Mexican on his mother's side and recognized the racism he would have faced if he had been named Venzor. "If I had my mother's name, there is no doubt I would have run into problems in those days, (given) the prejudices people had in Southern California."

2 Albert Baez was a brilliant scientist who helped develop the X-ray reflecting microscope as a graduate student at Stanford University in 1948. As the Cold War gripped the nation, he eschewed research for military purposes because of his Quaker beliefs and concentrated on education. Despite his accomplishments, he may still be better known as the father of folk singer Joan Baez.

3 Nearly 32 million Americans claimed Mexican heritage in the 2010 U.S. Census. Mexican-Americans represented 63 percent of the nation's Hispanic population, and saw the largest numeric growth from 2000 to 2010 of any Hispanic group. Although two-thirds live in California, Texas and Arizona, the next largest concentration is in Illinois.

4 Two ad campaigns around 1970 annoyed some Mexican-Americans. L&M highlighted its extra-long cigarettes by featuring a siesta-loving Mexican named Paco, who "never feenishes anything, not even the revolution." And the Frito Bandito loved corn chips so much that he robbed people to get more. Protesters weren't placated when Frito-Lay softened the Bandito's image by taking away his gold tooth, shaving his stubble and making him more friendly. He was retired after a four-year rampage of stereotype.

5 Don't be fooled by surnames. These Americans are at least partly of Mexican descent: quarterbacks Joe Kapp and Jim Plunkett, singer Vikki Carr, and actresses Catherine Bach, Lynda Carter and Yvette Mimieux.

6 The Treaty of Guadalupe Hidalgo in 1848 ended the Mexican-American War, added a huge swath of land to the United States and gave the 100,000 Hispanic Mexicans living in the new American Southwest—but not blacks and American Indians—one year to declare whether they wanted to be U.S. citizens. The territories piled on further restrictions as they applied for statehood so that America's newest citizens faced property seizures, abuse and even lynchings for decades after.

7 One of the best known Mexican-Americans, actress Salma Hayek, was born in Mexico, pursued a career in Hollywood and became a U.S. citizen. But her ethnic identity is more complex: Her father was a Lebanese immigrant, and the name Salma is Arabic for "peaceful" or "safe."

8 Who will be the first Mexican-American U.S. president? One Mexican-American with a political pedigree is George P. Bush, grandson of one president and nephew of another. The son of former Florida Gov. Jeb Bush and Mexican-born Columba Garnica Gallo, George P. was one of the grandkids affectionately called "the little brown ones" by George H.W. Bush. George P., who was born in 1976, was elected Texas Land Commissioner in 2014.

9 Comedian Louis C.K., creator of the sitcom "Louie," didn't speak English until he moved back to the United States when he was 7. His father's family still lives in Mexico, and he holds dual citizenship.

10 Sgt. Roy Benavidez simply refused to die. On May 2, 1968, in Vietnam, he rushed to aid a 12-man reconnaissance unit surrounded by a North Vietnamese Army battalion. Armed with just a knife and carrying a medic bag, Benavidez jumped from a hovering helicopter to reach the trapped unit. Over the next six hours, he was wounded 36 times but managed to save eight of the men and secure sensitive military documents as he called in airstrikes and held off the enemy. He was so badly injured that a medic declared him dead and started zipping up the body bag, until Benavidez spit in his face. He was awarded the Medal of Honor in 1981.

10 THINGS YOU MIGHT NOT KNOW ABOUT
CUBA

1 The shortage of cars and public transportation has made hitchhiking a must in Cuba, and those who drive government vehicles are expected to pick up people needing rides. In Cuba, hitchhiking is known as hacer botella, or "doing the bottle," because the way people hold their hand to thumb a ride is similar to the way they hold a bottle.

2 Sammy Davis Jr. used to tell people that his mother was Puerto Rican, but in fact she was of Cuban descent. Davis lied about Elvera "Baby" Sanchez Davis because he feared anti-Cuban feeling in the U.S. would hurt his career.

3 One of the most famous photographs in the world, Alberto Korda's portrait of Cuban revolutionary Che Guevara, went largely unnoticed for years. Korda covered a Havana rally in March 1960 as a freelancer for the newspaper Revolucion and snapped two shots of Che while concentrating on Cuban leader Fidel Castro and two French guests, Jean-Paul Sartre and Simone de Beauvoir. The newspaper printed the Castro photo but not the one of Che. Seven years later, the Che picture was widely circulated as a poster by Italian publisher Giangiacomo Feltrinelli, who was given the photo by Korda. Feltrinelli had another claim to fame: He was first to publish Boris Pasternak's "Dr. Zhivago."

4 The Desmarest's hutia, a Cuban rodent that is about the size of a rabbit and is known as a "tree rat," has a stomach divided into three chambers. In the Cuban countryside, it is a source of food, often cooked with nuts and honey.

5 The history of failed U.S. plots against Fidel Castro may seem too absurd to be true, but it's authentic. American spies either discussed or initiated attempts to kill Castro with a poison pen-syringe, deadly pills, a bomb-rigged seashell and a skin-diving suit treated to give him a skin condition, featuring a mouthpiece treated with tuberculosis bacteria. Other times the U.S. considered possible plots to simply embarrass him—once with a sprayed hallucinogenic drug that would disorient him during a radio appearance, another time with a depilatory chemical that was to be placed in his shoes so that his beard would fall out.

6 Granma, the Communist Party's newspaper, is named after the boat that carried Fidel Castro and his comrades from Mexico to Cuba in 1956 to launch the revolution. The boat got its name from its previous owner, an American who chose the name to pay tribute to his grandmother.

7 In 1992, Cuba changed its constitution to describe itself as "secular" rather than "atheist."

8 Castro banned Beatles music in 1964 as part of an attempt to root out decadent capitalist influences. But in 2000, Castro helped dedicate a statue of John Lennon in Havana. By that time, it was clear Castro and Lennon had something in common—as enemies of the U.S. government. Other noteworthy statues in Cuba depict Abraham Lincoln and Palestinian leader Yasser Arafat. A large statue of Jesus Christ was put up in Havana just weeks before a victorious Castro entered the city in 1959. The communists didn't dare take it down.

9 The first Latin-born baseball player in a U.S. professional league is believed to have been a Cuban: Steve Bellan of the American Association's Troy Haymakers. A slick infielder in the 1860s and '70s, Bellan was known as the "Cuban Sylph." He was followed by many other stars from the island, such as the Chicago White Sox's "Cuban Comet" (Minnie Minoso) and "Cuban Missile" (Alexei Ramirez). Current Sox superstar Jose Abreu is known in his native Cuba as "Pito," a Spanish word for whistle. The Mets' Yoenis Cespedes is nicknamed in Cuba as "La Potencia," the Power. (While we're talking about names, please note that American businessman Mark Cuban is not Cuban. His Russian Jewish immigrant grandparents changed the family name from Chabenisky to Cuban.)

10 In 1962, President John F. Kennedy expanded the U.S. trade embargo against Cuba to include cigars. But Kennedy, an avid cigar smoker, arranged for press secretary Pierre Salinger to buy 1,200 H. Upmann Petit Corona cigars the night before.

NORTH KOREA

1 The Korean War ended in 1953, right? Nope. An armistice was signed by the U.S.-led United Nations command, China and North Korea—but not by South Korea. That document established a truce "until a final peaceful settlement is achieved." But none ever was, leaving the combatants technically still at war.

2 The history of North Korea can be summarized in three words: Kim, Kim and Kim. The first leader of the communist North, Kim Il Sung, has been considered "Eternal President" since his death in 1994. His son, Kim Jong Il, known as "Dear Leader," ruled until he died in 2012. Now in charge is son Kim Jong Un, aka "Outstanding Leader." The Kims' cult of personality is demonstrated by an incident in June 2012 in which a 14-year-old girl drowned while trying to save portraits of the first two leaders during a flood. She was praised as a national heroine, with pledges to rename her school in her honor.

The history of North Korea can be summarized in three words: Kim, Kim and Kim.

3 The quality of life in North Korea has been so bad for so long that its people are now physically different from their South Korean cousins. A Seoul National University study published in 2005 found that northern young men were on average 2.3 inches shorter and young women 2.6 shorter. Another study found an even wider gap—nearly 5 inches—among children.

4 Despite its dismal record on many issues, North Korea is credited with an excellent literacy rate. The CIA's World Factbook lists that rate as 99 percent but notes the estimate is two decades old. (North Korea is unlikely to invite the CIA for a fact-finding visit to update its statistics.) But even if literacy remains top-notch, censorship severely limits what's available to read.

5 North Korea announced plans to build the world's tallest hotel. But the 105-story Ryugyong Hotel in Pyongyang has taken so long to construct—30 years and counting—that it missed out on the honor, surpassed by two taller hotels in Dubai that were started and finished in 2012. North Korea's rocket-shaped tower, which remained unfinished in early 2017, has been labeled by Esquire magazine as "the worst building in the history of mankind."

6 A country known for famine and forced-labor camps also features something cheerier: golf. The North Korea Amateur Open in May 2012 attracted a smattering of foreign tourists. And Kim Jong Un's wife, Ri Sol Ju, was introduced to the public that same year when the couple visited a miniature golf course. Like many Western golfers, North Korean duffers are prone to exaggeration: A golf pro at the nation's only course claimed Kim Jong Il once shot five holes-in-one during a single round.

7 If you want to learn more about North Korea, just visit. Yes, despite being a member of the "Axis of Evil," North Korea accepts American tourists, if only a few thousand annually. That said, the U.S. State Department offers up a lengthy warning to would-be tourists, noting among other things that it is a criminal act to show disrespect to the country's former or current leaders and that unauthorized picture taking or talking to the locals can be construed as espionage.

8 More than half of North Korean men smoke, a rate double that in the U.S., according to World Health Organization figures. The Pyongyang government has tried for decades to get people to quit, but the campaign wasn't helped by leader Kim Jong Un's clear love of a good smoke. (The nation apparently has cashed in on smoking: It has a reputation as an international counterfeiter of cigarette brands such as Marlboro, Dunhill and Benson & Hedges.)

9 Movie director Shin Sang Ok, known as "the Orson Welles of South Korea," found his studio shuttered when he got crossways with the South's government. But he was treated even worse by the North, which dispatched agents to kidnap him in 1978. Ordered to produce propaganda films for the North, he refused and was thrown in prison, where he ate grass to survive. After five years, he was released from prison, lavished with luxuries and allowed to make the movies he wanted. Even so, he eventually escaped. He later conceded, though, that he made his best film while in the North.

10 Kim Jong Un's succession to leadership may have been eased when another candidate who was his half brother embarrassed the family. Kim Jong Nam was caught in 2001 trying to enter Japan on a fake Dominican Republic passport. His suspected destination: Tokyo's version of Disneyland. Less amusing was the way Kim Jong Nam was finally removed as a rival—fatally poisoned by a nerve agent at a Malaysian airport in 2017, likely on the orders of his half brother.

CHINESE LEADERS

1 Di Xin, whose reign ended the Shang Dynasty around 1050 B.C., was remembered as a decadent leader who once threw a party featuring a pond filled with wine, allowing 3,000 guests to slurp up the booze like cattle.

2 Decades before Christopher Columbus sailed the ocean blue with fewer than 100 men in three small ships, a Chinese naval leader commanded 27,000 men in a fleet of more than 300 ships. Admiral Zheng He made seven famous voyages covering thousands of miles to points as far west as India, the Middle East and Africa. British historian Gavin Menzies even claims that part of the fleet sailed as far as both coasts of North and South America, Greenland and the Arctic Sea in 1421-1423.

3 When the philosopher Confucius served as an adviser to the Duke of Lu, a neighboring lord grew worried about Lu's power. To create a rift between the duke and his straight-laced counselor, the lord sent 100 good horses and 80 dancing girls to the duke, who spent three days ignoring his official duties and enjoying his gifts. A disgusted Confucius left his service.

4 Qin Shi Huang, possibly best known for being buried with his terra cotta army, was the first emperor of a unified China. During his reign from 221 B.C. to 210 B.C., he did much to modernize the country, including instituting standardized written language, currency and measurements, and building an extensive highway system. The flip side was that he was extremely cruel. He buried 400 Confucian scholars alive and ordered all books written before his Qin Dynasty to be burned.

5 Leadership has its privileges. When the Chinese first developed the seismograph in A.D. 132, it was kept at the emperor's palace. And when the Chinese invented toilet paper in the 14th century, it was for the emperor's household only.

6 Wu Zetian was China's only ruling empress. A woman of noble birth, she was a Buddhist nun before becoming the emperor's concubine. Through ruthless palace intrigue, she became the ruler herself in 690, displacing her own son. During her reign, peace prevailed, a merit system for government posts was encouraged—and women's rights advanced considerably.

7 Kublai Khan, the ruler of ancient China who is most famous in the Western world, was not even Chinese—he was a Mongol invader whose Yuan Dynasty controlled China for only a century. But that snapshot of China endured because it coincided with a visit from a Venetian traveler named Marco Polo.

8 Like other empires, China experienced betrayal and murder over the succession of its leaders. An emperor's son who was designated crown prince was sometimes marked for death. But the Qing Dynasty (1644-1917), created a countermeasure: No crown prince was publicly announced in most cases. Rather, an emperor on his deathbed would write his choice of successor on a piece of paper that was placed in a lockbox, to be opened by top government officials after the emperor's death.

9 Eager to avoid the cult of personality he saw in the Soviet Union with the permanent display of Vladimir Lenin's and Josef Stalin's bodies, Mao Zedong insisted that Chinese communist leaders be cremated. But when he died in 1976, the Politburo ignored his wishes and decided to preserve him. Unfortunately, the Chinese did not have the expertise, and the gruesome process saw the Chairman's corpse so badly bloated that formaldehyde oozed out of its pores. But it was eventually made presentable and displayed.

10 The Republic of China, the anti-communist government that was defeated by Mao's army and relocated to Taiwan in the late 1940s, has developed a more open political system. But democracy can sometimes be messy. Fistfights erupted among Taiwanese lawmakers in the '70s and '80s, and a 2004 lunch meeting of legislators turned into a food fight, with rice, meat, vegetables and hard-boiled eggs flying across the room. "My whole body smells like a lunchbox!" politician Chu Fong-chi said afterward.

SYRIA

1 Syria is commonly considered a Muslim country, but before the civil war it was about 10 percent Christian. One Syrian in 10 is non-Arab, including large numbers of Kurds and Armenians.

2 The Krak des Chevaliers ("The Fortress of the Knights") near Homs is considered a wonder of medieval military architecture and art. It threw off attack after attack during the Crusades, and even two earthquakes failed to dislodge the Knights Hospitallers. But in 1271, a Muslim army captured it in just a month. How? The sultan forged a letter from the Knights' allies warning them that no relief was on the way, and the defenders negotiated safe passage back to Lebanon.

3 Longtime Syrian leader Hafez Assad was something of a riddle: While orchestrating massacres and repression, he supported a constitution declaring the equality of women under the law. His heir apparent, eldest son Basil, died after driving his Mercedes into a road barrier in the fog. That left younger son Bashar, an eye doctor, to take over. When Hafez died in 2000, Bashar was only 34—six years under the constitutional minimum for president. No problem: The People's Assembly lowered the limit.

4 The New York Times reported that the Assad family paid public relations firm Brown Lloyd James $5,000 a month to facilitate Syrian first lady Asma Assad's March 2011 profile in Vogue headlined "Rose in the Desert." When Syria's image became less fashionable, Vogue took the profile off its website.

5 Emails attributed to Bashar and Asma Assad have been revealed by Britain's Guardian newspaper, depicting the first lady chatting about $4,000 Christian Louboutin heels and the president evading U.S. trade sanctions by getting a third party to order iTunes products, including Chris Brown songs and the video game "Real Racing 2."

6 One of this century's most admired people was Syrian-American—and didn't know it for most of his life. Steve Jobs' biological parents, University of Wisconsin student Joanne Schieble and Syrian-born teaching assistant Abdulfattah "John" Jandali, gave him up for adoption to Paul and Clara Jobs. While in his 30s, the consumer electronics genius tracked down his birth mother and learned he had a sister, novelist Mona Simpson. Jobs remained estranged from his biological father, who was working as a casino manager in Reno, Nev., when his famous son died in 2011.

7 Other Americans of Syrian descent are singer-dancer Paula Abdul (who calls herself a "Syrian-Brazilian-Canadian-American"), comedian Jerry Seinfeld (on his mother's side) and Indiana Gov. Mitch Daniels (on his father's side). Vic Tayback, who played the diner owner on TV's "Alice," was the son of immigrants from Aleppo. And the hero of Dave Eggers' Hurricane Katrina book "Zeitoun" is Syrian immigrant Abdulrahman Zeitoun.

8 Syria's capital, Damascus, makes a good claim to being the world's oldest continuously inhabited city. It is associated with both hard weapons and elegant cloth: Damascus steel and damask weaving.

9 Before the civil war, about a third of Syria's population was under age 15, and its median age (22.3) was far lower than in most surrounding countries, such as Turkey (30.5), Israel (29.7) and Lebanon (29.9). (The U.S. median age, by comparison, is 37.9.)

10 Syria does poorly in the Corruption Perceptions Index, in which a group called Transparency International uses polls and independent assessments to rank countries on the perceived level of public corruption. No. 1—viewed as least corrupt—are Denmark and New Zealand. No. 176—worst—is Somalia. While the U.S. is 18th, Syria has plummeted to 173 after years of civil war. All this talk about corruption reminds us of yet another famous Syrian-American: Antoin "Tony" Rezko, of Blagojevich scandal fame.

Syria ranks 173rd (out of 176) on Transparency International's Corruption Perceptions Index.

10 THINGS YOU MIGHT NOT KNOW ABOUT
RUSSIA

1 The Soviet Union at its height covered nearly one-sixth of Earth's land surface and was larger than the United States, Canada and Mexico combined. And while Russia is 2 million square miles smaller than that, it is still huge. Consider: If the westernmost tip of Russia were plopped on Los Angeles, and the country unrolled like a giant carpet, it would cross the continental U.S. and the Atlantic Ocean, roll over France, Germany, Austria and not run out till it got to Hungary.

2 Ivan the Terrible, the iron-fisted 16th-century ruler who was the first to officially take the title czar of all Russia, was indeed terrible from any modern viewpoint, torturing enemies and countrymen alike, and killing his son in an uncontrolled rage. But that's not what his nickname is referencing. His moniker—based on the Russian word grozny—is more accurately rendered as fearsome or formidable.

3 Vodka and cigarettes are among the culprits for a nearly 12-year gap in life expectancies between men and women in Russia—76.8 years for women and 65 for men. Russian men live shorter lives than those in Iran, Indonesia and Bangladesh. (In the U.S., average life spans are 82.1 for women, 77.5 for men.)

4 The surface area of Lake Baikal in Siberia is only about half as big as that of Lake Michigan, yet Baikal is so deep it holds one-fifth of the world's freshwater, about as much as the five Great Lakes combined.

5 In fall 1863, as the U.S. was embroiled in the Civil War, the Russian navy without warning sailed warships into the Northern ports of New York and San Francisco. Did it spark a panic? No, it was the occasion for extravagant parties. Before the Soviets were the Evil Empire, the Russians were America's fast friends. The fleets stayed the winter, and the strong show of support from a major European power was thought at the time to end talk of British or French intervention on the side of the Confederacy. It was later learned that the Russians, fearing an imminent fight of their own with Britain or France, needed to find a safe place to stow their warships.

6 Writer Vladimir Nabokov said he was raised in Russia as "a perfectly normal trilingual child"—speaking Russian, English and French—and initially was better at English than Russian. He wrote his most famous novel, "Lolita," in English, and translated it into Russian. A lover of wordplay, Nabokov created character names Vivian Darkbloom and Blavdak Vinomori using anagrams of his own name.

7 American-Russian culture clashes were common during the Cold War. When Soviet Premier Nikita Khrushchev visited Los Angeles in 1959, he was told he could not stop at Disneyland because of security concerns. That set off a Khrushchev rant: "What is it? Do you have rocket launching pads there? . . . What is it? Is there an epidemic of cholera there or something? Or have gangsters taken over the place that can destroy me? Then what must I do? Commit suicide?" (In Khrushchev's defense, it is difficult to understand why he was barred from the park; other world leaders were allowed to go there.)

8 Before the Soviets shocked the world by winning gold at the 1954 World Ice Hockey Championships and the 1956 Winter Olympics in Italy, they were nonentities in international hockey. How did they do it? A full-press national effort—and plenty of people who played bandy. That popular Russian sport is a mix of field hockey and soccer played on ice. The huge playing field requires great skaters, crisp passing and teamwork. In other words, Soviet-style hockey.

9 Lots of phrases used by Americans come from Russian names. There's the Molotov cocktail, a firebomb named by the Finns to ridicule Soviet Foreign Minister Vyacheslav Molotov. There's the fakery known as the Potemkin village, a phrase based on a tale about Russian official Grigori Potemkin building make-believe towns along Catherine the Great's travel route. Then there's Mikhail Kalashnikov's rifle. Not to mention Pavlov's dog, a reference to physiologist Ivan Pavlov's experiments with conditioned reflexes in canines. Also, the pavlova is a meringue dessert named after ballerina Anna Pavlova. And let's not forget diplomat Paul Stroganoff's beloved dinner, beef stroganoff.

10 Russian leader Vladimir Putin sang the Fats Domino song "Blueberry Hill" at a children's charity event in St. Petersburg in 2010.

10 THINGS YOU MIGHT NOT KNOW ABOUT
THE IRISH

1 In 1901, Chicago's top cop was a hard-nosed, aggressive Irishman, not that unusual for a force historically dominated by men who bled green. But Francis O'Neill was also arguably the world's pre-eminent expert on Irish folk music, collecting and preserving thousands of pieces of music, many of which would have been lost forever. Reporters who were used to his blunt, bordering on rude, manner at the office were amazed that the quiet scholar who lectured about music at his home was the same man.

2 While the origins of Notre Dame's nickname are lost in history, the moniker Fighting Irish was first used regularly around the turn of the last century. According to one account, university officials finally gave it their blessing in 1927 because they preferred it to the alternatives of Ramblers, Rovers and Nomads, coined because of the school's penchant for traveling far and wide to find opponents.

3 In 1845, 1 in 50 Bostonians were Irish-born. Ten years later, 1 in 5 were.

4 Friends of a young Dublin musician named Paul Hewson started calling him Steinvic von Huyseman, then just Huyseman, then Houseman. Later they named him after a hearing-aid store, Bonavox of O'Connell Street, perhaps in recognition that "bona vox" was Latin for "good voice." Ultimately he went simply by Bono, fronting a band called Feedback, then The Hype, then U2.

5 The third paragraph of Irish writer James Joyce's "Finnegans Wake" includes the word bababadalgharaghtakamminarronnkonnbronntonnerronntuonnthunntrovarrhun- awnskawntoohoohoordenenthurnuk. Joseph Campbell and Henry Morton Robinson, analyzing the novel, write that word is a "polylingual thunderclap" that represents "the voice of God made audible through the noise of Finnegan's fall." (Tim Finnegan is a character in a song who gets drunk, climbs a ladder and suffers an apparently fatal fall. But at his wake, an attendee splashes Finnegan with whiskey, and he jumps to life.)

6 Irish-Americans sometimes talk about past discrimination, including "NINA signs" declaring that "no Irish need apply" for jobs. As recently as 1996, Sen. Edward Kennedy, D-Mass., who grew up in a wealthy family, said he had seen NINA signs in stores when he was a boy. But according to 2002 research by Richard Jensen, a retired history professor at the University of Illinois at Chicago, such signs are an urban legend, and "no historian, archivist or museum curator has ever located one." Jensen concedes that "no Irish need apply" occasionally appeared in newspaper want ads. Several have been found in the Chicago Tribune in the 1870s.

7 The Irish turn up in the strangest places. Eliza Rosanna Gilbert was born in western Ireland in 1821, spent her childhood in India and England, married, had an affair, divorced, changed her name to Lola Montez and went on the London stage posing as a Spanish dancer. She later became the mistress of Bavaria's King Ludwig I, who was so infatuated that he named her a countess and let her dictate government policy, helping precipitate the revolution of 1848. The king abdicated, and Montez moved on to perform in gold-rush California and Australia, perfecting something she called the "Spider Dance." A lake northeast of Sacramento, Calif., is named after her.

8 John Patrick Hopkins, one of the first in a long line of Chicago mayors of Irish descent, took some flak on St. Patrick's Day 1894 when he didn't order the "green flag of old Ireland" to fly over City Hall, breaking with a long-standing tradition aimed to curry favor with what was already a sizable community in Chicago. The Tribune applauded the move, calling the practice a "cheap bit of demagogy" and declaring: "Mayor Hopkins is an Irish-American, with the American somewhat predominating."

9 The Irish Brigade was a U.S. Army unit made up mostly of Irish immigrants that fought famously for the Union at the Sunken Road in Fredericksburg and at Gettysburg. The heart of the brigade was the Fighting 69th, an infantry unit from New York. But its charismatic commander, Michael Corcoran, nearly missed the war after he refused a direct order in 1860 to parade his troops for the prince of Wales, who was visiting New York City. Corcoran, who was protesting English treatment of Ireland, was facing a court martial when the shots were fired at Fort Sumter, and the great recruiter was allowed to return to his command.

10 Italians are understandably proud of radio pioneer Guglielmo Marconi. But the Irish have a claim as well. Marconi's mother was Annie Jameson, from the family that founded the Jameson's brand of Irish whiskey.

10 THINGS YOU MIGHT NOT KNOW ABOUT

OHIO

1 Eight U.S. presidents have hailed from Ohio, and half have died in office. The last of them was likely the worst of them: Warren Harding, who was chosen as the 1920 Republican nominee by party bosses in the original "smoke-filled room" at Chicago's Blackstone Hotel. While Harding spent his career philandering, his cronies were busy filling their pockets. More sordid details emerged in 2014 when the Library of Congress unsealed Harding's love letters and poetry written to a secret paramour. Presidential scholarship would never be quite the same. To wit: "I love your poise / of perfect thighs / when they hold me / in paradise . . ." and "I love to suck / your breath away / I love to cling—/ There long to stay . . ."

Cleveland is a typo.

2 Cleveland is a typo. The city's founder was Moses Cleaveland, and even today there's no consensus for why the letter A disappeared in the 1830s. Among the theories: A local newspaper editor dumped the "A" because it didn't fit on the masthead; an early map contained a spelling error; or store signs posted by brothers named Cleveland made residents think that was the city's correct spelling.

3 Ohio once went to war with Michigan—and not just on the football field. The Toledo War of 1835 was a dispute over 500 square miles of land, including the town of Toledo. Militias from Ohio and Michigan confronted each other along the Maumee River, but reportedly the only injury was a single stab wound to the leg. The federal government settled the issue: Ohio got Toledo, and Michigan received the western Upper Peninsula.

4 Halle Berry, born in Cleveland, was named after the city's now-defunct Halle Brothers department store chain. The Oscar-winning actress is part of an impressive cast of African-Americans from Ohio. They include Nobel Prize-winning author Toni Morrison of Lorain; poets Paul Laurence Dunbar of Dayton and Rita Dove of Akron; Olympic hero Jesse Owens of Cleveland; and comedian Dave Chappelle, who lives on a farm outside Yellow Springs.

5 Chef Boyardee was no Betty Crocker or Aunt Jemima—he was a real person. Italian immigrant Hector Boiardi ran a restaurant in Cleveland whose spaghetti sauce was so popular that he began manufacturing it for home cooking.

6 Ohio wasn't officially admitted into the union until 1953. Back in 1803, Congress approved the state's constitution but neglected to adopt a resolution formally accepting it as the 17th state. A century and a half later, historians noticed the oversight, which was rectified by Congress and President Dwight Eisenhower.

7 Ohio is home to the Rock and Roll Hall of Fame, so you would think that the "official state rock song" would be world-class. Instead, it's "Hang On Sloopy," popularized by a Dayton group called the McCoys in 1965. The song is a favorite at Ohio State football games.

8 Among the greatest Ohioans were the Wright brothers, bicycle-makers from Dayton who made the first powered airplane flight. But while Orville and Wilbur are remembered as pioneers, they impeded the development of aviation by filing incessant lawsuits against business competitors. Some historians believe the lawsuit-happy Wrights are a major reason U.S. aviators in World War I had to fly foreign-made planes.

9 The Longaberger Basket Co.'s headquarters in Newark, Ohio, is a seven-story building shaped like a basket.

10 The logo of the Chicago International Film Festival features the eyes of an Ohioan named Theda Bara, the original "vamp" of silent films. Her movie studio invented an exotic back story for her, noting that her name was an anagram for "Arab Death" and claiming that her father was a French artist and her mother was an Arab princess. In truth, she was Theodosia Goodman, a bookish, middle-class Jewish girl from Cincinnati.

TEXAS

1 The congressional resolution that brought Texas into the union in 1845 allowed it to be sub-divided into five separate states. Such a partition has never been seriously considered, to the Democrats' relief. Otherwise, there might be 10 Republican senators from what is now Texas.

2 The Confederates won the last battle of the Civil War. It took place at Palmito Ranch, Texas, a month after the war effectively ended with Robert E. Lee's surrender at Appomattox Court House, Va. Three Union regiments attacked a rebel camp at Palmito Ranch and were driven back, with more than 100 soldiers killed.

3 The King Ranch in south Texas covers nearly 1,300 square miles—that's more than five times the size of Chicago.

4 The founders of Reklaw, Texas, wanted to call the town Walker, but that name was taken, so they spelled it backward. Same for the settlers of Sacul, whose first choice was Lucas. Then there's the town of Uncertain, Texas. According to one story, town fathers hadn't picked a name when they sent their application to the state, so they wrote "uncertain" on the form, planning to choose a name later.

5 Texas has produced some eccentric members of Congress. When newly elected Rep. J.J. Pickle arrived in Washington, President Lyndon Johnson sent a limousine to the airport and invited him to stay at the White House. Pickle sent the limo back empty, explaining that he had arranged to stay with a friend and it would be rude to change his plans. Then there's Rep. Sheila Jackson Lee, whom critics call "Hurricane Sheila" because she once complained that hurricanes didn't have distinctly African-American names. And let's not forget Rep. Tom DeLay, who posed for one of the happiest police booking shots ever. Accused of conspiracy and money-laundering, DeLay apparently decided that if he looked miserable in his mug shot, it would give comfort to his enemies.

6 Since 1976, more people have been executed for crimes committed in Texas' Harris County (home of Houston) than in any state outside Texas. During that time, about 4 in 10 U.S. executions have been in Texas. A state website once included a list of condemned prisoners' last meals, but it was removed after complaints of bad taste. According to the book "Texas Curiosities," one prisoner requested dirt as his last meal because he wanted to use it in a voodoo ritual. "He did not get dirt; he got yogurt," said Texas correctional spokeswoman Michelle Lyons.

Since 1976, about **4 IN 10** U.S. executions have taken place in Texas.

7 The Dr Pepper Museum is in Waco, which is appropriate because the soft drink was invented there and was originally known as a "Waco." There is no truth to the legend that the drink includes prune juice, but it is indeed true that there's no period after "Dr" in its name.

8 Texans love their nicknames, but not all of them are officially sanctioned. Gubernatorial candidate Richard "Kinky" Friedman was allowed to put his nickname on the ballot in 2006, but rival Carole Keeton "Grandma" Strayhorn had to drop her nickname. Poker legend Doyle Brunson became "Texas Dolly" after Jimmy "the Greek" Snyder tried to introduce him as "Texas Doyle." Either Snyder mispronounced the name or reporters heard it wrong. Either way, it was printed as "Texas Dolly," and the name stuck.

9 Two musical daughters of Texas who died too young, Janis Joplin and Selena, are well remembered. The slide rule that Joplin used in school is displayed at the Museum of the Gulf Coast in Port Arthur. A bronze statue in Corpus Christi honors Selena. Sculptor H.W. Tatum produced both a smiling Selena head and a solemn one. The family chose solemn. The smiling head resides at the Corpus Christi Museum of Science and History.

10 Texas has produced some of the nation's most famous TV journalists, including Walter Cronkite, Dan Rather, Linda Ellerbee, Bob Schieffer and Sam Donaldson. On the air, Rather once described Texas as "the big enchilada or, if not an enchilada, then a huge taco."

WISCONSIN

1 Wisconsin is known as the Badger State because of lead miners in the 1800s who were nicknamed badgers because they lived underground in tunnels and mine shafts.

2 Even when Wisconsin had the deadliest fire in American history, it was overshadowed by Chicago. The Peshtigo disaster in the Green Bay area began Oct. 8, 1871—the same day as the Great Chicago Fire, which dominated the nation's attention. Chicago's disaster killed about 250, while Peshtigo's death toll was at least 1,200, and perhaps twice that many.

3 The QWERTY keyboard layout was invented in Wisconsin. Christopher Latham Sholes, a Milwaukee printer and inventor, realized he could prevent his typewriter from jamming by separating the most popular keys.

4 Wisconsin traditionally sits near the top for its high school graduation rate, but also for its drunken driving rates. While the state legislature in 2017 toughened penalties for motorists caught driving while intoxicated, Wisconsin remains the only state where a first offense is not a criminal violation. The new law did make the *fourth* offense a felony regardless of when the third offense was committed. (Yes, before it was just a misdemeanor in some circumstances.)

5 Wisconsin rightfully boasts it is "America's Dairyland" on its license plates. In the late 1960s, it went one step further with a bright yellow version that people called "butter plates."

6 U.S. House Speaker Paul Ryan, who sits just two heartbeats away from being president, may be the most powerful Wisconsinite ever, depending on how you measure former Sen. Joseph McCarthy's Red-baiting reign of terror. But Ryan's legislative record is slim. According to a 2016 New York Times article, the 10-term congressman has proposed just three bills that have become law. One established a commission on "evidence-based policy making," another named a post office and the third changed a tax on arrows.

7 Madison is known as a center of political correctness, but it took a wrong turn in 2000 when the University of Wisconsin-Madison admissions office promoted diversity by digitally adding a black student into a photo of white people at a football game. The virtual spectator, Diallo Shabazz, said he'd never attended a UW game.

8 Before Tommy Bartlett thrilled thousands with his water-skiing show in the Wisconsin Dells, he worked in Chicago radio. He was just 17 in 1931 when he started at WBBM-AM, where he went on to host two very popular daytime programs targeted at housewives, "Meet the Missus" and "The Missus Goes to Market."

9 In 1951, divorced dressmaker Margaret Jorgenson of Oshkosh left nearly $100,000 in her will to a man after spending only four hours with him. The two began chatting in a hotel elevator while both were visiting Chicago, and they decided to have lunch together. Afterward, they parted, maintaining a correspondence but never again meeting face to face. Jorgenson's will left her relatives nothing, and they sued, winning more than half of the money intended for Jorgenson's four-hour friend.

10 Wisconsin boasts some funny names. There are places like Imalone, Ubet, Embarrass, Footville and Spread Eagle. Then there are people, such as the pride of Wisconsin Rapids, retired race car driver Dick Trickle.

10 THINGS YOU MIGHT NOT KNOW ABOUT
IOWA

1 The Ringling Brothers circus nearly expired in northeast Iowa in the 1880s. Bedraggled by bad luck and worse weather, the fledgling circus lurched through thick mud to Cascade at imminent risk of collapse. But Cascade's mayor, doubtless aware that the death of a circus wouldn't help Cascade's image, turned out huge crowds. The Ringlings were so appreciative of Cascade's generosity that they decreed free admission for Cascade residents—forever. The circus closed in 2017, some 130 years later, but reportedly stood by the brothers' promise until the end.

2 The University of Iowa Writers' Workshop boasts that it was the first creative writing degree program in the United States. Among its students: Stuart Dybek ("The Coast of Chicago"), John Irving ("The World According to Garp") and Flannery O'Connor ("Wise Blood"). The acerbic O'Connor once said: "Everywhere I go, I'm asked if I think universities stifle writers. I think they don't stifle enough of them."

3 The most famous thing about Riverside, Iowa, hasn't even happened yet. According to the "Star Trek" saga, the captain of the starship Enterprise was born in an unspecified Iowa town on March 22, 2228. Seeing that reference, Riverside postal worker Steve Miller persuaded town officials to call the town the "future birthplace of Capt. James T. Kirk," and "Star Trek" creator Gene Roddenberry reportedly went along with it. Today, the town's slogan is "Where the trek begins," and an annual Trekkie festival is held there.

4 One of the most dramatic U.S. air disasters occurred in Sioux City in 1989 when a Chicago-bound jetliner suffered catastrophic engine failure and crash-landed, killing 111. Heroic crew efforts saved 185 others. Iowa also was the scene of crashes fatal to boxer Rocky Marciano (1969, near Newton), members of the Iowa State women's cross-country team (1985, in Des Moines), and South Dakota Gov. George Mickelson (1993, near Dubuque). But none was as famous as the tragedy on Feb. 3, 1959, "The Day the Music Died." Buddy Holly, Ritchie Valens and the Big Bopper, J.P. Richardson, were lost in an air accident near Clear Lake.

5 Iowa wasn't 15 years old as the Civil War approached, and would never host a battle. Yet Iowa contributed a higher percentage of its men to war than did any other state, North or South: Of the 116,000 Iowa men subject to military duty, 75,000 fought for the Union, according to the Iowa Official Register, a state government factbook.

Iowa contributed a higher percentage of its men to the Civil War than did any other state.

6 Iowa's first-in-the-nation caucuses haven't always been so important in the presidential race. It wasn't until South Dakota's George McGovern and his campaign manager, Gary Hart, realized how, under new party protocols, the state's 1972 vote could launch his long-shot presidential bid that they rose to prominence. The campaign recruited many Iowans and convinced national political reporters to cover the caucuses. McGovern stole the show and headlines from front-runner Edmund Muskie. He won the nomination but lost to Richard Nixon in November. In 1976, an obscure Georgian named Jimmy Carter repeated the feat by shocking the Democratic field, but he went on to win it all.

7 Which of these show business figures was not born in Cedar Rapids: Ashton Kutcher ("Two and a Half Men"), Elijah Wood ("The Lord of the Rings"), Ron Livingston ("Office Space") or Fran Allison ("Kukla, Fran and Ollie")? The answer: Allison, who attended Coe College in Cedar Rapids but was born in La Porte City.

8 Drive from Dyersville to the "Field of Dreams" baseball diamond, and you'll traverse the same undulating farm-to-market roads that bring hundreds of vehicles to the site in the 1989 movie's final, twilight scene. How did filmmakers choreograph the movements of all those cars on crowded two-lane roads so they could shoot the scene from the sky? A radio station in Dubuque, 25 miles east, surrendered its airwaves for the evening: All the drivers tuned to WDBQ-AM for precision commands on when the enormous entourage should come forward toward the ballfield, or cautiously retreat in reverse gear.

9 A remarkable Iowan died in 2011: Norma "Duffy" Lyon, who fascinated Iowa State Fair visitors with her life-size butter sculptures of cows, Elvis Presley, Dwight Eisenhower and even Jesus Christ and his disciples at the Last Supper.

10 Iowans demand efficient government. Exhibit A is the Squirrel Cage Jail, which served Council Bluffs from 1885 until 1969 and is now a museum. The jail, a three-story Lazy Susan and the only one of its size ever built, allowed one jailer to control more than 60 inmates in pie-shaped cells that revolved at the turn of a hand crank. An 1881 patent noted that the design would provide "maximum security with minimum jailer attention." An inmate could exit his cell only when the jailer ratcheted it to the sole doorway on that level.

10 THINGS YOU MIGHT NOT KNOW ABOUT
SMALL TOWNS

1 Centralia was a vital little mining town in eastern Pennsylvania until Valentine's Day 1981, when the ground opened up and tried to swallow 12-year-old Todd Domboski. The town was sitting on an underground coal fire that had started some 20 years earlier, spread through the network of old mine tunnels and seemed intent on destroying the town. Todd was pulled to safety, but most residents fled in the 1980s. The state ordered the rest to leave in the 1990s. By 2016, 11 hardy residents remained.

2 Fruita, a town in western Colorado, hosts the annual Mike the Headless Chicken festival, inspired by a 1945 incident in which a farmer tried to slaughter a rooster for dinner and failed. The farmer's ax blade chopped off most of Mike's head but left the jugular vein and much of the brain stem intact, allowing Mike to survive, and even to peck for food and preen his feathers. Fed through an eyedropper, the rooster survived for 18 months, touring sideshows from coast to coast.

3 Do you fondly remember your youth growing up in an idyllic "urban cluster"? That's what the U.S Census Bureau calls a community of at least 2,500 but less than 50,000 people. According to the 2010 count, there are more than 3,000 such towns, but they hold just 9.5 percent of the population. Most U.S. citizens are residents of "urbanized areas," that is, city folk.

4 The southeastern Illinois town of Oblong, named after Oblong Prairie, was previously known as Henpeck, after general store owner Henry Peck.

5 Driving across America's vast open spaces, a motorist could ditch the map and simply hopscotch from water tower to water tower. Typically the tallest structure in town, it often stakes the community's claim to fame and becomes something of a tourist attraction. Circleville, Ohio, boasts a million-gallon water tower painted and shaped like a pumpkin, honoring its annual festival. The giant peach towering over Gaffney, S.C., made a cameo on the

Netflix series "House of Cards." But it is hard to beat Ogallala, Neb., for its flight of fancy. The town's tower is painted to look like a UFO, especially when lit at night.

6 Marfa, Texas, has just 1,981 souls, but it can boast seven Oscars. The town, about 50 miles from the Mexican border, was the setting for three movies—"Giant" in 1956, and in 2007 "There Will Be Blood" and "No Country for Old Men," which all together hauled in 26 Academy Award nominations. If that's not a big enough box-office draw, go for minimalist sculptor Donald Judd's vast art installation.

Marfa, Texas, has just 1,981 souls, but it can boast **SEVEN OSCARS**.

7 How small can a small town get? The 2010 census counted four incorporated towns with a single occupant. One was Monowi, in the northeast corner of Nebraska. Elsie Eiler became Monowi's single resident when her husband died in 2004. Eiler is now the town's mayor, bartender and librarian. Of course, she handles city business at "city hall," which is a desk at the end of the bar.

8 The lauded Andy Warhol tribute album "Songs for Drella" by Lou Reed and John Cale begins with the song "Smalltown," about the suffocating environment of Warhol's youth. What small town did Warhol grow up in? Pittsburgh, where he was one of 670,000 residents of the nation's 10th largest city. From a New York perspective, everywhere else must look small.

9 "The Terror of Tiny Town," a 1938 Western movie "with an all-midget cast," is often listed as one of the worst movies of all time.

10 The town of Mayberry, N.C., in "The Andy Griffith Show" was fictional, as was a nearby town mentioned in the series, Mount Pilot. But North Carolina does have a town called Pilot Mountain. Though many believed Mayberry was based on Griffith's birthplace of Mount Airy, he said: "Over the years a lot of people have come to believe that Mayberry is based on my hometown and, it is not, 'cause real towns have real problems that have to be dealt with. All of Mayberry's problems were solved in half an hour."

CHAPTER 6
Politics

CLOUT

1 Sidney Korshak, a Chicago native suspected of mob ties but never indicted, made his mark as a fixer for Hollywood moguls and Las Vegas hotels. When he entered negotiations, labor problems often disappeared. Film producer Robert Evans credited Korshak with persuading MGM executives to make Al Pacino available for "The Godfather." Korshak was also known for little favors. When comedian Alan King was told that a swanky European hotel had no rooms, he called Korshak from the lobby. Before King had hung up, a clerk tapped on the phone booth and told him his suite was ready.

2 A city councillor in York, England, made arrangements for her daughter's wedding in 2005—including switching nine sets of traffic lights to green so the bridal party could breeze through the usually traffic-clogged streets. The politician, Ann Reid, insisted that her main goal had been legitimate, to test the system that turns the lights green for emergency vehicles, and that the benefit to her daughter was just a bonus.

3 As Senate majority leader, Lyndon B. Johnson wielded unprecedented power, lording it over other senators and his aides. How did he get there? He identified the power brokers early and made himself indispensable. Sen. George Smathers of Florida described how Johnson did it: "He was ... so condescending, you couldn't believe it! I've seen him kiss Harry Byrd's ass until it was disgusting: 'Senator, how about so-and-so? Wouldn't you like to do this? Can't we do this for you?'"

4 In New York Police Department slang, a "rabbi" has nothing to do with religion. It's a term for a mentor, higher-up or otherwise connected person who can help an officer get ahead.

5 Bill Clinton's last day as president featured the controversial pardon of financier Marc Rich, who was convicted of tax evasion and illegal trading with Iran while it held American hostages. Rich's ex-wife, Denise, had donated more than $1 million to the Democratic Party and the Clinton library. Two lawyers in the case later gained wider fame. Lewis "Scooter"

Libby, who represented Rich until about a year before the pardon, became Vice President Dick Cheney's chief of staff and was convicted of perjury in the CIA leak case. Libby's prison sentence was commuted by President George W. Bush. Then there was Eric Holder, who as deputy attorney general gave a recommendation on the Rich pardon that was "neutral leaning favorable." Holder is now attorney general.

6 New York mobster Charles "Lucky" Luciano spent World War II in prison but maintained enough clout that U.S. authorities cooperated with him in something called "Operation Underworld" to aid the war effort. Luciano made sure there were no work stoppages or acts of sabotage on the New York City docks. In exchange, authorities moved Luciano to a prison closer to the city, and after the war they commuted his sentence and deported him to Italy.

7 Dan Quayle's nomination for vice president in 1988 led to disclosure of his successful effort to use his wealthy family's connections to get into the Indiana National Guard and avoid the Vietnam War. But Quayle insisted he got into the Guard "fairly." Asked why he didn't just go down to the Guard's office and apply, he said, "I do what any normal person would do at that age. You call home. You call home to mother and father and say, 'I'd like to get in the National Guard.'" That comment may have inspired the protest chant "Quayle, Quayle, called his mom, everyone else went to 'Nam."

8 Besides the sacks of cash, the clout of special interest groups such as the National Rifle Association, AARP and unions springs from their ability to mobilize armies of volunteers at election time to help friends and to punish enemies, much as political parties do. In Chicago, the Democratic army is often peopled by city workers. That reality was highlighted by a federal investigation that found a third of city employees in five targeted departments were absent on Feb. 25, 2003, the day of municipal elections. In fact, more workers took that day off than the Fourth of July or Christmas the year before. Said one Streets and Sanitation employee: "Garbage, we could take care of that some other time. We had to take care of the votes."

9 In 2009, Tribune reporters pored over 1,800 pages of emails and documents for the "Clout Goes to College" investigation of favoritism in University of Illinois admissions. One email exchange initially stumped reporters. A U. of I. staffer bemoaned the fact that "(redacted) was overlooked again," and a colleague responded that "poor (redacted) . . . should be in." The reporters finally figured out that the discussion was about Cubs great Ron Santo, who had been denied admission to the Baseball Hall of Fame. The U. of I. official who handled the redactions mistakenly thought Santo was a student applicant.

10 One of the most egregious abuses of power arose out of . . . (What? Are you speaking to us? Yes. No, we couldn't, really. Wow, how generous. We're flattered. Please give him our thanks.) Now, what were we talking about? Oh. Never mind.

10 THINGS YOU MIGHT NOT KNOW ABOUT
DIRTY POLITICS

1 When unscrupulous British political operatives show up at nursing homes with pre-marked absentee voter ballots, it's called "granny farming."

2 Once upon a time, Roman Catholics were very, very scary. Running for U.S. president in 1928, Catholic Al Smith, a Democrat, was called a "rum-soaked Romanist." His opponents circulated construction photos of New York's Holland Tunnel, saying they showed the beginnings of a tunnel to the Vatican.

3 In the 1946 Democratic primary race for Georgia governor, Eugene Talmadge appealed to white racists by hiring a look-alike of his opponent to campaign in a limousine with two cigar-puffing blacks in the back seat. It worked, but Talmadge died before Inauguration Day.

4 According to political lore out of Florida, Democratic primary challenger George Smathers defeated Florida Sen. Claude Pepper in 1950 by declaring Pepper was a "shameless extrovert" whose sister "was once a thespian" and who "habitually practiced celibacy" before his marriage. But that speech probably was apocryphal. A Time magazine article at the time cited it as a "yarn," but some believed it despite Smathers' denials.

5 Hairdressers, beware. When Republican Mike Taylor challenged Democratic Sen. Max Baucus in Montana in 2002, a Democratic ad cited financial irregularities in Taylor's hair-care business decades earlier. The ad featured old footage of Taylor with his shirt half-open while he applied lotion to a man's temples as disco music played. The Village People didn't appear in the ad, but the suggestion was obvious. Taylor, a father of two who had been married 22 years, was defeated.

6 Former Bush aide Karl Rove admitted a "youthful prank" in Chicago in 1970. As a 19-year-old, he stole campaign stationery for Alan Dixon, a Democratic candidate for Illinois treasurer, and printed 1,000 fliers promising "free beer, free food, girls and a good time" at a Dixon rally. The leaflet was distributed to street people, creating unexpected diversity at the event.

7 Dirty tricksters love telephone "push polls," which pretend to be surveys but ask leading questions, such as the one in the South Carolina 2000 primary: "Would you be more or less likely to vote for John McCain if you knew he had fathered a black child out of wedlock?" (The child was his adopted Bangladeshi daughter.) Another phone prank is the "Super Bowl scheme," in which a caller pretends to be from an opponent's campaign and annoys voters by interrupting them during the football game.

8 Many historians believe Chicago Mayor Richard J. Daley's Democratic machine stuffed the ballot box to win Illinois for John F. Kennedy in the 1960 race for the White House. But it's often wrongly assumed that Illinois was crucial. In fact, JFK would have captured the presidency without Illinois. After the election, a joke went around Washington: Kennedy, Secretary of State Dean Rusk and Daley were in a lifeboat with enough food for one. Two of them would have to jump overboard. But whom? Daley suggested the three of them vote on it and he won, 8-2.

9 It's known as "oppo," or opposition research, in which investigators hunt for damaging information. William Casey was a master. Working for Richard Nixon in 1960, he investigated John F. Kennedy's medical condition but was never directly tied to a break-in at the office of Kennedy's doctor. Two decades later, Jimmy Carter's debate briefing book went missing, and a congressional probe later cited Casey as the chief suspect, despite his denials. When Ronald Reagan defeated Carter, Reagan decided Casey was well-qualified for a key job: CIA director.

10 Whispering campaigns often label candidates as drunkards. But in Wisconsin in 1956, the opposite was true. Republican gubernatorial candidate Vernon Thompson was from Richland Center, which banned alcohol sales. His opponents went to taverns in resort areas and struck up conversations about how Thompson was from a dry town and wanted to turn the whole state that way. Thompson won, barely.

10 THINGS YOU MIGHT NOT KNOW ABOUT
CAMPAIGN SLOGANS

1 When Democrats sought to get Franklin Pierce elected president, they reminded voters of James Polk's win eight years earlier. The slogan: "We Polked you in 1844; we'll Pierce you in 1852."

2 "Sunflowers die in November" doesn't seem like a winning slogan in a presidential race, but it was. Franklin Roosevelt's campaign was referring to 1936 opponent Alf Landon's home state of Kansas and its official flower, which was featured on Landon's campaign buttons.

3 Candidates usually try to reassure the voters, but in 1997, Liberian rebel leader Charles Taylor intimidated them instead, suggesting that a civil war might be reignited if he was not elected president. Taylor's slogan: "He killed my ma, he killed my pa, but I will vote for him." (He won the election but was later arrested and convicted of war crimes.)

4 The 1884 U.S. election was by all accounts nasty. The Democratic candidate, New York Gov. Grover Cleveland, was considered an honest man who wasn't afraid to stand up to special interests. But it also came out in the campaign that he had had an affair years earlier and that he was financially supporting the woman and their illegitimate son. The Republicans enjoyed yelling, "Ma! Ma! Where's my Pa?" But the Democrats got the last laugh after Cleveland won with the rejoinder, "Gone to the White House. Ha! Ha! Ha!"

5 Some unglamorous Illinois politicians have tried to turn that deficit into an advantage. Gov. Richard Ogilvie used the slogan "Charisma isn't everything," but the voters were more charmed by Dan Walker in 1972. The grandmotherly looking Dawn Clark Netsch described herself as "more than just a pretty face," but she was less than a match for incumbent Gov. Jim Edgar in 1994.

6 When ethically challenged Edwin Edwards ran against former Ku Klux Klan grand wizard David Duke for Louisiana governor in 1991, the bumper stickers included "Vote for the crook—it's important" and "Vote for the lizard, not the wizard." (The lizard won.)

7 The second spot on the ticket rarely gets much respect, but Grover Cleveland's running mate, former Indiana Gov. Thomas Hendricks, surely had reason to complain when a sloganeer penned, "We'll shout for our man and his important appendix! We'll whoop'er up lively for Cleveland and Hendricks!"

8 Some slogans sound like they were doomed from the start. In 1952, Adlai Stevenson—facing World War II hero Gen. Dwight Eisenhower—went into battle with the jarring, passive-aggressive "You Never Had It So Good." And in 1968, Democrats for Humphrey asked, "Who but Hubert?"

9 It's a good thing for politicians that campaign slogans have an expiration date. Woodrow Wilson's 1916 claim "He kept us out of war" lasted only until April 6, 1917.

10 Barack Obama was the "hope and change" candidate in 2008, reflecting the optimistic American view that change is good. But in 1900, President William McKinley won re-election with the opposite slogan: "Let well enough alone."

"Let well enough alone."
—WILLIAM MCKINLEY CAMPAIGN SLOGAN

POLITICAL ADS

1 The star of the most famous political ad in U.S. history didn't see the ad until more than 35 years later. In President Lyndon B. Johnson's "Daisy" TV commercial in 1964, a scene of a little girl counting daisy petals morphs into the countdown to a nuclear explosion. The suggestion: If you vote for Barry Goldwater, this kid is toast. The girl was Monique Corzilius, whose parents didn't even know the commercial was about politics, according to interviews in Newsweek and on the Conelrad Adjacent website. Corzilius doesn't remember much about the commercial's filming, and she didn't see it until she stumbled onto it one day while web surfing.

2 "Daisy" aired as a paid ad only once but was replayed many times in news reports. These days, political ads sometimes are posted online and get mentioned in news reports without any ad buy at all. That used to be called "free media," but political consultants didn't like the perception that they were being paid good money for something that was "free." So they rebranded it as "earned media" because the consultants' cleverness had "earned" such notice.

3 It didn't take long for our esteemed Founding Fathers to go negative. The weapon of choice was the handbill. These campaign screeds were easily printed and widely distributed. In their personal, vicious and baseless attacks, they make today's TV ads seem downright friendly. Gen. Andrew Jackson was the target of particularly nasty attack handbills in the 1828 campaign against John Quincy Adams, who was seeking re-election. One called his mother a prostitute and his wife an adulteress. Another handbill, bordered in black and showing six coffins, labeled Jackson a murderer, claiming he killed six fellow soldiers in cold blood. The truth was that the six militiamen had not only deserted but had stolen military supplies and tried to stir up a mutiny. They were sentenced and executed.

4 One of the most unusual campaign ads ridiculed 1968 vice presidential candidate Spiro T. Agnew, known for ethnic slurs and the memorable quote "If you've seen one slum, you've seen them all." The ad—created by the man behind the "Daisy" ad, Tony Schwartz—showed a TV set with the words "Agnew for Vice-President?" while a person in the background laughed uproariously.

5 Political ads for Chicago Mayor Jane Byrne tried to explain her combative style in the context of femininity: "She was 24, her husband died, and she had to put her life back together. Today she still draws on that same determination, that same toughness. She's feisty, with a mother's protective instincts."

6 In Chicago's 1983 campaign that led to the election of Harold Washington as the city's first black mayor, white opponent Bernard Epton was blasted for his ad slogan "Before it's too late." Few accepted Epton's explanation that the slogan was not about race and was developed before the primary, when he thought his opponent would be Jane Byrne. Washington made his own appeal to race, with a TV commercial that showed images of the Ku Klux Klan and the John F. Kennedy and Martin Luther King Jr. assassinations and suggested that a defeat for Washington would be an act of intolerance leaving Americans "profoundly ashamed."

7 A TV ad for Illinois Gov. Adlai Stevenson's 1952 presidential bid featured a jazzy song called "I Love the Gov," with a woman singing:

> *I'd rather have a man with a hole in his shoe*
> *Than a hole in everything he says*
> *I'd rather have a man who knows what to do when he gets to be the prez*
> *I love the Gov, the governor of Illinois*
> *He is the guy that brings the dove of peace and joy*
> *When Illinois the GOP double-crossed*
> *He is the one who told all the crooks, "Get lost"*
> *Adlai, love you madly*
> *And what you did for your own great state*
> *You're going to do for the rest of the 48 . . .*

8 The 2010 U.S. Senate campaign in Delaware added a rule to the political playbook: Avoid issuing denials concerning witchcraft. In her book "Troublemaker," Republican candidate Christine O'Donnell writes that her "I am not a witch" TV ad was a matter of her "trusting a group of people I hardly knew and going against my better judgment." She said she hadn't seen the ad or approved it before it was leaked to The New York Times, forcing her hand.

9 Warren Harding is considered by some to be one of the nation's worst presidents. But in turning to Albert Lasker, a Chicago adman considered the father of modern advertising, he proved in 1920 to be a visionary political campaigner. One of Lasker's big breakthroughs was to enlist celebrities such as Al Jolson, Douglas Fairbanks and Mary Pickford to endorse Harding on newsreels and in newspaper advertisements. That tradition continues, notably in 2012 when Clint Eastwood talked to an empty chair at the Republican National Convention.

10 How much those celebrities actually sway voters is often unclear, but one YouTube ad in 2008 seems to have packed quite a punch in Iowa. Action star and cult hero Chuck Norris gave the little-known former Arkansas governor Mike Huckabee his full support in a humorous spot that had Huckabee saying, "My plan to secure the border? Two words: Chuck Norris" and "I'm Mike Huckabee and I approved this message . . . so did Chuck." An already surging Huckabee shocked many by winning the Iowa caucuses, beating Mitt Romney and John McCain.

10 THINGS YOU MIGHT NOT KNOW ABOUT
PRESIDENTIAL ALSO-RANS

1 A perennial presidential candidate in the mid-19th century was Leonard "Live Forever" Jones, a Kentuckian who believed that if people could find a way to live sinless lives, they would never die. Jones envisioned a city of immortals where cemeteries would be unnecessary, but that city was never built, and he never made much of an impact as the candidate of the High Moral Party. Jones, to his presumed embarrassment, died in 1868.

2 Victoria Woodhull, an Ohio native often described as the first female candidate for U.S. president, was an amazing public figure—an advocate for women's sexual freedom, a Wall Street broker, a spiritual healer and the first American publisher of "The Communist Manifesto." When she ran as the Equal Rights Party candidate for president in 1872, women didn't have the right to vote, and Woodhull hadn't yet reached the minimum age of 35. She spent Election Day in jail on a charge of sending obscene materials through the mail, and any votes she got apparently went uncounted. In 1877, Woodhull moved to England, and later became one of the first women there to own a car.

3 The anti-war protesters who descended on Chicago for the Democratic National Convention in 1968 were adept at publicity. Near the Picasso sculpture downtown, they appeared with a hog named Pigasus and announced him as their candidate for president. Seven protesters were arrested on charges of disturbing the peace and Pigasus was taken to the Anti-Cruelty Society, later to be adopted by a farmer in Grayslake. At the jail, a police officer told the suspects: "I've got bad news for you, boys. The pig squealed."

4 Samuel Tilden infamously lost the hotly contested 1876 election by one electoral vote to Rutherford B. Hayes, but that didn't stop Wichita Falls, Texas, from including him when it named streets after presidents, slipping Tilden Street between Grant and Hayes streets.

5 Harold Stassen started out as a prodigy, becoming the youngest governor of Minnesota at age 31. He ended up as a joke, running for the Republican presidential nomination nine times and coming up empty. Even so, he chalked up some impressive accomplishments, including appointing the first black officer in his state's National Guard and signing the United Nations Charter, one of eight Americans to do so.

6 Just one man, Franklin D. Roosevelt, has been American voters' choice for president more than twice. So say all the history books. But Grover Cleveland did capture the most votes in three consecutive elections: 1884, 1888, 1892. Unfortunately for Cleveland, Republican Benjamin Harrison grabbed more electoral votes—and the presidency—in 1888. Cleveland had to settle for being the only president to serve nonconsecutive terms.

7 New York Gov. Al Smith, the Democratic candidate in 1928, faced nasty campaign rhetoric targeting his Catholicism. One example: A photo of the Holland Tunnel linking New York and New Jersey was widely distributed with a caption claiming it secretly led to the Vatican. If that weren't enough, Smith also strongly opposed Prohibition, which put him in the wet camp. Naturally, his campaign buttons read: "Vote for Al Smith And Make Your Wet Dreams Come True." He lost in a landslide to Herbert Hoover.

8 Martin Van Buren's Free Soil candidacy in 1848 was America's first serious third-party movement, but its abolitionist stance was a nonstarter in the South. Still, when Van Buren was credited with nine votes in Virginia, his campaign cried foul—just nine votes out of 92,000 cast? A Virginian wit responded, "Yes, fraud, and we're still looking for the son-of-a-bitch who voted nine times."

9 The 1948 election saw Strom Thurmond, the States Rights Party candidate, spit virulent racism at every turn, but it was the Progressive Party's Henry Wallace who walked into the buzz saw of public disfavor. In the midst of a Red Scare, Wallace made the mistake of suggesting there was more than one way to deal with the Soviet Union. The blowback was staggering. The Pittsburgh Press published the names, addresses and workplaces of Wallace supporters. Other supporters were arrested, beaten and even killed. And in New York, a judge said support for Wallace could weigh against a parent in a child-custody case.

10 Bob Dole lost several bids for the presidency, but he never lost his sense of humor. After his defeats, he said, "I slept like a baby. Every two hours I woke up and cried."

10 THINGS YOU MIGHT NOT KNOW ABOUT
HOUSE SPEAKERS

1 As a representative and even as a senator, Lyndon B. Johnson often greeted his mentor, Sam Rayburn, the feared speaker of the U.S. House in the mid-20th century, by kissing the fellow Texan's bald head and saying, "How are you tonight, my beloved?"

2 Though the U.S. House speaker is second in line for presidential succession, only one has ever become president, and that was by a more indirect route. James K. Polk left the U.S. House to become governor of Tennessee, but voters booted him out after one term. As a dark-horse candidate in 1844, he won the White House with the promise—which he kept—of annexing Texas.

3 Chicago's Ashland Avenue is named after the Kentucky estate of U.S. House Speaker Henry Clay.

4 Tiny Hainesville, tucked between Grayslake and Round Lake, Ill., claims to be "Lake County's oldest village." It is named after Elijah Haines, a longtime Illinois state representative who served as the only Independent speaker in state history, selected as the compromise candidate by the equally matched Democrats and Republicans. It may be they rued that decision. When Haines died in 1889, the Tribune wrote: "It is a matter of history that he has created more confusion in Illinois Legislatures than any dozen of his contemporaries possibly could. . . . As a member he seldom manipulated legislation except by indirection, and as speaker his rulings were as devious as the winds."

5 Paul Powell, Illinois House speaker from 1949-51 and again from 1959-63, was Illinois secretary of state when he died in 1970, and his shoe box became famous in political lore. That shoe box was one of Powell's storage places for $800,000 in cash, an impressive sum for a public servant whose salary never exceeded $30,000. In addition to the money, Powell's hoard included 49 cases of whiskey, 14 transistor radios and two cases of creamed corn. No solid explanation for the creamed corn has emerged, but state Auditor Michael Howlett had this theory about the cash: "He must have saved his money when he was young."

6 William Redmond, speaker of the Illinois House from 1975-81, worked as a model as a child, appearing on calendars carrying a fishing pole and accompanied by a dog. When he was 5, his face was on the Sun-Maid Raisins package.

7 Amid pre-Civil War bickering on the U.S. House floor in 1858, Rep. Laurence Keitt of South Carolina called Rep. Galusha Grow of Pennsylvania, who was white, a "black Republican puppy," and Grow responded that "no negro-driver shall crack his whip over my head." A full-blown rumble erupted, with many members joining in. Mississippi Rep.

William Barksdale's hairpiece was knocked off, and he put it on backward, causing lawmakers on both sides to laugh, breaking the tension. After the war broke out, Keitt and Barksdale became Confederate generals and were mortally wounded—Keitt at the Battle of Cold Harbor and Barksdale at the Battle of Gettysburg. Grow was U.S. House speaker from 1861 to 1863.

8 Dennis Hastert's 2004 memoir, "Speaker," recounts him suffering a broken nose while boxing with a friend and trying unsuccessfully to hide the injury from his parents. In the context of his paying $1.7 million to cover up child sex abuse, his words take on a different tone. "I was never a very good liar," he wrote. "Maybe I wasn't smart enough. I could never get away with it, so I made up my mind as a kid to tell the truth and pay the consequences."

9 As U.S. House speaker from 2007-11, Nancy Pelosi was the highest-ranking woman in U.S. political history. She grew up amid power, with a father who was a congressman and mayor of Baltimore. Pelosi wrote that she first visited Congress when she was 6. Her brothers told her, "Nancy, look at the Capitol," and she asked, "Is it a capital A, B or C?"

10 Uncle Joe Cannon, who consolidated power by not only being speaker but also chairman of the powerful House Rules Committee, ruled the U.S. House with such an iron grip that he became known as Czar Cannon. The Illinois Republican served in the House for nearly half a century, and he knew something about politicians: "Sometimes in politics one must duel with skunks, but no one should be fool enough to allow skunks to choose the weapons."

10 THINGS YOU MIGHT NOT KNOW ABOUT
PATRIOTS

1 Two Illinois women named Mary made an enormous impact on the medical treatment of Union soldiers wounded during the Civil War. Mary Livermore, of Chicago, was a top official of the U.S. Sanitary Commission and was in charge of cleaning and supplying hospitals along the Mississippi River. Mary Ann Bickerdyke, of Galesburg, served on 19 battlefields and fought filthy hospital conditions, often clashing with the men running the facilities. When one official complained to Gen. William Sherman about her, he responded: "She outranks me."

2 The controversial 2001 law passed in the wake of the Sept. 11 attacks is known as the Patriot Act, but it's actually the USA PATRIOT Act, an acronym for Uniting and Strengthening America by Providing Appropriate Tools Required to Intercept and Obstruct Terrorism.

3 Next time you curse a jury summons, remember the story of George F. Porter. The Texas community college president had twice been summoned to jury service in Dallas and summarily sent home because he was black. When he was called a third time, in September 1938, he decided enough was enough. After refusing to leave, Porter was thrown down the courthouse steps by two thugs. He picked himself up, pushed his way through a crowd of angry white men and sprinted to the courtroom. He never did get to sit on that jury, but his story made national news, and a young NAACP lawyer took notice. His name was Thurgood Marshall. Just a few weeks after Marshall visited, the offending judge impaneled a black juror.

4 Abigail Adams was so adamant about women's rights that she threatened to revolt against the American revolutionaries. "Remember all men would be tyrants if they could," she wrote her husband, John Adams, in 1776. "If particular care and attention is not paid to the ladies, we are determined to foment a rebellion, and will not hold ourselves bound by any laws in which we have no voice or representation." Even so, full voting rights for women wouldn't come for nearly a century and a half. Common was the view of Thomas Jefferson, who wrote that "the tender breasts of ladies were not formed for political convulsion."

5 The Patriot Movement in the United States is often vehemently anti-government—and enjoying renewed popularity. According to the Southern Poverty Law Center, there was a dramatic spike in such groups after the election of President Barack Obama, jumping from 149 in 2008 to 1,360 in 2012. The center reported 663 groups in 2016. The movement, which emerged in the 1990s after the Ruby Ridge and Waco incidents, birthed Timothy McVeigh and Terry Nichols, who were responsible for the worst domestic terrorism attack in U.S. history: the Oklahoma City bombing in April 1995.

6 Louis Post was a paper pusher, but he also was a patriot. During the Red Scare in 1919, U.S. Attorney General A. Mitchell Palmer and his aide J. Edgar Hoover ordered widespread arrests and deportations of suspected radicals, and the paperwork fell to Assistant Labor Secretary Post. The bureaucrat determined that many of the actions were illegal, and he refused to endorse them. That courageous stand inspired calls for Post's firing, but it also blunted the so-called Palmer Raids, remembered today as one of the worst violations of civil rights in the nation's history.

7 U.S. history has sometimes overlooked blacks' military contributions, so it's worth noting that you may have an African-American named Jacob Peterson to thank for your July 4 holiday. In 1780, Peterson and another militiaman raised the alarm after spotting the British sloop Vulture in New York's Hudson River, and their comrades' cannon fire forced the ship downriver. That left British spy John Andre without a ride back to New York City after his secret meeting with Gen. Benedict Arnold, and Andre's capture unraveled Arnold's plot to surrender West Point. Had Arnold succeeded, the War of Independence might have ended quite differently.

8 Americans aren't the only people who are patriots. Russians refer to their victorious struggle against Nazi Germany as the Great Patriotic War. Ukraine, attempting to distance itself from Russia, decided in 2014 to stop referring to the Great Patriotic War in its textbooks and simply consider it part of World War II. In June 2015, Russian leader Vladimir Putin opened a theme park called Patriot Park, featuring heavy weapons for kids to climb on and army rations for lunch.

9 One of the darkest days in U.S. history was March 16, 1968, when U.S. soldiers murdered as many as 500 unarmed Vietnamese civilians, including women and children, in the My Lai massacre. One American serviceman, though, tried to stop the killing. Warrant Officer Hugh Thompson, a helicopter pilot, witnessed the bloodbath in progress and landed his chopper to protect villagers from fellow soldiers, ordering his crew to train their guns on a group of GIs until he led the civilians to safety. For his trouble and for testifying against his fellow soldiers, Thompson was vilified and ostracized by his brothers in uniform, the American public and officials who questioned his motives and his integrity. It wasn't until 1998 that Thompson was awarded the Soldier's Medal, for heroism not involving conflict with an enemy. Later he said, "Don't do the right thing looking for a reward, because it might not come."

> *"Don't do the right thing looking for a reward, because it might not come."* —HUGH THOMPSON

10 Historians generally agree that only a minority of the colonists actively supported the American Revolution. Most people in the colonies either avoided staking out a position or were loyalists. And since our Founding Fathers were officially British subjects, they were considered by many to be traitors, not patriots. Obviously, they got the last word.

10 THINGS YOU MIGHT NOT KNOW ABOUT
THIRD PARTIES

1 Nevada is the only state that includes "none of the above" as a ballot option. But if "none" finishes No. 1, the second-highest vote-getter wins.

2 A high point for third parties was 1912, when Teddy Roosevelt tried to win a third term in the White House because he was disgruntled with his successor, William Howard Taft. Roosevelt's Bull Moose Party beat Taft but lost to Woodrow Wilson. Roosevelt won 27 percent of the popular vote and got 88 electoral votes.

3 In 1967, the citizens of Picoaza, Ecuador, were treated to a series of advertisements with slogans such as "For Mayor: Honorable Pulvapies" and "Vote for any candidate, but if you want well-being and hygiene, vote for Pulvapies." The honorable Pulvapies was elected mayor by write-in votes, but could not take office. Why? Because Pulvapies was a foot powder.

4 For nearly seven years, former Alaska Gov. Sarah Palin's husband, Todd, was a registered member of the Alaskan Independence Party, which advocates that state residents be allowed to vote on seceding from the United States.

5 Socialist Party presidential candidate Eugene Debs finished third in 1920 with 913,664 votes—about 3.5 percent of those cast—even though he couldn't go on the campaign trail or even vote for himself. Debs had been thrown in prison because he protested against American involvement in World War I.

6 When President Richard Nixon visited communist China in 1972, right-wing California politician John G. Schmitz quipped: "I have no objection to President Nixon going to China. I just object to his coming back." Schmitz was the American Independent Party's 1972 presidential candidate, winning more than 1 million votes. Many more millions have heard of Schmitz's daughter, whom he nicknamed "Cake." She is Mary Kay Letourneau, the teacher who was imprisoned for having sex with an underage pupil and married him upon her release.

7 By definition, the third-party route is an uphill battle. But for the crusading Victoria Claflin Woodhull, it was particularly daunting. Running as the Equal Rights Party presidential candidate in 1872, her most likely supporters—women—couldn't even vote.

8 Jesse Ventura, a former professional wrestler who shocked the political establishment in 1998 when he won the Minnesota gubernatorial race, may have been the first political candidate to launch his own action figure. One of his campaign ads featured two boys playing with custom-made Ventura action figures dressed in a suit. It didn't take long before the dolls were available for sale.

9 A third-party presidential candidate has never won a general election in Illinois—not even Rockford native Rep. John B. Anderson, who ran as an independent in 1980 against President Jimmy Carter and Ronald Reagan. Anderson, who won just 7 percent of the vote in his home state, had become considerably more liberal since first being elected to the U.S.

House in 1960. Early in his career, he repeatedly pushed a constitutional amendment that would have recognized "the law and authority of Jesus Christ."

10 When H. Ross Perot announced on "Larry King Live" in February 1992 that he would run for president if supporters got him on the ballot in all 50 states, the most surprised person may have been his wife, Margot.

THE U.S. SUPREME COURT

1 Nicknames for justices include "Old Bacon Face" (Samuel P. Chase, who had a reddish complexion), "Scalito" (Samuel Alito, characterized as a mini-me of Antonin Scalia), "The Lone Ranger" (William Rehnquist, for his contrarian positions) and "Hugo-to-Hell" (Hugo Black, a strict sentencing judge). But if you see a reference to Thurgood Marshall as "Thoroughgood," that's not a nickname—that's the first name he was born with, before changing it in the second grade.

2 While delivering a speech to the Utah Bar Association in 1982, Justice Byron White was attacked by a man who shouted "Busing and pornography don't go!" and hit the judge. After the man was hauled away, White referred to his younger days as a University of Colorado running back, quipping, "I've been hit harder than that before in Utah."

3 Protestants dominated the Supreme Court for most of its history, so much so that for the first half of the 20th century, court watchers talked about the "Jewish seat" and the "Catholic seat." In 1985, the Supreme Court had no Jews and one Catholic, but by the time John Paul Stevens retired a quarter century later in 2010, the court had flipped completely and would have no Protestant member for the first time ever. Now, with the appointment of Neil Gorsuch, who was raised Catholic but attends an Episcopalian church, court wags ask if there's a "Protestant seat."

4 Jimmy Carter was a tough-luck president, with crises at the gas pump and in the embassy at Tehran. So it's little wonder that Carter was shut out at the Supreme Court, becoming the only president in U.S. history to serve at least a full term without making a high court nomination.

5 When conservative Robert Bork was nominated to the court in 1987, all aspects of his life were examined, even his video rentals. A leaked list of his videos included nothing sexually explicit and many classics, such as Alfred Hitchcock's "North by Northwest" and Orson Welles' "Citizen Kane." Among the surprises: Federico Fellini's "8½." Bork also rented "The Star Chamber," a film about a secret society imposing vigilante justice. Bork's nomination was rejected, but it left legacies such as the term "Borked," based on the nominee's rough treatment, as well as a federal law banning disclosure of video rentals.

6 Douglas Ginsburg withdrew his nomination to the court in 1987 amid revelations that he had smoked marijuana. Within a few years, that was no longer a fatal flaw. Our last three presidents have smoked pot, as has at least one current justice, Clarence Thomas. When Thomas was nominated only four years after the Ginsburg debacle, the White House confirmed that Thomas had smoked marijuana "several times" in college and "perhaps once" in law school. "We believe this matter is inconsequential," said White House spokeswoman Judy Smith, and she turned out to be right.

7 The chief justice of the United States earns $263,300, while associate justices get $251,800. When Justice John Paul Stevens stepped down in 2010, he continued collecting his salary for life under a policy that applies to all federal judges who retire at age 65 or later with at least 15 years of service. The idea is that federal judges never fully retire and are available as needed.

8 President Richard Nixon, smarting from the rejection of nominee Clement Haynsworth, presented Harrold Carswell in 1970 as his second choice for justice. When critics called Carswell mediocre, Sen. Roman Hruska, R-Neb., issued a most unhelpful defense: "Even if he were mediocre, there are a lot of mediocre judges and people and lawyers. They are entitled to a little representation, aren't they, and a little chance?" Carswell, forever cast as a symbol of mediocrity, was rejected by the Senate. Six years later, he was fined $100 for making sexual advances to an undercover police officer in a shopping mall restroom in Tallahassee, Fla.

9 Former Justice Scalia, who was considered one of America's finest legal minds, was rejected by the college of his choice. "I was an Italian boy from Queens, not quite the Princeton type," Scalia said. He went to Georgetown instead.

10 Historians generally agree that the court's low point came in 1857 when it ruled that Dred Scott must remain a slave. But the second worst? Perhaps the case of Chicagoan Myra Bradwell, who passed the Illinois bar exam in 1869 but was denied a license because of her sex. Bradwell appealed to the U.S. Supreme Court but lost, with Justice Joseph Bradley writing: "The paramount destiny and mission of woman is to fulfill the noble and benign offices of wife and mother. That is the law of the Creator." About two decades later, Bradwell finally won her law license, retroactive to 1869.

CHAPTER 7
Language & Letters

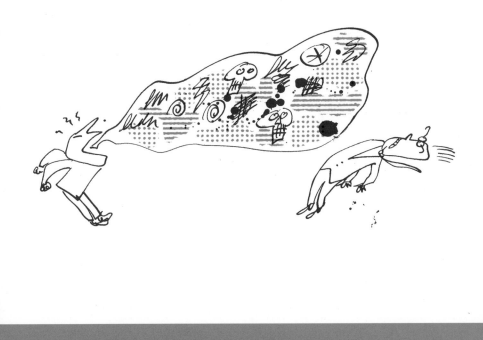

INSULTS

1 In some countries, shaking a person's hand while your other hand is in your pocket is considered an insult. A photo of Microsoft's Bill Gates doing just that while meeting with South Korean President Park Geun-hye caused an uproar in that country in 2013.

2 The traditional African-American game of "the dozens"—in which two people trade outrageous insults, often for an audience, and frequently about each other's mother—has more than a dozen other names. A 1972 study found it was called "sounding" in New York, "woofing" in Philadelphia, "joning" in Washington, D.C., and "signifying" in Chicago. Some say the term "the dozens" comes from an expectation that each person would throw 12 insults. There's also the theory that it refers to the unlucky roll of 12 in craps. Still others believe the phrase comes from the slavery era, when the 12 least desirable slaves to survive a trans-Atlantic journey were sold as a "dirty dozen."

3 Anthony Weiner's repeated sexting scandals made him a punching bag in the New York mayor's race. But Weiner punched back, calling 69-year-old rival George McDonald "grandpa" and ridiculing British reporter Lucy Watson by feigning a British accent and wondering whether he had "stepped into a Monty Python bit." McDonald called Weiner a "punk" and a "self-pleasuring freak." And mayoral candidate Erick Salgado declared that Weiner's sexting pseudonym, Carlos Danger, was an insult to Latinos.

4 Tony Curtis' famous insult of Marilyn Monroe—"It's like kissing Hitler"—came out of frustration over her lateness and inability to say her lines during filming of "Some Like It Hot." And indeed, her behavior was decidedly unattractive. It once took her 47 takes to properly say a single sentence. Director Billy Wilder tried pasting the line inside a dresser drawer, but she opened the wrong drawer. So Wilder had the line pasted in every drawer.

5 When a politician starts out by saying, "My staff tells me not to say this . . . ," it's a good sign he's about to offend people. Such was the case when then-Senate Majority Leader Harry

Reid, D-Nev., observed in 2008 that before the opening of the U.S. Capitol Visitor Center, people had to stand out in the summer heat and "you could literally smell the tourists coming into the Capitol."

6 The Lincoln-Douglas debates in 1858 are considered remarkable examples of political discourse, but that doesn't mean the participants didn't fling a few insults. Abraham Lincoln described one of Stephen Douglas' arguments as "explanations explanatory of explanations explained," but possibly even more bitingly, "as thin as the homeopathic soup that was made by boiling the shadow of a pigeon that had been starved to death."

7 Feel free to take offense if an Australian calls you a bushpig, dapto, drongo or doodlehead.

8 In the early 19th century, some prickly Southern gentlemen were wound so tightly that even the slightest perceived insult—a thrown snowball, a sideways glance at a new hat or being jostled in a theater lobby—could result in a duel. In notoriously duel-happy New Orleans, where one traveler reported there were 15 duels one Sunday morning alone, even the honor of the Mississippi River was defended after a foreigner called it a "mere brook."

9 William Shakespeare was a master of the insult. In "King Lear," he opted for the kitchen-sink approach. In Act 2, Scene 2, Oswald asks Kent, "What dost thou know me for?" Kent's reply is a mouthful: "A knave; a rascal; an eater of broken meats; a base, proud, shallow, beggarly, three-suited, hundred-pound, filthy, worsted-stocking knave; a lily-livered, action-taking knave, a whoreson, glass-gazing, super-serviceable finical rogue; one-trunk-inheriting slave; one that wouldst be a bawd, in way of good service, and art nothing but the composition of a knave, beggar, coward, pandar, and the son and heir of a mongrel bitch: one whom I will beat into clamorous whining, if thou deniest the least syllable of thy addition." If Oswald wasn't offended by being called a whoreson or a knave, being an "eater of broken meats" must have boiled his blood. After all, he surely didn't enjoy other people's leftovers.

10 A boring person once cornered painter James McNeill Whistler and told him he had recently passed by the artist's house. Whistler replied: "Thank you."

10 THINGS YOU MIGHT NOT KNOW ABOUT
PROFANITIES

1 A "grawlix" is a cluster of typographical symbols that substitutes for profanity, as any #$@%* should know.

2 The first f-bomb in U.S. television history was dropped in February 1981 on "Saturday Night Live." Charles Rocket threw it out there in the final minutes of a show plugging into the "Who shot J.R.?" craze. He was fired. Of course, the British beat us to that cultural, uh, landmark, by 16 years. Writer Kenneth Tynan used the word in November 1965 on a BBC show during a discussion about whether sexual intercourse was appropriate in a theater production. This singular "accomplishment"—which he planned ahead of time—ended up overshadowing his life's work as a theater critic.

3 Voted the No. 1 movie line of all time by the American Film Institute in 2005 was "Frankly, my dear, I don't give a damn" from the 1939 film "Gone With the Wind," starring Clark Gable and Vivien Leigh. It was said by Gable, as Rhett Butler, in his final words to Scarlett O'Hara. The line was a big deal back then because profanity was generally not allowed in films during that era.

4 Tourette syndrome has been called the cursing disease, but involuntary swearing and inappropriate outbursts occur in less than 15 percent of people diagnosed with the disorder.

5 How can we stop 8-year-olds from cursing when the nation's leaders do it? Former Vice President Joe Biden whispered near a microphone that the health care reform law was "a big (expletive) deal." President Richard Nixon and his Watergate tapes set the blue standard for potty-mouthed presidents—a far cry from George Washington, who issued "General Orders on Profanity" in 1776, urging his troops to avoid the "foolish and wicked practice."

6 The American politician most associated with cursing—Chicago's own Rahm Emanuel— lost part of the middle finger on his right hand working a meat slicer at Arby's. Former President Barack Obama famously joked that the injury "rendered him practically mute."

7 Men curse more often than women, but they curse much less when women are present. Women, on the other hand, don't reduce their swearing as dramatically in the presence of men, and at least one study found they cursed more often when men were around.

8 The ever-adaptive English language loves a good swear word, but it can also create or adopt other words to avoid them. It appears donkey (about 1784) and rooster (about 1775) came about so polite early Americans didn't have to use words for those animals that were also slang for private parts.

9 Swear words come and swear words go, and few words illustrate that like "hell." Once the granddaddy of curses, an exclamation that carried the actual, terrifying threat of eternal damnation has been watered down to the equivalent of a shrug ("for the hell of it") or used so often as to be meaningless ("haircut from hell").

10 The Dutch curse at you with diseases. The Dutch words for cancer and cholera are as flexible as the f-word is in the U.S. and used as verb, noun, adjective, etc. Or you can go with the straight up, "May you go get syphilis!"

10 THINGS YOU MIGHT NOT KNOW ABOUT
MISSPELLINGS

1 Google got its name from a misspelling of the word googol, which is the number "1" followed by 100 zeros.

2 Have you ever misspelled a Web domain name? Of course you have, and "typo-squatters" know that. They buy domain names similar to popular ones, except with a typo. Legal fights have erupted over sites such as gacebook.com (just one keystroke from facebook.com) and arifrance.com (two transposed letters away from airfrance.com).

3 Properties in the game Monopoly are named after places in the Atlantic City, N.J., area. But a misspelling was inserted early in the game's development. It should be Marven Gardens, not Marvin Gardens.

4 Buddy Holly's name was Charles "Buddy" Holley until it was misspelled on an early recording contract and he decided to go along with it, losing the "e."

5 Some misspellings are embarrassing. Some cost $40,000. That's what Ottawa County in Michigan had to pay to reprint ballots in 2006 that spelled "public" without the "l."

6 F. Scott Fitzgerald and Ernest Hemingway were good friends who carried on a spirited rivalry about many subjects, including spelling. Hemingway claimed to be the better speller, though that's hard to judge. While Fitzgerald liked "ect." instead of "etc.," Hemingway was fond of "loveing" and "its-self." Fitzgerald probably lost this one, if only because he regularly wrote about his friend "Hemmingway" and even "Hemminway."

7 Markings on the street that misspell the word "school" have appeared all too frequently in the U.S. in recent years. Some of the errors said "shcool" (Kalamazoo, Mich., in 2007; Guilford County, N.C., in 2010; New York City in 2011; and Salt Lake City in 2012). But various Florida locations have featured a variant—"scohol" (in 2007, 2009 and 2011).

*Criminals
are often
lousy spellers.*

8 Criminals are often lousy spellers. The Manson family misspelled a Beatles song as "Healter Skelter" when writing it in blood at a murder scene. David Berkowitz, the "Son of Sam" killer, wrote police that he was not a "weman-hater." And one of the pieces of evidence linking Bruno Richard Hauptmann to the Lindbergh baby's kidnapping was that he misspelled words the same way as the writer of the ransom notes—"boad" instead of "boat," for example.

9 Marketers sometimes like to spell words wrong for effect. Examples include Froot Loops and Mortal Kombat. There's even a name for that practice—sensational spelling.

10 Alfred Mosher Butts was a self-proclaimed poor speller. Who was Butts? The inventor of Scrabble.

10 THINGS YOU MIGHT NOT KNOW ABOUT
OBSCURE WORDS

1 A dozenalist is a person who advocates for society to adopt a base-12 counting system rather than the current base-10 system. According to the argument, dozenal math would be easier because 12 can be divided by 2, 3, 4 and 6 while 10 is divisible only by 2 and 5. And besides, some aspects of our daily lives are already dozenal—our clocks, for example.

2 This one isn't in many dictionaries yet, but an afterism is a clever retort that you come up with too late. The French refer to it as "staircase wit" (l'esprit de l'escalier), a quip that comes to you after your conversation is over, when you're on the stairs leaving. Another English-language term is "escalator wit."

An **AFTERISM** is a clever retort that you come up with too late.

3 The brougham was a horse-drawn carriage—and early automobile model, for that matter—with an enclosed passenger compartment but an open-aired driver's seat. The phaeton, named after the out-of-control chariot driven by the wayward son of the Greek sun god, was a carriage or auto with or without a cloth canopy. Not to be confused with the cabriolet or the drophead coupe, two names for the convertible.

4 You may have wondered what you call that grooved place between your nose and upper lip. Well, it's your philtrum. Adolf Hitler had a philtrum mustache, also known as a toothbrush mustache.

5 The universal language Volapuk was anything but obscure in the late 1800s. It was invented by a Roman Catholic German priest who said he was told by God to create a language that was easy to master to bring people together. It was referenced in the Chicago Tribune dozens of times in that period, especially the 1890s, though word of its demise followed closely thereafter. A 1910 story used the term to mean any universal language.

6 Sfumato is a painting technique in which one tone blends into another, without sharp outlines. Leonardo da Vinci's "Mona Lisa" is an example. According to the Encyclopaedia Britannica, sfumato comes from the Italian sfumare, meaning "to tone down" or "to evaporate like smoke."

7 A quincunx is the arrangement of five things in which four of them form a square and the fifth is in the center. The number five on throwing dice is expressed as a quincunx. Something that is in such a configuration is called quincuncial.

8 If your uncle spent a good deal of time in the bridewell, he was likely the black sheep of the family. This generic term for jail comes from a mid-16th-century prison near St. Bride church in London. The city of Chicago called its house of corrections the bridewell for more than a century, beginning as early as the 1850s.

9 When a leader assigns incompetent underlings to a minor task to get them out of the way, the leader has stellenbosched them. The word comes from the Second Boer War, when the British sent unproven officers to the South African town of Stellenbosch to mind the horses and handle other chores away from the front lines. (The verb stellenbosch is a toponym, a word derived from a place name.)

10 A person who collects beer bottle labels is a labeorphilist.

10 THINGS YOU MIGHT NOT KNOW ABOUT
SIGNATURES

1 A flourish at the end of a signature is called a paraph.

2 Bogus signatures on candidate petitions are as Chicago as peppers on a hot dog. A common tactic is "roundtabling," in which people sit around a table and take turns signing petitions, using names from a phone book or making them up. We might have had a different president in 2008 if Illinois state Sen. Alice Palmer's petitions had been better in 1996. Instead, they had names like "Superman," "Batman" and "Pookie." A newcomer named Barack Obama filed a challenge, knocked the incumbent off the ballot and went on to win his first elective office.

3 For a time in the 1980s, Steve Martin didn't give autographs. Instead, he passed out cards that included a copy of his signature and the words "This certifies that you have had a personal encounter with me and that you found me warm, polite, intelligent and funny." But he gave it up because "I found people didn't quite get it."

4 Joseph Cosey was one of the most famous forgers in U.S. history. Working in the early 20th century, he specialized in faking the signatures and penmanship of Abraham Lincoln and Mark Twain, but he also inked an entire original draft of the Declaration of Independence by Thomas Jefferson. His forgeries themselves became collectors' items, selling for hundreds of dollars.

5 John Hancock's signature on the Declaration of Independence has been shrouded in myth. Many think the Founding Fathers signed in unison on July 4, 1776, with Hancock penning an oversized signature and declaring, "I guess King George will be able to read that." But, in fact, most of the delegates signed the document Aug. 2, and others waited even longer—as late as 1781. Hancock's supposed quote didn't make it into the literature until well after the events—a likely sign that it was invented.

6 As the Soviet army fought its way into Berlin in April 1945, a middle-aged bureaucrat-turned-soldier named Walter Wagner was brought to a bunker. There he officiated at the marriage of a couple he had never met, Adolf Hitler and Eva Braun. When Braun signed the marriage certificate, she started to use her old name and had to cross out the B and write "Hitler." Wagner also had trouble with his signature—he wrote a double A in his own last name, which historian John Toland attributes to his nervousness.

7 For years, one of the most frequent tax return errors was forgetting to sign it. The signature was so important that even with the advent of electronic filing in 1986, the IRS still required e-filers to send in a form that included their signature. It wasn't until 2002 that the government allowed a PIN to supplant the taxpayer's authentic John Hancock.

8 William Shakespeare's father signed documents with a mark—a drawing of glover's tools—rather than his name. Some believe he knew how to read but not to write.

9 The first national group dedicated to collecting autographs was formed in Chicago in 1948. Despite being called the National Society of Autograph Collectors, the group wanted to make one thing clear: Its members were serious historians. The Tribune first reported about the group in a short story headlined, "Do you collect autografs, or merely names?" The group's first secretary, E.B. Long, answered that question, calling name collectors "bobby-soxers who run around asking people for their signatures." The NSAC changed its name to The Manuscript Society in 1953 to further emphasize that its members "are not just autograph seekers."

10 When Chicago author Nelson Algren signed his autograph, he liked to include a drawing of a cat.

10 THINGS YOU MIGHT NOT KNOW ABOUT
LISTS

1 Theodor Seuss Geisel, aka Dr. Seuss, wrote most of "The Lorax" while sitting poolside at a Kenyan hotel and watching a herd of elephants. He wrote on the nearest available paper: a laundry list.

2 Author Edmund Morris noted that the guest list at a White House lunch on Jan. 1, 1907, included "a Nobel prizewinner, a physical culturalist, a naval historian, a biographer, an essayist, a paleontologist, a taxidermist, an ornithologist, a field naturalist, a conservationist, a big-game hunter, an editor, a critic, a ranchman, an orator, a country squire, a civil service reformer, a socialite, a patron of the arts, a colonel of the cavalry, a former governor of New York, the ranking expert on big-game mammals in North America and the president of the U.S. All these men were named Theodore Roosevelt."

3 One of America's most emotion-evoking lists, the Vietnam Veterans Memorial in Washington, contains more than 58,000 names of those killed and missing in the Vietnam War. But according to the Vietnam Veterans Memorial Fund, as many as 38 names on the wall may be survivors listed erroneously.

4 A Brooklyn child actor named Richard Selzer went to Hollywood, changed his name to Dick Ellis, changed it again to Richard Blackwell, then gave up acting and went into fashion. As Mr. Blackwell, he produced an annual Hollywood worst-dressed list that was both detested and devoured in a town full of insincere praise. Brigitte Bardot was "a buxom milkmaid reminiscent of a cow wearing a girdle" and Barbra Streisand was "Ringo Starr in drag," while Sinead O'Connor was "the bald-headed banshee of MTV" and Madonna was the "bare-bottomed bore from Babylon."

5 The most-wanted criminals list was born in Chicago. Frank Loesch, Chicago Crime Commission president, was fed up with rampant gang crime in the 1920s, and was also offended by the public's worship of the gang lords. He issued the first list of public enemies in an attempt to turn public sentiment against them. Public Enemy No. 1? Al Capone, of course. Inexplicably, the Tribune printed that first roster of 28 hooligans on April 24, 1930, in alphabetical order, and Capone was fourth on the list.

6 On July 21, 1972, comedian George Carlin performed his "Seven Words You Can Never Say on Television" routine at Milwaukee's Summerfest and was arrested for disorderly conduct. The charges eventually were dropped, but Carlin made the most of it, often calling the list the "Milwaukee Seven."

7 Some of the oldest writing ever found came from Sumer (now modern Iraq) some 5,000 years ago. What did these ancient people write? Lists. Tax payments, goods sold and bought, inventory, rationed food: all lists.

8 CBS-TV's Daniel Schorr was reporting on the Watergate hearings in 1973 when a colleague handed him a newly released copy of an "enemies list" kept by the Nixon White House. Schorr read the 20 names live on-air without looking them over first. No. 17 was familiar: his own. "I tried not to gasp," he recalled in a PBS interview. "So I read on: 'Mary McGrory, Paul Newman, now back to you.' . . . I read it without a comment. I just tossed it right back. I wanted to collapse."

9 Perhaps the most famous list in human history is the Ten Commandments. But different faiths list the 10 differently, and other details are also in conflict. Movies and paintings often depict Moses carrying two tablets with five Commandments on each, but some scholars believe each tablet had all 10. And then there's the Mel Brooks version, in which there were 15

Commandments until Moses dropped one of his three tablets and it broke into bits, leaving him with 10.

10 Comedy writer Steve O'Donnell told the Tribune's Phil Rosenthal that he devised the idea of David Letterman's Top 10 list to ridicule the many silly lists in the media. A particular inspiration, he said, was a Cosmopolitan magazine "eligible bachelors" list that included CBS boss William Paley, who was in his 80s.

10 THINGS YOU MIGHT NOT KNOW ABOUT
VICTORY SPEECHES

1 After President Bill Clinton's victory speech in 1996, ABC-TV's David Brinkley declared it was "one of the worst things I've ever heard." He also opined that the president "is a bore, and always will be a bore." Brinkley thought he was off the air. He wasn't.

2 Many victors use their election night speeches to call for unity. Not Rep. Justin Amash, a Michigan Republican. After his August 2014 primary win, he aimed remarks at challenger Brian Ellis: "You owe my family and this community an apology for your disgusting, despicable smear campaign." Addressing former Rep. Pete Hoekstra, an Ellis backer, Amash said: "You are a disgrace. And I'm glad we could hand you one more loss before you fade into total obscurity and irrelevance."

3 The difference between victory and defeat can be slim. When Neil Armstrong, Edwin "Buzz" Aldrin and Michael Collins blasted off for the moon, the White House had two eerily similar speeches ready. From President Richard Nixon's long-distance call with the astronauts to salute the victory, he said: "For one priceless moment in the whole history of man all the people on this Earth are truly one—one in their pride in what you have done and one in our prayers that you will return safely to Earth." From the never-needed backup speech: "In their exploration, they stirred the people of the world to feel as one; in their sacrifice, they bind more tightly the brotherhood of man."

4 Washington Nationals manager Matt Williams brought class to the locker room when he addressed his team after it clinched the division in September 2014. "Congratulations. But we've got promises to keep. And miles to go before we sleep," he said, in a reference to Robert Frost's poem "Stopping by Woods on a Snowy Evening."

5 President George W. Bush's "Mission Accomplished" speech on the aircraft carrier USS Abraham Lincoln in May 2003 is considered a prime example of a premature claim of victory. Bush did indeed put a "win" on the scoreboard: "Major combat operations in Iraq have ended. In the battle of Iraq, the United States and our allies have prevailed." But the president did not say the war was over: "We have difficult work to do in Iraq. We are bringing order to parts of that country that remain dangerous." That attempt to bring order continued for years.

6 Bush's "Mission Accomplished" speech may have been ill-advised, but it was prudent compared to the pronouncements of Iraqi spokesman Mohammed Saeed al-Sahhaf, aka "Baghdad Bob," whose declarations of Iraqi success in the early days of the war were ludicrous. "There are no American infidels in Baghdad. Never!" he declared as U.S. tanks rolled into the capital.

7 Democrat Harold Bennett's victory in 1996 in an East Hampton, N.Y., board of trustees race was so unexpected, supporters had to find him on election night. After they tracked him down, the lobsterman's speech was short and salty: "If you're lucky, (obscenity) will do for brains. If you're not lucky, you have to be one smart son-of-a-bitch. Thank you."

8 Former Chinese tennis star Li Na was famous for her humorous comments after big victories. After a 2011 Australian Open match, she joked that she struggled early because her husband's snoring kept her up all night. She topped that performance at the 2014 Australian Open when she won the singles title. After thanking her agent for making her rich, she thanked her husband for giving up everything to travel with her, to "be my hitting partner, fix the drinks and fix the rackets." She then served up: "So thanks a lot. You're a nice guy. And also you are so lucky to find me."

9 The Academy Awards show is known for memorable victory speeches. From Joe Pesci's short and sweet, "It's my privilege. Thank you," in 1991 to F. Murray Abraham's blatant honesty in 1984, "It would be a lie if I told you I didn't know what to say, because I've been working on this speech for about 25 years." In 1994, Tom Hanks inadvertently outed his high school drama teacher as gay while accepting the best actor Oscar for "Philadelphia." Rawley Farnsworth said he was "elated" to be mentioned. "I don't mind going public now," said the retired teacher then. "I didn't think I had anything to lose. But if I still was in professional life I don't know how I would have reacted."

10 Lance Armstrong made history by winning consecutive Tour de France races from 1999 to 2005. In light of the fact he was stripped of those seven titles in 2012 and banned for life for doping, his comments take on new meanings. After his first win in 1999, he said, "This is an awesome day. This is beyond belief." In 2003: "I came into this race very confident I'd win." In 2004: "Everything went perfectly. The tactics, the training, everything." And in 2005, with rumors and doping accusations hounding him, he said, "The last thing I'll say to the people that don't believe in cycling, the cynics, the skeptics, I'm sorry for you. I'm sorry you can't dream big, and I'm sorry you don't believe in miracles."

10 THINGS YOU MIGHT NOT KNOW ABOUT
LITERARY ENIGMAS

1 In September 1849, Edgar Allan Poe left Richmond, Va., headed for New York. A week later, he was found delirious on a Baltimore street and was taken to a hospital, where he died. The cause of death is unknown, but some have suggested it was alcoholism or epilepsy or heart disease or rabies or carbon monoxide poisoning or murder by men who disapproved of Poe's relationship with their sister. There's even an intriguing theory that since it was Election Day, Poe was a victim of "cooping," a practice in which gangs kidnapped potential voters, threatened them and fed them drugs and drink, and then took them to the polls to vote a certain way.

2 Thomas Pynchon, whose postmodernist masterpiece "Gravity's Rainbow" was deemed by the Pulitzer Prize board to be unreadable when it declined to honor the novel in 1974, is so famously elusive that some have rumored him not to exist. He refuses all interviews and avoids all cameras. But the author deigned to appear twice on "The Simpsons"—with a bag over his cartoon face.

3 A young William Faulkner desperately wanted to fight in World War I. After being rejected by the U.S. military, he lied his way into the Canadian Air Force. Fortunately for literature, the war ended during his training. That didn't stop him from later telling tall tales about harrowing acts of derring-do, stories that proved embarrassing when he gained fame as an author. But he never really disowned them. Why? His brother John explained, "Anyone who writes spends a lot of his time in an imaginary world. . . . It's even enough for him to become someone he is not. . . . Bill was about the best at it I ever saw."

4 Did Ernest Hemingway really win a bet at the Algonquin round table by producing a story in only six words—"For sale, baby shoes, never worn"? It's doubtful. Those who have investigated the anecdote, including snopes.com and quoteinvestigator.com, note that the story linking the quote to Hemingway cropped up in the 1990s, three decades after his death. Similar quotes attributed to others were common decades earlier.

5 J.K. Rowling of Harry Potter fame began writing detective novels as Robert Galbraith because "I was yearning to go back to the beginning of a writing career in this new genre, to work without hype or expectation and to receive totally unvarnished feedback." Agatha Christie, likewise, took the pen name Mary Westmacott for six romantic novels unlike her murder mysteries. Christie's secret lasted nearly 20 years; Rowling's only three months. Dr. Seuss, aka Ted Geisel, employed the name Theo LeSieg ("Geisel" backward) for books that he wrote but did not illustrate.

6 A catchphrase in the film "All the President's Men" was "Follow the money," but it never appeared in the book by Carl Bernstein and Bob Woodward. So who put those words in the mouth of anonymous source Deep Throat? At first, scriptwriter William Goldman said he thought Woodward had told him about it, but Woodward checked his notes and the phrase was not there. More recently, Goldman has acknowledged inventing the phrase, but his inspiration is unclear. Some think the phrase should be credited to the late Henry Peterson, a Justice Department official involved in the Watergate investigation, who urged his staffers to follow the money.

7 When James Tiptree Jr. burst on the science fiction scene in the late 1960s, he was acclaimed for not only his action-packed stories of aliens, sex and alien sex but also for his nuanced handling of relationships and gender issues. In 1976, the science fiction community was shocked to learn he was "nothing but an old lady in Virginia" named Alice Sheldon. It's unlikely anyone was more shocked than Robert Silverberg, who was one of Tiptree's close correspondents. Just the year before, in rejecting rumors that Tiptree was a woman, he wrote that it was "a theory that I find absurd, for there is to me something ineluctably masculine about Tiptree's writing."

8 The "Iliad" and "Odyssey" are credited to the Greek poet Homer, but some scholars question whether Homer ever existed.

9 Clement Clarke Moore wrote "The Night Before Christmas," right? Well, maybe. Nearly two centuries after the poem was first published anonymously in a New York newspaper, scholars are still arguing about the authorship. A rival claim comes from the family of Col. Henry Livingston Jr., who died in 1828, a few years after the poem's first publication and before Moore publicly claimed the work. Some experts say the poem's style matches Livingston's more than Moore's, but others dispute that.

10 As the story goes, Percy Shelley's heart simply refused to burn during his cremation, and a friend grabbed it from the smoldering remains. True or not, Mary Shelley, the famous Englishman's wife and the author of "Frankenstein," believed the tale. Odder still, Leigh Hunt, a popular writer of the day who was a close friend of the Shelleys, obtained the alleged organ and for a time refused to give it up. By some accounts, after Mary did get a hold of the Romantic poet's heart, she kept it in her home as a sort of personal relic. It is believed to be buried with their son who died in 1889.

10 THINGS YOU MIGHT NOT KNOW ABOUT
FICTIONAL MOTHERS

1 The death of Bambi's mother in Walt Disney's 1942 animated film was so sensitive that Disney kept her actual killing off-screen. Disney was deeply worried about audience reaction—about "sticking a knife in their hearts," as he put it. When he took his 8-year-old daughter,

Diane, to an early screening of "Bambi," it only reinforced his worries: She cried afterward and complained that he should have spared Bambi's mom.

2 Barbara Billingsley became America's mom as June Cleaver in the classic TV show "Leave It to Beaver." Cleaver famously wore pearls and high heels as she cleaned, cooked and dispensed wisdom to poor Beaver, but the shoe choice served a pragmatic purpose also. When the show debuted, Billingsley wore flats, but she switched to heels in later seasons to stay taller than Tony Dow (Wally) and Jerry Mathers (Beaver).

3 Louisa May Alcott was never a mother, but she gave birth to one of the most admirable maternal characters in literature—Mrs. March, aka "Marmee," in the novel "Little Women." Alcott's own mother, Abigail "Abba" May Alcott, was clearly an inspiration. Through her, Louisa was related to a most interesting ancestor: Samuel Sewall, one of eight judges to sentence 20 women to death as the witches of Salem, Mass. Of the eight, only Sewall publicly expressed regret later.

4 Cruel stepmothers were abandoning sons and poisoning daughters in stories and plays long before the Brothers Grimm. In fact, it was such a common plotline for the ancient Greeks and Romans that the Latin word for stepmother—noverca—was also military jargon for a site that was too dangerous to use as a camp.

5 Angela Lansbury, who played the evil mother in the 1962 film "The Manchurian Candidate," was only three years older than Laurence Harvey, who played her son.

6 Actress Greer Garson married actor Richard Ney about a year after he played her son in the 1942 film "Mrs. Miniver." (She was 38; he was 26.) But another theatrical mother-son relationship is sometimes overstated: "Brady Bunch" mom Florence Henderson did not really "date" Barry Williams, who played her stepson in the show. They went out to dinner when he was a teenager and she was a married mother in her 30s with four kids. Williams' older brother drove them.

7 Younger readers may have trouble believing there was ever a series called "My Mother the Car." But indeed there was. Airing for one season in the mid-1960s, the show told the story of a man whose antique car was the reincarnation of his dead mother and spoke to him through the car radio. Sometimes listed among the worst TV shows of all time, its writers included Allan Burns and James L. Brooks, who went on to create one of the most admired shows ever, "The Mary Tyler Moore Show."

8 What fictional mother character has had the most impact on American history? You could argue that it's Eliza, the slave in "Uncle Tom's Cabin" who escapes with her young son to the North. The scene where Eliza and her son flee from slave catchers across the partly frozen Ohio River took only two paragraphs in Harriet Beecher Stowe's novel, but it was a spectacular scene in the play and left audiences in tears. The story's emotional impact moved the nation toward the deadliest war in its history, which led to the abolition of slavery.

9 Real-life superhero mothers are quite common, as we all know, but fictional superhero mothers aren't. In the mainstream comic universe, Mrs. Incredible was something of a galactic anomaly when she arrived in 2004: a mother shown caring for her children. On the other side of the ledger, Mystique dropped one son off at an orphanage after realizing he didn't have special powers—and literally threw the other son away.

10 Clair Huxtable, the elegant, smart and loving mother played by Phylicia Rashad on "The Cosby Show," was also a successful lawyer—the equal counterpart to Cliff Huxtable's obstetrician. But in Bill Cosby's original vision for the show, Cliff was a chauffeur—and Clair was a plumber.

10 THINGS YOU MIGHT NOT KNOW ABOUT
FICTIONAL FATHERS

1 Among the most admired fictional fathers is Atticus Finch, the widower lawyer in Harper Lee's novel "To Kill a Mockingbird." The character, played by Gregory Peck in the film, was based on Lee's father, Amasa Lee. One day on the set, Peck saw the novelist crying as she watched a scene. Thinking "we just got to her something terrific," Peck stopped to talk. She told him: "Oh, Gregory, you've got a little potbelly just like my daddy!"

2 Chevy Chase plays Clark Griswold in four "Vacation" feature films, but Clark's two kids are played by different actors in each. In the fourth movie, "Vegas Vacation," Griswold declares: "You guys are growing up so fast, I hardly recognize you anymore!"

3 Imagine Gene Hackman as the father in "The Brady Bunch." Impossible? Lucky for him, he lacked celebrity, so he was passed over for the role. In stepped Robert Reed, who considered himself a real actor and feared being typecast as a sitcom dad. The show was so silly, Reed said, "I do not want it on my tombstone."

4 Pat Conroy's abusive character Lt. Col. "Bull" Meecham in the novel "The Great Santini" was based on his own fighter-pilot father. But Conroy said the truth was even worse—he toned down the depiction because he was afraid readers would find it incredible. Yet when the book came out, Don Conroy reformed himself. "My father may be the only person in the history of the world who changed himself because he despised a character in literature who struck chords of horror in himself that he could not face," the novelist wrote.

5 Gay fathers are no longer controversial on television shows. Will became a father on the "Will & Grace" series finale in 2006; Kevin Walker on "Brothers & Sisters" adopted a surrogate child during the 2010-11 season, and Mitchell and Cam did the same on "Modern Family" in 2011-12. The first sympathetic depiction of a gay relationship and of a gay father on network TV likely was more than three decades earlier on ABC's Movie of the Week. It was a much different time. The writers of "That Certain Summer," starring Hal Holbrook as a gay father who struggles to come out to his 14-year-old son, not only had to include a reference to homosexuality as a "sickness," but also had to fight to keep the simple declaration that Holbrook and his partner, played by Martin Sheen, "love each other."

6 Some commonly quoted movie lines never really appeared in films. Among them is "Luke, I am your father," supposedly said by the evil Darth Vader in "The Empire Strikes Back." The actual line is "No, I am your father."

7 Laurence Fishburne and Cuba Gooding Jr. played father and son in the 1991 film "Boyz N the Hood" even though they're only six and a half years apart.

8 Before he was Howard Cunningham, everybody's favorite dad on "Happy Days," Tom Bosley acted with Paul Newman at the Woodstock Opera House in Woodstock, Ill. Bosley, who was born in Chicago and grew up in Glencoe, served in the Navy during World War II.

9 In John Irving's novel "The World According to Garp," the protagonist is conceived when his mother, a nurse, has sex with a dying, brain-damaged patient named Technical Sergeant Garp. In real life, Irving did not know his biological father and told his mother that if she did not tell him the circumstances of his conception, he would make them up. "Go ahead, dear," she said.

10 "Father Knows Best" started as a radio sitcom in 1949 as "Father Knows Best?" When it moved to TV in 1954, the producers were apparently more confident in dad's wisdom and the question mark was left behind.

10 THINGS YOU MIGHT NOT KNOW ABOUT
ACRONYMS

1 WWILF stands for "What was I looking for?" It's not the queen's English, but it is the basis for a British slang word, "wilfing," which means aimless internet searching, especially at work.

2 DFAC is a "dining facility" in the military. It's pronounced dee-fak. If you call it a "chow hall" or "mess hall," you're old school. Another military term is TRATS, for tin-tray rations that the Army sometimes uses in the field.

3 OTM is used by U.S. border control officials for "other than Mexican."

4 KGOY means "kids getting older younger." This is used by both social scientists and toy-makers to describe the perception that children are embracing more mature interests earlier, which is bad news for dollmakers, among others. Some people believe it's also bad for society, and they blame the advertising industry for turning young girls into sexual objects.

5 BSOs are "bright, shiny objects"—anything new and intriguing, especially in technology. The acronym is often used negatively, with the suggestion that BSOs distract a person from what is truly important.

6 "Get Smart," the classic television series from the 1960s that inspired the 2008 Steve Carell movie, has two fake acronyms: The good-guy spy agency, CONTROL, and the evil agency, KAOS, appear to be acronyms but don't stand for anything.

7 EGR is a Christian term for a sinful or difficult person. It stands for "extra grace required."

8 You've heard of NIMBYs ("not in my backyard") and LULU ("locally unwanted land use"). Well, NOTEs go a step beyond: "not over there either." There's also NOPE ("not on planet Earth").

9 An anachronym is a word that started out as an acronym but no longer is thought of that way. Examples include laser (light amplification by stimulated emission of radiation) and scuba (self-contained underwater breathing apparatus), even when worn by dogs such as Hooch the Daredevil.

10 There's also the opposite—a backronym, a word that didn't start out as an acronym but was given such a meaning on the back end. Wiki, the word for media created and edited by users, comes from a Hawaiian word for quick, but some people have alleged that it stands for "what I know is." Another example is bimbo, which most likely comes from the Italian word for baby but has been turned into a backronym: "body impressive, brain optional."

10 THINGS YOU MIGHT NOT KNOW ABOUT
DOUBLE TALK

1 During the George W. Bush administration, homeland security adviser Frances Townsend rejected the idea that the United States' inability to capture Osama bin Laden was a "failure." Instead, she said, it was "a success that hasn't occurred yet."

2 Trying to take the sting out of the recession, employers shy away from the word "layoff." The alternatives: smartsizing, decruitment, involuntary attrition, employee simplification, corporate outplacing, negative employee retention and career-change opportunity. In 2009, Nokia Siemens Networks announced a "synergy-related head count restructuring."

3 The U.S. War Department ceased to exist in the late 1940s and was absorbed into a new agency called the Defense Department. Since then, not a single American military engagement has begun with a formal declaration of war. More than 100,000 Americans have died in warfare since the War Department disappeared, many of them in a "police action" in Korea and a "conflict" in Vietnam. More recently, former President Barack Obama dumped the George W. Bush-era phrase "global war on terror" in favor of the more bureaucratic and less warlike "overseas contingency operations."

4 Warfare is prime time for euphemists. The accidental killing of comrades is known as "friendly fire." Dead soldiers are "nonoperative personnel." A retreat is a "redeployment." The simple act of reinforcement is a "surge." During World War II, U.S. airmen lost in action assumed the acronym of NYR—not yet returned.

5 In polite company after the American Civil War, the bitter conflict that left about a half million soldiers dead was referred to as "The Late Unpleasantness."

6 When leaders of the anti-war demonstrations during the 1968 Democratic National Convention were tried in Chicago two years later, defendant David Dellinger uttered an eight-letter word in court that likened a police officer's testimony to the waste product of a bull. Dellinger was reprimanded and his bail was revoked. New York Times reporter J. Anthony Lukas called his editor, urging that the Times print the word. The editor suggested that it simply be called an obscenity, but Lukas worried that readers would imagine even worse words than the one that was spoken. "Why don't we call it a barnyard epithet?" the editor suggested. And so they did.

7 Let's hope that the marketing person who rebranded adult diapers as "discreet active wear" got a nice bonus.

8 Because of South Carolina Gov. Mark Sanford and his secret trip to Argentina in June 2009 for an extramarital affair, the phrase "hiking the Appalachian Trail" means much more than enjoying the great outdoors.

9 Remember when you were a kid and went to "phys ed" or "gym"? In some school districts, they're extinct. The preferred term now is "kinetic wellness."

10 On the internet, retailers tout their "wooden interdental stimulators." Also known as toothpicks.

10 THINGS YOU MIGHT NOT KNOW ABOUT
PUNCTUATION

1 First of all, let's explain why the serial comma is important to some people. A blog on econ-omist.com cites an apocryphal example: "I'd like to thank my parents, Ayn Rand and God." Without a comma after "Rand," the writer has a mighty unusual parentage.

2 Maybe it's not surprising that New York City, capital of the U.S. publishing industry, has plenty of lore about semicolons. When former Mayor Fiorello LaGuardia was annoyed by an overeducated bureaucrat, he used the insult "semicolon boy." When the Son of Sam killer put a semicolon in a note, police speculated he might be a freelance journalist. (Killer David Berkowitz was a security guard and cabdriver.)

3 Union Gen. Joe Hooker got his nickname because a newspaper printer left out a dash. The label headline that was supposed to read "Fighting—Joe Hooker" became "Fighting Joe Hooker." He hated it, but it stuck.

4 It could be said that the first blow that led to the Russian Revolution was over punctua-tion. Moscow printers went on strike in 1905, insisting they be paid for typing punctua-tion marks as well as letters. That led to a general strike across the country and to Czar Nicholas II granting Russia its first constitution.

5 Emoticons, punctuation marks arranged to form smiley or sad faces, predate texting and the internet. Puck magazine published such typographical art in 1881.

6 The most rudimentary punctuation is the dot between words. Romans' ancient texts often ran together without spaces using all capital letters, which meant readers had to start decoding from the first line every time. The introduction of the dot suddenly rendered a block of text legible. The dot between words and numbers engraved on buildings is a legacy of this.

7 Playwright George Bernard Shaw hated apostrophes, writing: "There is not the faintest reason for persisting in the ugly and silly trick of peppering pages with these uncouth bacilli."

8 Unnecessary use of quotation marks drives some people so "batty" that they have "posted" more than 1,000 examples of "quotation mark abuse" on the photo sharing site Flickr. Our favorites are signs reading: "Cleaning lady 'available'" and "Best 'food' on 'Route 66.'"

9 People get awfully philosophical about punctuation. Said author Kurt Vonnegut: "When Hemingway killed himself he put a period at the end of his life; old age is more like a semicolon." Comedian Gracie Allen is credited with the aphorism, "Never place a period where God has placed a comma."

10 In 1899, French poet Alcanter de Brahm proposed an "irony mark" (point d'ironie) that would signal that a statement was ironic. The proposed punctuation looked like a question mark facing backward at the end of a sentence. But it didn't catch on. No one seemed to get the point of it, ironically.

10 THINGS YOU MIGHT NOT KNOW ABOUT
MADE-UP WORDS

1 An idiot's journey through life can be called an "idiodyssey."

2 "Hasbian" is a term for a former lesbian.

3 When two words are blended to form one—such as "bromance" or "mockumentary" or "spork"—it's called a portmanteau or a portmanteau word. A portmanteau is also a type of suitcase that opens into two halves. (And the plural of portmanteau is correctly written two ways: portmanteaus and portmanteaux.)

4 "Hatriot" is used to describe an extremist member of a militia group, a person who greatly distrusts the current government, or a liberal who is always critical of the country. It is also used by football fans who don't like the team from New England.

5 If you've been "dixie-chicked," your own fans or customers have turned on you, as the country music group Dixie Chicks discovered in 2003 when they denounced then-President George W. Bush and the invasion of Iraq.

6 "Anticipointment" is a television and marketing term that was popular circa 1990, describing the feeling of consumers when a product is hyped but doesn't deliver.

7 The word "gerrymander" was invented in 1812 to describe a legislative district whose contours were grossly manipulated to favor one side. One such district in Massachusetts resembled a salamander, and the governor at the time was Elbridge Gerry. Thus, gerrymandering had occurred.

8 A "nagivator" is an auto passenger who nags instead of navigates.

9 Without the cell phone, "approximeeting" wouldn't work. That's when you make plans to meet someone but don't firm up the details until later, when you're on the move.

10 A college student who dates only people in his residence hall commits "dormcest."

CHAPTER 8
Rich & Famous

DONALD TRUMP

1 Donald Trump's family name was previously Drumpf. According to author Gwenda Blair, the Drumpfs became Trumps in 17th century Germany. Trump's German grandfather, Friedrich, immigrated to the U.S. in the 1880s. Trump's mother emigrated from Scotland in 1930, and her original language was Scottish Gaelic.

2 Trump wrote that when he was in second grade, "I punched my music teacher because I didn't think he knew anything about music." He gave the teacher a black eye, he said, adding, "I'm not proud of that, but it's clear evidence that even early on I had a tendency to stand up and make my opinions known in a very forceful way."

3 In 2003, Donald attended a fashion show with his son, Donald Jr., then 25. The proud father spied an attractive woman. "Hi, I'm Donald Trump. I wanted to introduce you to my son, Donald Trump Jr." The three attempted a short conversation. It didn't go well. A bit later, Donald again spotted a nice-looking woman. "I don't think you've met my son, Donald Trump Jr.," he said. The woman, Vanessa Haydon, replied, "Yeah, we just met five minutes ago." Donald Jr. and Vanessa were married two years later.

4 Trump's sister Maryanne Trump Barry, who makes meatloaf for him on his birthday, is a senior federal appellate court judge.

5 Trump sued the Chicago Tribune and its architecture critic Paul Gapp for $500 million in 1984 after Gapp called Trump's plan to build the world's tallest building in Manhattan "one of the silliest things anyone could inflict on New York or any other city." The suit was dismissed.

6 Donald Trump is famous for playing hardball in financial matters. His own family can vouch for that. In March 2000, Donald and his surviving siblings cut off medical benefits for nephew Fred Trump III—who a week earlier had sued his uncles and aunt in an inheritance dispute—even though Fred's infant son was born with a rare neurological disorder and needed constant care. "These are not warm and fuzzy people," Fred said.

7 After Jennifer Hudson's mother, brother and nephew were murdered in Chicago in October 2008, Donald Trump let the star and some of her relatives stay for free at the Trump International Hotel & Tower. "She's a great girl," Trump said, according to People magazine. "And we're protecting them well."

8 Donald Trump speaking in 2012: "Hillary Clinton, I think, is a terrific woman. . . . She really works hard, and I think she does a good job." Donald Trump three years later: "Hillary Clinton was the worst secretary of state in the history of the United States."

9 Though he ran as a political neophyte in capturing the White House in 2016, Trump had won presidential primaries years earlier—in the Reform Party's elections in California and Michigan in 2000.

10 Real estate executive John H. Myers tells this story in Robert Slater's book about Trump: Myers and Trump stepped out of a limousine and walked up to a newsstand where a screaming New York Post headline quoted future Trump spouse Marla Maples as saying her relationship with Trump offered the "BEST SEX I'VE EVER HAD." Myers said Trump read the headline and told him: "This is what sells condominiums in New York."

10 THINGS YOU MIGHT NOT KNOW ABOUT
ELVIS PRESLEY

1 Elvis liked to shoot things. Famously, he shot out his own TV because Robert Goulet was on the screen. Less famously, he sat beside his pool and ate watermelon while squeezing off rounds with his .22-caliber pistol to blast light bulbs floating in the water.

2 Elvis used to speak sentences backward as a code with his friends.

3 Elvis' manager, who called himself Col. Tom Parker, was a Dutch illegal immigrant born Andreas Cornelis van Kuijk. He served in the U.S. Army, but "colonel" was an honorary title conferred by Louisiana Gov. Jimmie Davis. Before meeting Elvis, Parker operated a carnival act in which chickens danced because Parker hid a hot plate under the sawdust in their cage. Parker was known for charging Presley extraordinary fees. British journalist Chris Hutchins said he once asked Parker, "Is it true that you take 50 percent of everything Elvis earns?" Parker's answer: "No, that's not true at all. He takes 50 percent of everything I earn."

4 Elvis liked his meat well-done. One of his favorite expressions was "That's burnt, man." Whether he was talking about a steak or a song, something "burnt" was good.

5 When John Lennon heard Elvis had died, he caustically remarked: "Elvis died the day he went into the Army."

6 Was Elvis' middle name Aaron or Aron? The answer: both. The King's middle name was in honor of his father's friend Aaron Kennedy, but the Presleys used the Aron spelling to match the middle name of Elvis' stillborn identical-twin brother, Jesse Garon Presley. Even so, Aaron is the spelling on the Graceland grave site. Either spelling is OK, according to the official elvis.com website.

7 Elvis salted his food before he even tasted it.

8 Elvis got his first name from his father, Vernon Elvis Presley. But it's unclear where Vernon got it. The name of a 6th century Irish saint was variously spelled Elvis, Elwyn, Elwin, Elian and Allan. Wherever the name came from, it has caught on. Modern-day Elvii include singer Elvis Costello (originally Declan Patrick McManus), film critic Elvis Mitchell, salsa star Elvis Crespo and Canadian skater Elvis Stojko.

9 The "catfish incident" occurred at a concert in Norfolk, Va., on July 20, 1975. The apparently drug-addled Elvis insulted his audience by complaining that the 11,000 people in the crowd were breathing on him. Then he said he smelled green peppers and onions and suggested that his quartet of black female backup singers, the Sweet Inspirations, had been eating catfish. Two of the "Sweets" walked offstage in disgust. Some took Elvis' comment as a racial insult, but it was more likely the culmination of bizarre remarks Elvis had made to his female backup singers—both black and white—during the tour. The offended Sweets returned the next night, and Presley publicly apologized.

10 The last food that Elvis Presley ate was four scoops of ice cream and six chocolate chip cookies. The last book that Elvis read—and may have been reading on the toilet when he died—was "A Scientific Search for the Face of Jesus," by Frank O. Adams, a slim volume about the Shroud of Turin.

The last food that Elvis Presley ate was four scoops of ice cream and six chocolate chip cookies.

10 THINGS YOU MIGHT NOT KNOW ABOUT
OPRAH WINFREY

1 Oprah Winfrey's mother intended to name her Orpah, after the sister-in-law of Ruth in the Bible. But the "P" and the "R" got switched. Biographers have described it as a paperwork error, but Winfrey has said that the people around her in Kosciusko, Miss., simply pronounced it wrong.

2 As a teen, Winfrey was Miss Fire Prevention of Nashville.

3 Winfrey, hired as a news anchor in Baltimore at age 22, was a disaster. She cried while reporting on a fatal house fire. She annoyed the news writers by ad-libbing. She mispronounced "Canada" three times in the same newscast. Her hair fell out after a bad perm. The station yanked her off the nightly news and assigned her to co-host a morning show, "People Are Talking." It was not a disaster.

4 Movie critics Gene Siskel of the Tribune and Roger Ebert of the Sun-Times appeared on Winfrey's Baltimore show. The guest ahead of them was a chef demonstrating how to make zucchini bread. He knocked over a blender, spraying pureed zucchini on the interview couch. During a commercial break, Winfrey turned over the couch cushions and wiped off the back of the couch with a copy of the Baltimore Sun. Then she told Siskel and Ebert: "OK, boys, sit down and don't mention the zucchini."

5 Winfrey once dated Ebert.

6 For a 1984 episode on blindness during her first year as host of "A.M. Chicago," Winfrey wore a blindfold for most of a day. That included dinner at Yvette's. The Tribune's Inc. column noted that "she didn't try soup."

7 Oh, to be a fly on the wall of a Southern California restaurant on Jan. 28, 1985, when Winfrey dined with Maria Shriver and her boyfriend, Arnold Schwarzenegger. Winfrey, a growing force in Chicago, was in California to make her first appearance on NBC's "Tonight Show," hosted by Joan Rivers. Her friend Shriver was on the "CBS Morning News" at the time. Schwarzenegger's first "Terminator" movie had recently debuted. As they sat in a booth, Schwarzenegger pretended he was Rivers and interviewed Winfrey. She recalled: "He kept pumping me. 'Why are you successful?' 'Why did you gain weight?'"

8 The idea of casting Winfrey in "The Color Purple" came from a TV set in a Chicago hotel room in 1984. Quincy Jones, co-producer of the film, was in Chicago to testify for Michael Jackson in a lawsuit over his song "The Girl Is Mine." While eating a room-service breakfast, Jones saw the talk show hosted by Winfrey, whom he already knew. He realized immediately that she should be Sofia.

9 In the audience of Winfrey's TV show, women outnumbered men 19 to 1.

10 Oprah.com may be the only website that gives advice on tax deductions, relationships, avoiding myriad scams, G-spot orgasms and more than 10 pages of articles on William Faulkner.

10 THINGS YOU MIGHT NOT KNOW ABOUT
ABRAHAM LINCOLN

1 Abraham Lincoln detested the nickname "Abe," and his friends and family avoided using it in his presence.

2 The Lincoln's Sparrow is not named after Abraham but for Thomas Lincoln, a man from Maine who shot the bird so that John James Audubon could draw it. Also not named after the 16th president are the towns of Lincoln in Alabama and Vermont, and the Lincoln counties in Georgia, Kentucky, Missouri, North Carolina and Tennessee. They're named after Benjamin Lincoln, the Revolutionary War general who accepted the British surrender at Yorktown.

3 Lincoln wanted African-Americans to be free—to leave the country. He supported proposals that they be sent to Africa, Central America and Haiti. But when U.S. financing of a black colony on Ile-a-Vache, off the Haitian coast, led to disaster, Lincoln became disillusioned with deportation proposals. He turned to Massachusetts' governor, writing him that if "it be really true that Massachusetts wishes to afford a permanent home within her borders for all or even a large number of colored persons who wish to come to her, I shall be only too glad to know it."

4 Lincoln's famed Bixby Letter was intended to express sympathy to a Boston mother who had lost five sons in the Civil War. The eloquent letter was featured in the film "Saving Private Ryan" and read by President George W. Bush at ground zero. But in fact, Lydia Bixby lost only two sons in battle. A third got an honorable discharge, a fourth deserted and a fifth was captured and later listed as a deserter. Mrs. Bixby, a Southern sympathizer suspected of running a house of prostitution, may have claimed all her sons were dead to elicit sympathy—and donations. It's not even certain that Lincoln wrote the sympathetic letter; some believe the author was his secretary, John Hay.

5 Lincoln declined the King of Siam's offer to supply elephants to the U.S. government, writing in 1862 that his country "does not reach a latitude so low as to favor the multiplication of the elephant."

6 Who lived in Lincoln's log cabin? How about Jefferson Davis? The cabin that sits inside a marble temple near Hodgenville, Ky., is just as likely the Confederate president's as Lincoln's. Back in the late 1800s, when an entrepreneur bought the Lincoln property, no cabin remained on the site. Instead, he found a cabin nearby that legend had it—and he claimed—was the original home and had it taken apart and moved back. Regardless of its authenticity, he later put that cabin and one said to be Davis' boyhood home on tour and exhibited them together in Nashville, Tenn., and Buffalo, N.Y. The logs from the two homes were intermingled and stored in a New York warehouse. They were resurrected for the historic site, which opened in 1911.

7 Lincoln was offered the governorship of the Oregon Territory in 1849 but turned down the job.

8 The story that Lincoln wrote his brilliant Gettysburg Address on a scrap of brown paper during a train ride on the way to the battlefield is complete bunk. Much of the blame can be laid at the feet of "The Perfect Tribute," an article by Mary Raymond Shipman Andrews that ran in Scribner's Magazine in 1906 and became a best-selling book. Lincoln, a careful, gifted writer, by all accounts started the speech weeks before on White House stationery. Interestingly, a Chicago Tribune article decried the scrap-of-paper myth in 1877, nearly 30 years before "The Perfect Tribute."

9 In May 1864, a New York journalist named Joseph Howard invested in gold and then forged phony news dispatches about how war setbacks were forcing Lincoln to draft 400,000 soldiers. Howard figured the bad news would inflate the price of gold. Two newspapers printed the bogus report, and Lincoln ordered the papers closed and their editors arrested, even though they were simply victims of the "Gold Hoax." Lincoln was especially angry because he indeed planned a major new draft and felt compelled to delay it because of the hoax.

10 When Lincoln was 10, a horse kicked him in the head, and for a short time young Abe was feared dead. Lincoln had been trying to get the family mare to work faster, whipping her to keep her moving and yelling, "Git up, you old hussy." As he said "git up" one last time, the horse knocked him senseless. The story has a rather apocryphal ending, repeated by many biographers, including Carl Sandburg: When Lincoln finally regained consciousness, he finished the sentence, "you old hussy!"

10 THINGS YOU MIGHT NOT KNOW ABOUT
ROYAL MOTHERS

1 The next time your mother tells you to eat hearty, try to forget that Roman Emperor Nero's mother, Agrippina the Younger, was suspected of killing her husband, Claudius, with a plate of poison mushrooms.

2 After Japan's Empress Nagako gave birth to four daughters, the pressure was on to produce a male heir. Her fifth child's birth in 1933 was a matter of great public suspense: If the child was a girl, the sirens would sound for a minute. If the child was a boy, that first minute of sirens would be followed by 10 seconds of silence and then another minute of the sirens. The siren's resumption, heralding the birth of Crown Prince Akihito, set off a celebration featuring the clanging of bells and the playing of the national anthem on radio. Emperor Hirohito was so overjoyed he ordered a prisoner amnesty, including commutation of death sentences.

3 A queen mother is the mother of the sitting monarch. A dowager queen is a king's widow, who may also be a queen mother. A queen regent rules as guardian of a child monarch, but a queen regnant is a queen in her own right, and she may or may not be a mother.

4 When British colonial rule in West Africa became intolerably oppressive in 1900, Queen Mother Yaa Asantewaa led the uprising. She famously exhorted a council of chiefs, "If you, the chiefs of Asante, are going to behave like cowards and not fight, you should exchange your loincloths for my undergarments."

5 America's unofficial royal family for much of the 20th century was named Kennedy, and its matriarch was Rose, who died in 1995 at age 104. Her famous children—including a U.S. president, two U.S. senators, the founder of the Special Olympics, a U.S. ambassador and a World War II Navy hero—remembered a loving but strict mother. To keep her nine headstrong children in line, she employed spankings, whacks with a ruler or a coat hanger and timeouts in a dark closet, apparently quite liberally. According to Teddy: "I stood in the darkness feeling sorry for myself, until I realized I was not alone: Jean was standing beside me, serving out her own time for some infraction of the rules."

6 In 1533, Catherine de Medici traveled from Italy to France, where she married king-to-be Henry and later gave birth to three future French monarchs. But her greatest impact may have been in spreading Italian cuisine. She is credited with promoting artichokes and parsley—and persuading the French to use forks.

7 British Queen Victoria found breast-feeding so repellent that when her daughter Alice decided to nurse, she called her a cow and renamed one of the animals in the royal dairy herd after her.

8 China's Empress Dowager Cixi, born in Beijing in 1835, was a low-ranking concubine of Emperor Xianfeng who became much more after bearing his only son. Xianfeng died at age 30, and Cixi assumed a powerful position as regent to their 5-year-old son, Emperor Tongzhi. But the son died at age 18, leaving no heir. (One of his concubines was pregnant, but she died mysteriously in what court officials called a suicide.) That led to the ascendancy of Tongzhi's cousin, Guangxu, who was only 3. His adoptive mother and regent? Cixi, one of the most powerful Chinese women in history, with political influence lasting nearly half a century.

9 The marriage of Britain's Caroline and the future King George IV in 1795 was anything but happily ever after. They lived apart, and their only child, Charlotte, was raised by her governess. The lonely Caroline fostered a number of orphaned neighbor children and saw to their day-to-day needs but visited with her own daughter just once a week. She claimed the limited time together actually was preferred. "If I were to have the child with me every day," Caroline rationalized, "I would be obliged sometimes to speak to her in a tone of displeasure, and even of severity. As it is, we remain, in some measure, new to each other."

10 In Disney's "Snow White and the Seven Dwarfs," actress Lucille La Verne provided the voice of the evil queen, Snow White's stepmother. The queen, in her plot against Snow White, transforms herself into an old hag and gives the heroine a poisoned apple. La Verne also was the voice of the hag, and produced a different voice through an unusual technique—by taking out her false teeth.

10 THINGS YOU MIGHT NOT KNOW ABOUT

FOUNDING FATHERS (AND MOTHERS)

1 Paul Revere did not shout "The British are coming!" Stop and think about it—he was a British subject at the time. In fact, he said the "regulars" were coming—regular uniformed troops. But regulars had one too many syllables for poet Henry Wadsworth Longfellow.

Paul Revere in fact said the "regulars" were coming—regular uniformed troops.

2 Before President Josiah "Jed" Bartlet on "The West Wing," there was Josiah Bartlett, a signer of the Declaration of Independence. The New Hampshire physician is credited with saving the lives of people suffering from diphtheria by breaking with the common practice of bloodletting or sweating and treating them with Peruvian bark, which contains quinine.

3 The phrase "Founding Father" is widely credited to President Warren Harding, who said it at the 1916 Republican National Convention in Chicago when he was still a senator. (And by Harding, we mean Judson Welliver, a campaign aide who wrote his speeches.)

4 Phillis Wheatley, whose first name came from the slave ship that brought her from Africa as a child, was too frail for housework but brilliant at poetry. She wrote patriotic verse honoring George Washington and was welcomed at his headquarters—a remarkable meeting considering she was a slave and he a slaveowner. (Four of the first five U.S. presidents owned slaves, the exception being John Adams.)

5 You probably haven't heard of Button Gwinnett unless you're an avid autograph collector. The Georgia politician, a signer of the Declaration of Independence, died violently during the Revolutionary War—but in a duel, not while fighting the British. That early demise makes his signature quite rare, and some say it's the most valuable of any American's. A Gwinnett letter fetched $722,500 at auction in 2010.

6 Francis Hopkinson, another signer, most likely designed the U.S. flag, the Stars and Stripes. He was never paid, though, and in 1780 he asked the government for "a quarter cask of the public wine" as a "reasonable reward." He never got it.

7 Speaking of American flags, there's little reason to think Betsy Ross sewed the first one. Her legend gained popularity long after the purported events, when her grandson addressed a Philadelphia historical group in 1870 and presented relatives' sworn statements that they had heard Ross tell the story.

8 Like the Ross legend, the Molly Pitcher story was popularized many decades after the fact. But the tale of a woman operating a cannon in place of her fallen husband matches the real exploits of at least two women: Mary Ludwig Hays at the battle of Monmouth and Margaret Corbin at the battle of Fort Washington. The badly wounded Corbin was the first woman to earn a U.S. military pension.

9 Samuel Adams wasn't such a good brewer (he ran his family's business into the ground), but he was a tireless revolutionary. One of the earliest colonists to argue for independence, he wrote hundreds of letters to newspapers promoting the cause. And he signed the letters with myriad fake names so it appeared the countryside was teeming with rebels.

10 What battlefield commander was most vital to American victory in the Revolution? Probably Benedict Arnold. His audacious attacks in upstate New York and Canada protected New England early in the war, and the victory at Saratoga (in which he suffered a grievous leg wound) led to the alliance with the French that made all the difference. OK, so Arnold later committed treason. Nobody's perfect.

OK, so Arnold later committed treason. Nobody's perfect.

10 THINGS YOU MIGHT NOT KNOW ABOUT
DICK CHENEY

1 We've been pronouncing former Vice President Dick Cheney's name wrong all these years. The Cheney family's preferred pronunciation rhymes with genie, not zany. Cheney told the Chicago Sun-Times' Lynn Sweet in 2000 that people got it right when he was growing up out West, but when he moved East, they pronounced it differently. "I'll respond to either," he said. "It really doesn't matter."

2 Cheney often is depicted as the elder regent who presided over the reign of a boy king named Dubya. But Cheney is only 5½ years older than former President George W. Bush. And Bush has a better academic record. Bush earned his undergraduate degree from Yale; Cheney flunked out of Yale. Bush earned a master's degree in business administration at Harvard; Cheney got his bachelor's and master's at the University of Wyoming, but left the University of Wisconsin without completing his doctoral studies.

3 Cheney has suffered five heart attacks—a fact so well known that it's fodder for comedians. It's less well known how Cheney battled back from his first heart attack at age 37 while making his first run for Congress. He sent a letter to every registered Republican in Wyoming announcing that he was staying in the race and would quit smoking. (He was a three-pack-a-day man.) It worked. In March 2012, at the age of 71, he received a heart transplant.

4 When Bush chose Cheney as his running mate in 2000, there was one problem: They both lived in Texas. The Constitution prohibits a state's electors from voting for both a president and vice president from their state. So four days before the announcement, Cheney changed his official residency back to Wyoming—an action later challenged in court but upheld.

5 His middle name is Bruce.

6 Cheney's parents were New Deal Democrats. As Joan Didion recalled in the New York Review of Books, Cheney's father told him during his first run for Congress as a Republican, "You can't take my vote for granted."

7 In her book "Now It's My Turn," Mary Cheney says she told her parents she was gay when she was a high school junior. After breaking up with her first girlfriend, she was so upset that she wrecked the family car, then told her parents the whole story. At first, she says, her mother thought it might just be "the world's most creative excuse for a car accident." But both parents quickly accepted her sexual orientation.

8 For a couple of hours, Cheney was leader of the free world. While Bush underwent a colonoscopy from 6:09 a.m. to 8:24 a.m. Central time on June 29, 2002, Cheney served as "acting president."

9 He met his wife, Lynne, at age 14. She is the author or co-author of 15 books, holds a doctorate in 19th century British literature and is former chairwoman of the National Endowment for the Humanities. Her mother was a deputy sheriff in Casper, Wyoming.

10 Cheney uttered the F-word on the Senate floor on June 22, 2004. He was annoyed by comments from Sen. Patrick Leahy (D-Vt.) about Halliburton's no-bid contracts in Iraq. A Cheney spokesman called it a "frank exchange of views."

10 THINGS YOU MIGHT NOT KNOW ABOUT
THE DALAI LAMA

1 "Dalai" is a Mongolian word for ocean, and "lama" is a Tibetan word for a monk of high rank. The Dalai Lama's wisdom is said to be as broad as an ocean.

2 The boy who would become known as the Dalai Lama (and as Kundun, meaning "The Presence") was born on the floor of a cowshed on his family's farm in the northeastern

Tibetan village of Taktser in 1935. He was named Lhamo Dhondrub. His parents, who met for the first time at their wedding ceremony, had 16 children, but only seven survived past infancy.

3 The leadership of Tibetan Buddhism is transferred through reincarnation, adherents believe. When a dalai lama dies—as the 13th one did in 1933—monks begin the search for a boy who is his new embodiment. According to various accounts, including the book "Kundun" by Mary Craig, the discovery of the 14th Dalai Lama occurred like this: Members of a Buddhist search party arrived in Taktser disguised as traders. The group's leader was dressed as a servant but was wearing a rosary that had belonged to the 13th Dalai Lama. Two-year-old Lhamo Dhondrub asked for the rosary and was told he could have it if he guessed who he was talking to. The boy said correctly that the man dressed as a servant was a "Sera aga," a lama from the Sera monastery. The boy also impressed the visitors by knowing other details about them, and he later identified more possessions of the 13th lama.

4 In the film "Caddyshack," the golf course groundskeeper played by Bill Murray describes how he caddied for the Dalai Lama. An excerpt: "I give him the driver. He hauls off and whacks one—big hitter, the Lama—long, into a 10,000-foot crevice, right at the base of this glacier. . . . So we finish the 18th and he's gonna stiff me. And I say, 'Hey, Lama, hey, how about a little something, you know, for the effort, you know.' And he says, 'Oh, uh, there won't be any money, but when you die, on your deathbed, you will receive total consciousness.' So I got that goin' for me, which is nice."

5 The great monk has plenty of celebrity admirers, including Richard Gere, Steven Seagal and Carmen Electra. Model-actress Elle Macpherson said in 2007 that she was considering a lawsuit against model Heidi Klum for allegedly appropriating her nickname, "The Body," but after meeting with the Dalai Lama, she dropped any plans to sue. "A few people have made me stop in my tracks, and the Dalai Lama would be one of them," Macpherson said.

6 The Dalai Lama is fascinated by science and has said that if he had not become a monk, he would have become an engineer. He is especially interested in neuroplasticity, the study of how the brain rewires itself. The Dalai Lama spoke to the Society for Neuroscience in 2005 despite some members' objections about mixing religion and science. The

"If surgery of the brain could provide the same benefit as hours of meditation, I would do it."
—THE DALAI LAMA

Dalai Lama declared that "if a surgery of the brain could provide the same benefits as hours of meditation daily, I would do it," according to the Agence France-Presse news service.

7 Rock star Patti Smith was keenly interested in the Dalai Lama when she was 12. She studied Tibet for a yearlong school project, and she prayed that the nation would become newsworthy. When China's oppression became so severe that the Dalai Lama fled in 1959, "I felt tremendously guilty," she told the Shambhala Sun, a Buddhist magazine. "I felt that somehow my prayers had interfered with Tibetan history. I worried about the Dalai Lama. It was rumored that his family had been killed by the Chinese. I was quite relieved when he reached India safely." (The Dalai Lama has been based in Dharamsala, India, since then.)

8 He served as a guest editor for an issue of French Vogue magazine in 1992.

9 Tibetans often change their names after major events, such as recovery from illness or the visit of a great lama. When the boy named Lhamo Dhondrub was recognized as the reincarnated leader of his people, he was renamed Jetsun Jamphel Ngawang Lobsang Yeshe Tenzin Gyatso (meaning Holy Lord, Gentle Glory, Compassionate, Defender of the Faith, Ocean of Wisdom). His people sometimes call him Yeshe Norbu (the Wish-fulfilling Gem).

10 What will happen when the Dalai Lama, an octogenarian, dies? He has left open the possibility that the tradition of the dalai lama will end. But more likely, he says, there will be rival dalai lamas—one found among the Tibetan exile community, and another appointed by the Chinese.

10 THINGS YOU MIGHT NOT KNOW ABOUT
THE KENNEDYS

1 The Kennedys' matriarch, Rose, was the daughter of a Boston mayor and visited President William McKinley at the White House as a child. But raising nine children might have been more intimidating. She maintained a system of index cards listing her children's weights, shoe sizes and medical conditions. She scheduled meals in two shifts: one for the young children and another for the older children and adults. The family sometimes went through 20 quarts of milk in a day.

2 Considering the liberal reputation of the Kennedy family, some might be surprised that the patriarch of the family, Joseph Kennedy Sr., was friends with red-baiting Sen. Joseph McCarthy of Wisconsin. McCarthy was a guest at the Kennedys' home, hired Robert as a Senate staffer, and even dated two Kennedy sisters, Patricia and Eunice.

3 President John F. Kennedy commonly went through three or four shirts a day.

4 When John F. Kennedy received the Roman Catholic sacrament of confession, he attempted anonymity. Visiting a church, he would line up with a group of Secret Service agents who were Catholic and would try to slip into the confessional unrecognized. That sometimes worked, but on one occasion Kennedy entered the booth and the priest greeted him with "Good evening, Mr. President." Kennedy answered, "Good evening, Father," and quickly left.

5 Chicago's Northwest Expressway was renamed the Kennedy Expressway a week after President John F. Kennedy's assassination in 1963. Chicago's Wilson College was renamed Kennedy-King College in 1969 in the wake of the assassinations of Robert Kennedy and Martin Luther King Jr.

6 Benjamin Smith was the ultimate seat warmer. When John F. Kennedy was elected president in 1960, his replacement in the Senate was his old college pal—Smith, the mayor of Gloucester, Mass. Two years later, Smith chose not to run for the seat, clearing the way for JFK's brother Ted, who had just reached the minimum age of 30.

7 When the Kennedys played touch football, Eunice was a quarterback. The four Kennedy men all played football at Harvard. Joe Jr. and John were not outstanding, nor was Robert, who broke his leg crashing into an equipment cart during practice. Ted was the best, a tight end who received a smattering of interest from the Green Bay Packers but chose politics instead.

8 The last of Robert Kennedy's 11 children, Rory, was born six months after her father's 1968 assassination.

9 Air travel has always been a curse for the Kennedys. In 1999, JFK's son, John Kennedy Jr., was killed with his wife and sister-in-law when the Piper Saratoga he was piloting crashed off the coast of Martha's Vineyard. But there are other major accidents that are less well-known. Ted Kennedy broke two ribs and three vertebrae in a 1964 crash. His sister Kathleen died in a 1948 plane crash in France. The first-born son, Joe Jr., volunteered for a World War II mission called Operation Aphrodite in which he flew a bomber laden with 21,170 pounds of high explosives. The idea was for the crew to bail out and for the bomber to be directed by radio controls to its target in France. But it exploded prematurely, killing the first great hope among the Kennedy brothers.

10 In her elder years, Rose Kennedy sometimes played golf all by herself at the Hyannisport Club, carrying her own clubs for nine holes.

10 THINGS YOU MIGHT NOT KNOW ABOUT
MICHAEL MOORE

1 As a teenager, documentary filmmaker and activist Michael Moore attended a seminary for a year. One of the main reasons he dropped out was that he wasn't allowed to watch the Detroit Tigers, who went to the World Series that year.

2 What does Moore have in common with former President Gerald Ford and businessman Ross Perot? All were Eagle Scouts. For his Eagle project, Moore put together a slide show on pollution by local businesses.

3 Moore grew up in the middle-class suburb of Davison, Mich., outside Flint. At age 18 he was elected to the school board on a platform of removing the principal and assistant principal at his high school. Both eventually left.

4 Moore quit college because he couldn't find a parking space. As he told the Tribune's Julie Deardorff: "The first semester of sophomore year of college I was at a commuter campus at the University of Michigan, Flint. I drove around for what seemed to be an hour, looking for a parking space. After an hour, I said, 'The hell with it!' and gave up and drove home . . . and I haven't been back since."

5 One of Moore's early benefactors was singer Harry Chapin, who held benefit concerts to help finance a youth hot line and alternative newspaper run by Moore in the Flint area.

6 Moore got his start in filmmaking when he was hired by documentary director Kevin Rafferty to interview Ku Klux Klan members. Rafferty, who was cinematographer for Moore's first film, "Roger & Me," is the cousin of former President George W. Bush.

7 Moore was fired twice within two months in 1986. After less than half a year as editor of Mother Jones magazine, he was dismissed. He took a job as a writer for a Ralph Nader newsletter but was fired again.

8 Staff Sgt. Raymond Plouhar, one of the Marine recruiters in Moore's "Fahrenheit 9/11," was killed in 2006 by a roadside bomb in Iraq.

9 Moore's interview with actor and gun advocate Charlton Heston in "Bowling for Columbine" prompted criticism that the filmmaker was taking advantage of a sick man. (After the interview, but before the film's general release, Heston announced he had Alzheimer's-like symptoms.) Moore once considered—and rejected—the idea of running against Heston for the presidency of the National Rifle Association.

10 Move over, David Hasselhoff—Germany's in love with Michael Moore. At least two of Moore's books—"Downsize This!" and "Stupid White Men"—sold more than 1 million copies each in Germany, and Moore's following there was once compared to comedian Jerry Lewis' fame in France.

Moore once considered running for the presidency of the National Rifle Association.

10 THINGS YOU MIGHT NOT KNOW ABOUT
SARAH PALIN

1 Former Alaska Gov. Sarah Palin inspires both positive and negative nicknames like few other people in modern history. The names include Sarah Barracuda, Caribou Barbie, Disasta from Alaska, Wasilla Godzilla, Thrilla from Wasilla, Moosealini, Dick Cheney in Lipstick, Dan Quayle with an Up-do, Snowjob Squareglasses, June Cleavage, the Pit Bull with Lipstick, Hockey Mom and the Quitter on Twitter.

2 Sarah Heath (later to be Palin) learned to shoot a firearm at age 8 and hunted for rabbits and ptarmigans. What's a ptarmigan? It's a type of grouse whose name comes from Scottish Gaelic and is pronounced TAR-migan, with the "P" silent.

3 Much has been made of Palin leading her Wasilla High School basketball team to the state championship. Though she was certainly an important part of that team, her state tournament performance was limited. Suffering from an ankle injury, she scored only nine of her team's 170 points in the three tournament games.

4 Part of Palin's popular appeal is her willingness to risk humor in public. While campaigning for vice president at a North Carolina bar in October 2008, a patron handed her his cell phone and urged her to say hello to his wife. Palin asked the wife: "Libby, why is your husband here drinking beer without you?"

5 At the 2008 Republican National Convention in St. Paul, Minn., Palin accepted the vice presidential nomination with a speech declaring, "I told the Congress, 'Thanks, but no thanks,' for that Bridge to Nowhere. If our state wanted a bridge, we'd build it ourselves." But Palin was once a solid supporter of spending more than $200 million in federal funds for the bridge linking Gravina Island with the town of Ketchikan. Like others, Palin backed off when the political heat got intense.

Palin named her pet bloodhound AGIA, an acronym for the Alaska Gasoline Inducement Act.

6 Palin never tried to establish her foreign policy credentials by saying, "I can see Russia from my house!" That was actress Tina Fey, doing a parody of Palin on "Saturday Night Live." Palin had merely cited Alaska's proximity to Russia—and trade missions between them—in a discussion about foreign policy experience. But Fey's impersonation was so spot-on that some people attribute the remark to Palin.

7 When Sarah and Todd Palin eloped, they forgot to bring any witnesses to the courthouse in Palmer. So two witnesses were recruited from the nursing home next door, one in a wheelchair and another using a walker.

8 A few years ago, Palin set up a marketing and consulting firm, but it hasn't done business. She called it Rouge Cou—playfully using the French words for "red" and "neck." But in proper French, "red neck" would have been cou rouge, with the adjective coming after the noun.

9 Palin does not particularly like cats but is fond of dogs. While governor, she named her pet bloodhound AGIA, an acronym for the Alaska Gasoline Inducement Act.

10 The Palins picked unusual names for their five children—Track, Bristol, Willow, Piper and Trig. Their first-born, Track, got his name because it was track season. Palin joked that if it were basketball season, he would've been Hoop, and if it were wrestling season, he would've been Mat.

CHAPTER 9
Military & War

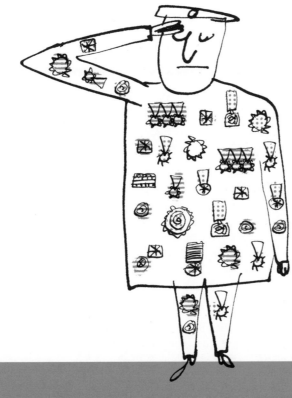

TERRORISM

1 France has been a primary target of radical Islamist attacks, and it's also the birthplace of the word "terrorism." At first the word referred to actions by the French government, not by insurgents. In a period of chaos after the French Revolution, the country's leaders instituted an official Reign of Terror that sent thousands to the guillotine. Some of the official French executioners even called themselves "terrorists."

2 A Chicago park honors an advocate of terrorism. Lucy Parsons, whose husband, Albert, was hanged after the 1886 Haymarket bombing, was more bellicose than her spouse but was spared, probably because she was a woman. In anarchist essays, Lucy Parsons urged Southern blacks to commit arson and called on Chicago's homeless to bomb the rich. "Learn the use of explosives!" she wrote. When a Northwest Side park was named after Parsons in 2004, the police union protested. Mayor Richard M. Daley, who may not have understood Parsons' politics, said: "Please don't blame the wife because of her husband's actions. That is sexist."

3 Since 9/11, more Americans have been killed by toys than by terrorism on U.S. soil, according to a comparison of figures from the Consumer Product Safety Commission and the New America Foundation.

4 Guy Fawkes was a most successful failure. The Catholic revolutionary was captured as he helped hide 36 barrels of gunpowder under Britain's House of Lords in 1605, intending to kill the country's Protestant leaders. But he did manage to thwart his own hanging. He leaped from the ladder leading to the hanging platform, breaking his neck and dying instantly. In modern times, he has become a well-known symbol for confronting tyranny, thanks to the graphic novel and film "V for Vendetta," featuring the Guy Fawkes mask. In Britain, there's a popular saying that Fawkes was "the only man to enter Parliament with honest intentions." One more Fawkes fact: Though his first name was Guy, he preferred to be called Guido.

5 The Ku Klux Klan's image as a white supremacist terrorist group includes the intimidating symbol of a fiery cross. But the original Klan, founded after the Civil War, did not burn crosses. When Thomas Dixon wrote about the early Klan in his 1905 novel "The Clansman," he embellished the tale by adding the tradition from medieval Scotland, where crosses were burned to summon troops. A new version of the Klan organized in 1915 and adopted the fake cross-burning tradition from the novel.

6 One of the worst bombings in U.S. history is unsolved and almost forgotten. Four days after Christmas in 1975, a blast rocked the baggage claim area at LaGuardia Airport in New York, killing 11 people and wounding about 75. Because the motive is unknown, it's not even a certainty that it was terrorism. But some suspect a group of Croatian nationalists who were later captured after hijacking a New York-to-Chicago jet. In that 1976 incident, the hijackers successfully demanded that a communique be published in U.S. newspapers, including the Chicago Tribune, and that leaflets be dropped over U.S. cities, including Chicago. Then they surrendered and were charged and convicted.

7 Stories about people predicting the 9/11 attacks are common on the internet—some serious, some not. In a 1997 episode of "The Simpsons," Lisa holds a publication with "$9" on the cover next to a picture of the Twin Towers, which look like "11." Then there's the 1985 film "Back to the Future," featuring a digital clock that reads "911" (well, if you look at it upside down, it does). Two novels have eerie references: In Tom Clancy's "Debt of Honor" (1994), a pilot flies a jetliner into the U.S. Capitol. And Jack Kerouac's "On the Road" (1955) included this passage: "Dean had a sweater wrapped around his ears to keep warm. He said we were a band of Arabs coming in to blow up New York."

8 Terrorists typically use bombs or guns to commit their assaults, but in 1984 a group in Oregon employed a most unusual weapon: salad bars. The Rajneeshee cult brought salmonella into restaurants in The Dalles and poisoned their salad bars, sickening about 750 people. The cult's goal was to make people too ill to vote in local elections, allowing the cult to take power. But the locals suspected as much and got to the polls. Cult leaders were convicted in the bioterrorism plot.

9 People who worry about the threat of terrorism might take comfort in the stupidity of some plotters. The group that committed the first World Trade Center bombing in 1993 was detected after Mohammad Salameh rented a van in his own name, used it in the bombing, assumed it would be vaporized and untraceable, and then showed up at the rental agency claiming the van had been stolen and demanding his $400 deposit back. A fellow terrorist later was secretly recorded slamming Salameh as "the stupidest, the stupidest, the stupidest of God's creatures!"

10 A San Francisco man's attempt in March 2016 to make a $374 payment to his dog walker was blocked by his bank and referred to the U.S. Treasury Department because he wrote "Dash" in the memo line. Someone at the bank thought that might mean "Daesh," a name used to describe Islamic State terrorists. But Dash, in fact, was the dog's name.

10 THINGS YOU MIGHT NOT KNOW ABOUT
WAR HEROES

1 Pfc. Leonard M. Kravitz's platoon was attacked by overwhelming Chinese forces in Korea in 1951 and was ordered to retreat. But Kravitz stayed at a machine gun to cover his platoon's withdrawal, saving the unit at the cost of his life. Kravitz's bravery was noted at the time, but the highest honor was given belatedly—in March 2014. The Medal of Honor ceremony was attended by Kravitz's nephew and namesake, famed rock guitarist Lenny Kravitz.

2 Robert Smalls was born into slavery in South Carolina and gained considerable skill working on ships. During the Civil War, when the Union Navy blockaded Southern ports, Smalls was on the crew of the Confederate steamship Planter in Charleston Harbor. The white crew went ashore for an evening in 1862, and Smalls and other slaves made off with the ship. They chugged past five gun batteries, with Smalls wearing a captain's hat and giving the proper signals. Then they surrendered to the Union Navy, and Smalls went on to become an advocate for African-American participation in the Union Army. After the war, he served in Congress.

3 There are many routes to heroism. For Daniel Bissell, it meant lying, subterfuge and being arrested as a deserter. Even after Gen. George Washington confirmed his story that he was spying on the British, he struggled to reclaim his reputation. For the dangerous work and the important intelligence, Bissell was one of just three soldiers to receive the Badge of Military Merit, one of the oldest U.S. military decorations, for his "unusual gallantry" and "extraordinary fidelity."

4 Democrat George McGovern was a decorated World War II bomber pilot, but his 1972 presidential campaign decided not to run ads focusing on that fact. The thinking was that it was off-message since McGovern was the anti-war candidate. He was crushed by Republican Richard Nixon.

5 It's often said that Americans are still fighting the Civil War, so it makes sense that we're still giving out medals for it too. The Confederate Medal of Honor has been awarded about 50 times since 1977, most recently in 2013 to Maj. James Breathed, a Virginian who fought valiantly at the Battle of Spotsylvania Courthouse.

6 A World War I carrier pigeon named Cher Ami won France's Croix de Guerre with Palm for delivering messages around Verdun. She also became an American hero for carrying a message that helped rescue the so-called Lost Battalion of the 77th Infantry Division, which had been isolated in the Argonne. Cher Ami was shot while carrying the Lost Battalion's note and arrived with the message capsule hanging from a ligament of her shattered leg. She died of her wounds in 1919.

7 Russell Johnson, who played the professor on TV's "Gilligan's Island," was a bombardier on a B-24 Liberator when his plane was shot down in the Philippines during World War II. Johnson broke both his ankles in the crash-landing, earning a Purple Heart.

8 Ruby Bradley, who wanted to be remembered as "just an Army nurse," was lauded as an "Angel in Fatigues" while trying to ease the suffering of fellow prisoners captured in the Philippines during World War II. She lost so much weight sharing her meager rations with the sick and the children that she was able to smuggle more food, medicine and surgical equipment in her baggy clothing. Nearly starving in a Japanese prison camp didn't deter Bradley from returning to service for the Korean War, where she again showed great courage in 1950, making sure her injured and ill charges were successfully evacuated as enemy troops descended on her position. Bradley was the last person to board the plane; moments later the ambulance she used was blown up. When she left Korea in 1953, Bradley was given a full-dress honor guard ceremony, the first woman ever to receive such an honor.

9 It's not a crime to pose as a war hero, though it was before the U.S. Supreme Court struck down the Stolen Valor Act in 2012 as an infringement on free speech. A revamped version of the act, passed last year, bans false claims about military service or honors if the aim is to get money or other tangible benefits. A private group, Guardian of Valor, has a "hall of shame" identifying people who make false service claims, and the federal government lists recipients of major medals at valor.defense.gov.

10 Ted Williams was not only a great baseball hitter but also a Marine fighter pilot. He lost three seasons to World War II at the height of his career and missed parts of two other seasons for the Korean War. Once when he was in Korea, his plane caught fire and he had to belly-land it. "Everybody tries to make a hero out of me over the Korean thing," Williams said. "I was no hero. There were maybe 75 pilots in our two squadrons and 99 percent of them did a better job than I did."

10 THINGS YOU MIGHT NOT KNOW ABOUT
THE AFGHAN WAR

1 The U.S. authorized $686 billion to fund the war in Afghanistan through fiscal year 2015—enough for every man, woman and child in Chicago to buy 65 iPad Pros, 100 Kindle Fires, Bulls season tickets, dinner at Alinea every night for a year and still have money left for a fully loaded Mercedes Benz C300.

2 CIA operatives occasionally offered Viagra to elderly tribal chieftains to secure their cooperation.

3 Very little was known about the elusive Taliban leader Mullah Mohammad Omar, who died of tuberculosis in 2013—except that he had one eye. According to Abdul Salam Zaeef, a former high-ranking member of the Taliban, Omar lost his eye fighting the Soviets in hand-to-hand street fighting in the 1980s. Zaeef wrote that the next day, Omar had to be persuaded to get treatment rather than continue the fight.

4 The story of Pat Tillman, who quit a $3.6 million NFL contract to join the Army, was often obscured after his death in Afghanistan. The military covered up the fact that he died from friendly fire, and speakers at his memorial service invoked the deity even though Tillman was either an agnostic or atheist and had requested no chaplain at his funeral. Also little publicized after his death was the fact that he was opposed to the war in Iraq. Writing about Iraq in his diary, he declared that "we have little or no justification other than our imperial whim."

5 More than four dozen countries committed troops to the NATO-led International Security Assistance Force in Afghanistan. In 2011, while the United States deployed 90,000 service personnel in ISAF, others were less invested: Austria kicked in 3 troops, compared with Iceland's 4, Ireland's 7, Luxembourg's 11 and El Salvador's 24.

6 Afghanistan lost two popular leaders at a crucial time. Two days before the Sept. 11 attacks, anti-Taliban guerrilla leader Ahmad Shah Massoud was killed by assassins posing as journalists. Sept. 9 is now Massoud Day, a national holiday in Afghanistan. Seven weeks after Massoud's death, another admired leader, Abdul Haq, was captured and executed by the Taliban after riding into the country on horseback to lead a popular revolt without U.S. support.

7 A "jingle truck" or a "jingly" was a vehicle used by Afghans to deliver goods to Western troops. Often brightly painted, they had trinkets or tassels hung from the truck frame so that they jingled. Some troops also use the term "jinglies" to refer to the Afghans themselves.

8 John Walker Lindh, the "American Taliban" captured in Afghanistan, is imprisoned near Terre Haute, Ind., in the same federal correctional complex where terrorist Timothy McVeigh was executed and where former Illinois Gov. George Ryan was held. (The ex-governor was in a low-security camp separate from Lindh's facility.)

9 The Javelin missile was so expensive ($75,000, by one account) that British soldiers in Afghanistan referred to firing a Javelin as "throwing a Porsche at them."

10 Former Afghan President Hamid Karzai's signature headwear, the karakul hat, was praised as stylish and denounced as a product of animal cruelty. The karakul is made from the pelt of a newborn lamb or—in the case of the more expensive ones—a lamb fetus that is removed when a pregnant ewe is cut open.

OBSCURE WARS

1 The War of Jenkins' Ear was so named because British politicians angry at Spain publicized an incident in which English sea captain Robert Jenkins' left ear was cut off by Spanish coastal guards near Havana. The war began in 1739, and three years later became part of the less interestingly named War of the Austrian Succession.

2 America's Founding Fathers were grateful for French help during the Revolutionary War. But after the French underwent their own revolution, they fell into a dispute with the Americans over debts and trade. Thus ensued the Quasi-War, or Half-War, fought largely at sea from 1798-1800. It ended so quietly it barely makes the history books.

3 The Milk War of October 1935 spilled hundreds of thousands of gallons of milk and not an inconsequential amount of blood. Sparked by a very low price of milk, a faction of dairy farmers in northwest Illinois and southern Wisconsin tried—and nearly succeeded—in blocking all milk deliveries to Chicago and Elgin. Before you scoff at the idea of a farm dispute being called a war, know that before it was all said and done, at least two people were killed, many were beaten, two bridges were burned down and a railroad track was blown up. And for a two-week period much of the milk delivered into Chicago was accompanied by armed guards.

4 It's said that Americans and Canadians share the "world's longest undefended border," but 150 years ago both the Americans and the Canadians were fortifying the frontier to try to stop invasions into Canada by a private Irish-American army. The Fenian Brotherhood, seeking to pressure the British to free Ireland, launched a series of raids from the U.S. (1866-71) with hundreds of fighters. The Fenian Raids failed miserably, and had an unintended result—helping push Canada's provinces toward unification.

5 When people talk about the War Between the States, they probably don't mean the Toledo War or the Honey War—two disputes that pitted U.S. states or states-to-be. The Toledo War was fought in 1835-36 over the Toledo Strip, claimed by both Michigan territory and the state of Ohio. Hundreds of men took up arms, but only one fighter was wounded and none killed. Ohio got the strip; Michigan received the Upper Peninsula instead. The Honey War, an 1839 dispute over how the border was drawn between Iowa territory and the state of Missouri, was even less bloody, with no casualties except for three trees containing beehives, which were cut down by Missouri tax agents. Iowa prevailed in the U.S. Supreme Court.

6 Yes, the Punic Wars between Rome and Carthage from 264-146 B.C. are quite famous among ancient conflicts—think Hannibal and his elephants—but here's an obscure fact: These hostilities make a strong claim to being history's longest. It wasn't until 1985 that the mayors of the two cities signed a peace treaty, officially ending a 2,249-year-old conflict.

The mayors of Rome and Carthage signed a peace treaty in 1985, officially ending a **2,249-YEAR-OLD** conflict.

7 Everyone knows the Crusades involved Christian armies marching to the Holy Land to seize it from the Muslims. But one offshoot of the Second Crusade took the fight much closer to home. In the Wendish Crusade of the mid-12th century, crusaders attacked non-Christian Slavic peoples (collectively called the Wends) in what is now Germany. They were given the choice of converting—or dying.

8 There are justifiable reasons to go to war. And then there's what happened in 1325 in Italy. The 12-year War of the Oaken Bucket between the city-states of Modena and Bologna started when soldiers from Modena stole a wooden bucket from Bologna. After Bologna demanded it back, the dispute escalated into war and thousands of people died before cooler heads prevailed. Modena displays the bucket to this day. (This shouldn't be confused with the annual Old Oaken Bucket Game between Purdue and Indiana universities, though that bucket also is proudly displayed by the winner.)

9 Reconstruction after the Civil War led to new wars. The Jaybird-Woodpecker War in Texas' Fort Bend County in 1888-89 pitted two white factions—"Woodpeckers" who were allied with African-Americans and "Jaybirds" who were not. After a gun battle, the Jaybirds prevailed. In two North Carolina counties, Alamance and Caswell, attacks by the Ku Klux Klan prompted Gov. W.W. Holden to declare martial law in 1870 and send in militia under former Union Col. George Kirk. The so-called Kirk-Holden War was so controversial that Holden was impeached.

10 Don't mess with the French about cuisine. A French pastry chef in Mexico, annoyed because local soldiers had looted his shop, complained to France's King Louis-Philippe. In 1838, the king demanded compensation and sent a fleet, which fought the Mexicans around Veracruz and won a promise of payment. The brief conflict was called the Pastry War.

10 THINGS YOU MIGHT NOT KNOW ABOUT
MILITARY SPEAK

1 During World War II, American troops referred to canned milk as "armored cow."

2 Because the 33rd Illinois volunteers in the Civil War had a lot of college graduates, they became known as the Brains Regiment.

3 Acronyms have overrun modern military language. A CHU (containerized housing unit) is a trailer used for housing. If it has a bathroom, it's known as a wet CHU. When a person on a military aircraft has no clear job, he might be called a BLOB—big lump on board. And no one wants a BCD, a bad conduct discharge, even when it's described with the slang term "big chicken dinner."

4 The handsome black satchel that is never far from the president's side is called the nuclear football not because five specially trained aides from the military services hand it back and forth. No, the nickname came about shortly after the Cuban Missile Crisis—as part of a war plan that was code-named Dropkick.

5 Possibly the most famous example of military speak is snafu, which started as an acronym (the sanitized meaning being "situation normal, all fouled up"), but has since become a word meaning mix-up or mishap. Reportedly coined by U.S. soldiers in World War II, snafu both mocked the Army's use of acronyms and explained the GIs' jaded view of life. Far from shying from that assessment, the Army embraced it with a series of cartoons in 1943-45

When a person on a military aircraft has no clear job, he might be called a BLOB—big lump on board.

featuring a Pvt. Snafu. The often-bawdy cartoons—produced by an all-star cast including Frank Capra, Theodor "Dr. Seuss" Geisel, Friz Freleng, Chuck Jones and Mel Blanc—aimed to educate illiterate GIs to avoid booby traps, breaches of secrecy and the like. You know—snafus.

6 The Bay of Pigs fiasco (aka Operation Zapata) didn't dampen U.S. officials' fervor to undermine Fidel Castro. In the subsequent years, they whipped up various schemes, including Operation Good Times (distributing doctored photos showing an obese Castro cavorting with beautiful women and gorging on expensive food); Operation Free Ride (air-dropping one-way plane tickets out of Cuba); and Operation Dirty Trick (blame Castro if John Glenn's historic orbiting flight failed and use it as a pretext to invade).

7 Many phrases in American English have obscure military origins. When you say you "heard it through the grapevine," you're using an expression from the Civil War, when telegraph wire was strung haphazardly from trees or was laid on the ground. Soldiers would attribute rumors to the "grapevine telegraph." Another American word with a war origin is "boondocks." It comes from Marines fighting Philippines guerrillas around 1900 and adopting the Tagalog word bundok, for mountain.

8 Eponyms—words based on people's names—include shrapnel, which originated with British artillery shell inventor Henry Shrapnel.

9 British Prime Minister Winston Churchill issued instructions on the naming of operations during World War II. They should not have boastful names with words like "triumphant," he said, nor should they have an "air of despondency" with words like "massacre" and "pathetic." And they should never be "frivolous," he commanded, explaining that he didn't want "some widow or mother to say that her son was killed in an operation called 'Bunnyhug' or 'Ballyhoo.'"

10 According to The Wall Street Journal, the name Operation Inherent Resolve, the U.S.-led effort begun in summer 2014 to defeat the Islamic State, was greeted with cynical humor among the military. Noting that Islamic State guerrillas were using seized U.S.-made equipment, one Pentagon jokester suggested it would be better called Operation Hey That's My Humvee.

10 THINGS YOU MIGHT NOT KNOW ABOUT
WOMEN AT WAR

1 Historians believe hundreds of women, disguised as men, fought on both sides of the American Civil War. Among them was Loreta Velazquez, a Confederate soldier who reportedly wore a specially padded uniform and fake facial hair. According to her memoir, she fought in the first battle of Bull Run and at Shiloh. Her disguise was discovered when she was treated for shrapnel wounds.

2 Soviet sniper Lyudmila Pavlichenko was credited with killing 309 Germans in World War II. Forced out of action by her wounds, she went on a publicity tour in 1942 and boasted about her exploits. "Dead Germans," she said, "are harmless."

3 Israel's compulsory military service includes women. But after the nation's initial war in 1948, they were barred from close combat. Retired U.S. Lt. Col. Dave Grossman, in his book "On Killing," cites two problems the Israelis encountered with women in combat: The sight of a female soldier being killed or wounded seemed to trigger "uncontrolled violence" among her male comrades. Also, Arab fighters were reluctant to surrender to a woman. Since the 1990s, Israel has liberalized its policies on women in combat.

4 In modern times, Vietnamese women have been especially fierce fighters, according to David E. Jones in his book "Women Warriors." A unit of markswomen supporting the South Vietnamese government had a policy of wounding Viet Cong fighters with a single shot, then beating them to death with their rifle butts to save bullets. Ming Khai, an anti-French Vietnamese fighter in the 1940s, wrote a poem in blood on her prison cell wall. The last lines were: "The sword is my child, the gun is my husband."

"The Army is not a monastery. More like a fraternity. Or a massive frat party. With weapons." —ARMY SGT. KAYLA WILLIAMS

5 Joice Mujuru, a former vice president in Zimbabwe who became a vocal opponent of strongman Robert Mugabe, commanded guerrillas in the fight against white rule in the 1970s and claimed that she single-handedly shot down a helicopter with an AK-47. She was given the nickname Teurai Ropa, which means "Spill Blood."

6 Women's contributions to America's military numbers have soared since 1973, when the U.S. went to an all-volunteer force. Back then, women represented 2 percent of enlisted personnel and 4 percent of officers. Now it's 16 percent of enlisted personnel and 17 percent of officers.

7 U.S. Sen. Tammy Duckworth lost both legs when the Black Hawk helicopter she was piloting was hit by a rocket-propelled grenade north of Baghdad in 2004. Her public image is well-known. Her private pain was described by husband Bryan Bowlsbey: "It was necessary to tell her that she had lost her legs, as she felt the phantom pain in the appendages, and didn't understand why the pain meds weren't taking that away."

8 An Iraq war veteran, former Army Sgt. Kayla Williams, wrote a racy 2005 memoir called "Love My Rifle More Than You" that was frank about sexual activity between male and female soldiers. "The Army is not a monastery," she wrote. "More like a fraternity. Or a massive frat party. With weapons."

9 The problem of sexual assault against female soldiers has gained great notice. On salon.com in March 2006, journalist Helen Benedict quoted Spec. Mickiela Montoya as saying that she kept a knife with her at all times: "The knife wasn't for the Iraqis. It was for the guys on my own side."

10 The unplanned pregnancy rate for the general U.S. population was 45 for every 1,000 women in 2013, disturbingly high among developed nations. But for women in the U.S. military, it was even higher: 72 in 1,000, according to Ibis Reproductive Health. Yes, the military has maternity uniforms.

WORLD WAR II

1 On May 5, 1945, Elsie Mitchell took five neighborhood children on an outing to Gearhart Mountain, Ore., where they encountered a strange object. One of them touched it, and suddenly all six were dead. It was one of at least 6,000 "balloon bombs" launched by the Japanese to drift toward the U.S., and that single bomb caused the only known American war deaths on the U.S. mainland.

2 U.S. Gen. George Patton was nearly sent stateside because he slapped a hospitalized soldier suffering from shell shock in Sicily. But another action by Patton—unreported at the time—was far worse. Before the Sicily fighting, Patton told his troops that enemy soldiers who continued to fight as Allied forces drew within 200 yards of them should not be taken prisoner and should instead be killed even if they surrendered. This, of course, was a violation of international law, but such killings happened several times in areas of Sicily controlled by Patton.

3 According to British Field Marshal Bernard Montgomery, the biggest quarrel he ever had with Prime Minister Winston Churchill was over two dentist chairs delivered to Normandy shortly after D-Day. Churchill thought the delivery was frivolous; Monty believed that a soldier with a toothache could not fight effectively.

4 After the Germans were driven from Paris, French authorities detained fashion diva Coco Chanel because of her affair with a German official a dozen years younger than her. Chanel, in her early 60s, told a French interrogator, "Really, sir, a woman of my age cannot be expected to look at his passport if she has a chance of a lover." She was freed.

5 The German 6th Army, encircled by the Russians at Stalingrad, was starving and freezing to death in the winter of 1942-43. Food, clothing and fuel were desperately needed. But an airlift was badly disorganized. Thousands of right shoes arrived without left shoes. Four tons of spices were delivered. And when soldiers opened one shipment, they were stunned to discover millions of condoms.

6 The British showed impressive courage and common purpose, but there were exceptions. In 1943, a stampede at a London air raid shelter killed 173 people in 90 seconds.

7 Poison gas is associated with World War I. But during World War II, neither side trusted the other to resist using gas, so both kept stockpiles. When German bombers attacked the port of Bari, Italy, in December 1943, they struck an Allied ship loaded with 100 tons of mustard gas, fatally poisoning scores if not hundreds of Allied troops. Doctors who treated victims of the gas noticed it had a specific effect on white blood cells, and they realized it might be useful to treat some cancers. After the war, doctors at the University of Chicago and two other universities produced the world's first cancer chemotherapy, based on mustard gas.

8 Alan Magee was a ball turret gunner on an American B-17 bomber that was shot up and began spinning out of control over France on Jan. 3, 1943. Magee's parachute was unusable, but he jumped anyway, losing consciousness as he fell about 20,000 feet. He crashed through the glass skylight of the St. Nazaire train station and suffered severe injuries. Yet Magee recovered, enjoying backpacking until his death at age 84. Magee's 4-mile plunge was well-documented, but it's not clear how he survived. Some believe the angle of the skylight deflected his fall.

9 Few human beings saw as much history as Mitsuo Fuchida. The Japanese flight commander led the first wave at Pearl Harbor and sent the signal "Tora! Tora! Tora!" that indicated his pilots had achieved complete surprise. Six months later, before the battle of Midway, Fuchida underwent an emergency appendectomy aboard the carrier Akagi. Unable to fly, he was on the ship when U.S. planes attacked. An explosion broke both of his legs, and the Akagi was so badly damaged it had to be sunk. Later in the war, Fuchida visited Hiroshima but left the city a day before the atomic bomb fell. After the war, he raised chickens, supplying eggs for a U.S. artillery unit that was part of the force occupying Japan.

10 An American-Canadian force attacked the Aleutian island of Kiska in 1943 to root out Japanese occupiers. Amid confused combat in the fog, at least 28 Allied troops were killed and 50 wounded. But the attackers later realized that every casualty was caused by booby traps or friendly fire. The Japanese had left the island weeks earlier.

D-DAY

1 War photographer Robert Capa, who said, "If your pictures aren't good enough, you aren't close enough," landed at Omaha Beach on D-Day. He took more than 100 pictures, but when the film was sent to London, a darkroom technician dried it too quickly and melted the emulsion, leaving fewer than a dozen pictures usable. Even so, those shaky and chaotic photos tell the story of Omaha Beach. A decade later, Capa got too close: He died in 1954 after stepping on a land mine in Indochina.

2 In the weeks before D-Day, British intelligence was highly concerned about crossword puzzles. The London Daily Telegraph's recent puzzle answers had included Overlord and Neptune (the code names for the over-all operation and the landing operation), Utah and Omaha (the two American invasion beaches) and Mulberry (the code name for the artificial harbors planned after the invasion). Agents interrogated the puzzle-maker, a Surrey school headmaster named Leonard Dawe. Turns out, it was just a coincidence.

3 The people who planned D-Day were bigots. That was the code word—bigot—for anyone who knew the time and place of the invasion. It was a reversal of a designation—"to Gib"—that was used on the papers of those traveling to Gibraltar for the invasion of North Africa in 1942.

4 The Allied effort to hoodwink Adolf Hitler about the invasion was code-named Fortitude, and it was nearly as elaborate and detailed as the invasion itself. The Allies went so far as to parachute dummies, outfitted with firecrackers that exploded on impact, behind enemy lines as a diversion. Under an effort code-named Window, Allied airplanes dropped strips of aluminum foil cut to a length that corresponded to German radar waves. The effect created two phantom fleets of bombers out of thin air—and ingenuity.

5 Among those who landed at Normandy on D-Day were J.D. Salinger (who went on to write "Catcher in the Rye"), Theodore Roosevelt Jr. (the president's son, who died of a heart attack a month later) and Elliot Richardson (attorney general under President Richard Nixon).

6 D-Day secrets were almost exposed in Chicago. A package from Supreme Headquarters in London arrived at a Chicago mail-sorting office a few months before D-Day and was accidentally opened. Its contents—including the timetable and location of the invasion—may have been seen by more than a dozen unauthorized people. The FBI found that a U.S. general's aide of German descent had sent the package to "The Ordnance Division, G-4" but had added the address of his sister in Chicago. The FBI concluded that the aide was overtired and had been thinking about his sister, who was ill. But just to be safe, the Chicago postal workers were put under surveillance and the aide was confined to quarters.

7 In a 1964 interview, Dwight Eisenhower said a single person "won the war for us." Was he referring to Gen. George Patton? Gen. Douglas MacArthur? No—Andrew Higgins, who designed and built the amphibious assault crafts that allowed the Allies to storm the beaches of Normandy. The eccentric boat builder foresaw not only the Navy's acute need for small military crafts early on, but also the shortage of steel, so he gambled and bought the entire 1939 crop of mahogany from the Philippines. His New Orleans company produced thousands of the unimpressive-looking—but vital—boats for the war effort.

8 While U.S. forces were conducting a training exercise off the southwestern English coast to prepare for the landing on Utah Beach, German torpedo boats ambushed them. More than 700 Americans were killed—a toll far worse than when U.S. forces actually took Utah Beach a few months later.

9 Woe be unto a politician who commits a gaffe during a D-Day remembrance. In 2004, Canadian Prime Minister Paul Martin referred to the "invasion of Norway" when he meant Normandy. In 2009, speaking at an event with President Barack Obama, British Prime Minister Gordon Brown cited "Obama Beach" when he meant "Omaha Beach."

10 France wasn't the only theater of action in early June 1944. On June 5, the B-29 Superfortress flew its first combat mission; the target: Bangkok. The day before that, U.S. forces were able to capture a German submarine off the African coast because they had broken the Enigma code and learned a sub was in the vicinity. On the eve of D-Day, the U.S. couldn't risk that the Germans would realize the code was cracked. So they hid away the sub and its captured crew until the end of the war, and the Germans assumed the vessel was lost at sea. But the U-505 would survive to become one of the most popular attractions at Chicago's Museum of Science and Industry.

CHAPTER 10
Science & Technology

10 THINGS YOU MIGHT NOT KNOW ABOUT
DRONES

1 For centuries, the word "drone" referred primarily to a male honeybee that mates with the queen. Because a drone is not a worker bee, the word also was applied to a lazy person. And perhaps because of the insect connection, "drone" became a synonym for monotonous talk, like a bee's hum. The use of the word for unmanned vehicles has another bee connection: In the 1930s, the British showed the U.S. military a remote-controlled aircraft called the Queen Bee that was used for anti-aircraft practice. The Americans decided to build their own, and they called it a drone.

2 The first instance of a human surrendering to a drone is believed to have occurred in February 1991 during the Persian Gulf War, when Iraqi soldiers waved a white flag at a Pioneer drone flying over Kuwait's Faylakah Island.

Serbian-American genius Nikola Tesla invented a drone more than a century ago. The Navy dismissed the idea as impractical.

3 Serbian-American genius Nikola Tesla invented a drone more than a century ago. At an 1898 exhibition in New York City's Madison Square Garden, Tesla used radio waves to maneuver a boat in a tank of water. Tesla downplayed the military applications in public but privately pitched the Navy on a fleet of remote-controlled torpedo boats that could "destroy a whole armada." The Navy dismissed the idea as impractical.

4 A British actor named Reginald Denny (you might know him as Sir Harry Percival in the Jane Fonda movie "Cat Ballou") started Radioplane, a company that built target drones for U.S. military training during World War II. A Radioplane plant in California hired a young woman named Norma Jeane Dougherty to spray varnish on the drones' fuselage fabric. Dougherty later found more lucrative work in Hollywood after changing her name to Marilyn Monroe.

5 Martha Stewart is an unabashed drone fan, in a fashion all her own. In a July 2014 column she wrote for Time magazine, she gushed about how she received one for her birthday and "in just a few minutes I was hooked." She loved taking aerial photos: of herself on the beach, of her 153-acre farm in Bedford, N.Y., and of her horse paddocks, greenhouses and cutting garden. And she wondered what landscape architect Andre Le Notre could have done with it while designing the Versailles palace gardens.

6 It must have seemed like a good idea to Brenton Lee Doyle at the time. Use a drone to deliver a phone, tobacco and marijuana into maximum-security Lee Correctional Institution in Bishopville, S.C. But the drone failed to clear the 12-foot razor-wire fence with its payload. Though the contraband never made it into prison, Doyle did: He was sentenced in January 2015 to 15 years for the attempt.

7 Palestinians in Gaza refer to Israeli drones as zenana, which translates roughly to "buzz." In nearby Egypt, zenana is a slang term for a nagging wife.

8 During the Vietnam War, U.S. drones known as Lightning Bugs were used to conduct reconnaissance, jam radar, serve as decoys and even drop propaganda leaflets. They also carried "SAM sniffers" to detect surface-to-air missiles. Just before one of the Bugs was destroyed by a SAM, it relayed the missile's signal back to base, allowing the U.S. military to develop a way to warn pilots when a SAM's signal was active near them. The Bugs weren't so good at landing by parachute, though. To prevent drones from being damaged upon landing, U.S. helicopters conducted "air snatch" missions, grabbing them in midair.

9 When Raija Ogden competed in a 2014 triathlon in Geraldton, Australia, little did she know that her fiercest opponent would be a drone. The unmanned aircraft plummeted toward her, and she went down with a head injury. The operator insisted that the drone simply startled Ogden and she fell. But Ogden said the drone hit her, and "the ambulance crew took a piece of propeller from my head." In any case, the operator was fined for flying the drone too close to people.

10 Drones aren't all about death. Activists envision hunting down rhino poachers in South Africa, and a restaurateur in Singapore wants to use them to deliver drinks. Businesses see huge potential to monitor large construction sites, assess crop growth, map mines, or inspect skyscrapers and towers. And one Belgian entrepreneur has plans for an "ambulance drone" that's basically a flying defibrillator.

GENIUSES

1 "Genius" is a vague, debatable term. But in the 1920s, Stanford professor Edward Terman used IQ scores to select more than 1,000 children as subjects in his Genetic Study of Genius. The participants—nicknamed "Termites"—have generally remained unidentified. But among them were Edward Dmytryk, who directed the film "The Caine Mutiny," and Norris Bradbury, who ran the Los Alamos National Laboratory. Two children whose IQ scores didn't meet Terman's standards were William Shockley and Luis Alvarez. Those rejects grew up to win the Nobel Prize in Physics.

2 Shortly after Albert Einstein died on April 18, 1955, his brain was sliced and diced and photographed in an effort to see what made him so darn smart. But it wasn't until 2010 that newly rediscovered photos and advances in brain research offered some answers to that question. Certain sections of Einstein's brain were more developed, and it had more wrinkles and loops and ridges—which is good in a brain—but the key may have been his huge corpus callosum, the dense network of nerve fibers that connects the different areas of the brain. Einstein, as it turns out, had a superhighway running through the center of his noggin, likely explaining his astonishing creativity and genius.

3 Vivien Thomas, a 19-year-old black man in Nashville, Tenn., found his hopes of going to college dashed by the Depression in 1930. So he took a job as a lab assistant to white surgeon Alfred Blalock of Vanderbilt University. Despite Thomas' lack of higher education, he became a brilliant surgical technician and research partner who helped Blalock develop pioneering methods of treating shock and operating on the heart. Yet for years Thomas was classified as a janitor and paid at that level when he was doing the equivalent of postgraduate work. Thomas even worked as a bartender at Blalock's parties to earn extra money. Ultimately, Thomas' vital role in the medical breakthroughs was widely recognized, and he received an honorary doctorate from Johns Hopkins in 1976.

4 Eureka moments are strokes of genius that have produced a number of scientific breakthroughs, including Alexander Fleming's discovery of penicillin and Philo Farnsworth's invention of the television. When Swiss inventor George de Mestral pulled burrs from his dog in 1941, his aha moment not only eventually gave the world Velcro, but also one of the first examples of biomimetics, or biological mimicry.

5 When Polish physicist and chemist Marie Sklodowska married Frenchman Pierre Curie and became "Madame Curie," she handled the grocery shopping and cooking with scientific precision. But the woman who would win two Nobel Prizes was confused by a recipe and had to ask her sister a difficult question: What exactly is a "pinch"?

6 Hedy Kiesler Markey received a patent in 1942 for her work with George Antheil to develop a frequency-hopping technique allowing radio-controlled torpedoes to avoid detection and jamming. The technological advance had major implications beyond World War II, fostering development of wireless communications. Markey was brilliant in another field as well, performing in movies under the name Hedy Lamarr.

7 It seemed like a great idea: a Nobel Prize sperm bank. But the 1980 brainchild of Robert K. Graham, who made millions off shatterproof plastic eyeglasses, quickly ran into trouble when he announced that the first Nobelist to donate was none other than William Shockley, an inventor of the transistor and also a notorious racist who promoted voluntary sterilization for less-intelligent people. Though it survived until 1999 and produced 215 babies, the Repository for Germinal Choice, as the bank was officially known, couldn't shed the taint it was a Nazi-like scheme to create a master race. It also never persuaded more than a few Nobelists to donate. The bank's operations couldn't have instilled great confidence either. The catalog used colors to mask donor identities but was rife with misspellings. How could a prospective mother envision her own baby Einstein coming from a donor named Corral, Turquois and Fucshia?

8 Hungarian physician Dr. Ignaz Semmelweis had a controversial medical theory that many of his fellow doctors refused to accept. Frustrated, Semmelweis lashed out publicly and was fired from his job. Ultimately, he was committed to a mental asylum, where the guards reportedly beat him and he died in 1865. Semmelweis' unpopular brainstorm: that doctors should wash their hands before treating patients.

9 If you find yourself a bit bored at your next meeting of Mensa International, the club for people with IQs in the highest 2 percent, maybe it's time to apply to the Top One Percent Society or even the Triple Nine Society, representing the 99.9th percentile. If that proves less than stimulating, you may be ready for the Prometheus Society, which restricts membership to the 99.997th percentile and up, or the Mega Society, for those with an IQ of 176 or more, the top 99.9999th percentile of the population. Then again, being a genius, you know there are serious doubts about the accuracy of tests trying to measure IQs above 140.

10 Physicist Tsung-Dao Lee has wrestled with such complex issues as parity violation and nontopological solitons, but when the Columbia University professor shared the 1957 Nobel Prize, his favorite Chinese restaurant in New York put up a sign with a simple explanation for his triumph: "Eat here, win Nobel Prize."

10 THINGS YOU MIGHT NOT KNOW ABOUT

POISON

1 In August 1982, a 30-year-old Navy lieutenant named George Prior embarked on a healthy activity, playing 36 holes of golf at the Army-Navy Country Club in Arlington, Va. Within weeks, four-fifths of his skin had peeled off and his organs were failing. After his death, the culprit was identified as a fungicide named Daconil that had been sprayed on the golf course.

2 Chocolate is poisonous to dogs because it contains caffeine and a related chemical called theobromine, which your pet can't metabolize fast enough. While a human might get a slight buzz for just a few minutes, a dog that eats too much chocolate (the darker the worse) will be affected for hours, possibly leading to heart failure. Another food that is selectively poisonous: avocados for most pet birds.

3 Mr. Yuk, the cartoon character with his tongue sticking out who appears on poisonous products to signal their danger, was developed at the Children's Hospital of Pittsburgh. A more traditional warning symbol, the skull and crossbones, wasn't considered effective in Pittsburgh because of worries that it would remind children of the Pirates baseball team.

4 Arsenic has long been known as a killer—and a cure. Charles Darwin, who used an arsenic product to treat skin outbreaks, often complained of physical ailments, and medical historians note that many of his symptoms match those of arsenic poisoning. Arsenic was an effective treatment for syphilis, and was used by Karen Blixen, who wrote "Out of Africa" under the name Isak Dinesen. Some have theorized that plotters slowly poisoned Napoleon Bonaparte with arsenic, and indeed hair taken from him at his death showed high levels of the poison. But studies of Napoleon's hair samples from many years earlier also showed high levels, suggesting that there was no murder conspiracy and that the arsenic may have come from hair ointment, gunpowder or wallpaper paste.

5 America's war in Vietnam might never have happened if the Hanoi poison plot of 1908 had succeeded. Vietnamese rebels sought to kill the French garrison in Hanoi by spiking their dinners, but they used the wrong poison or the wrong amount, leaving 200 soldiers ill but still able to defend themselves. The revolt fell apart, 13 plotters were executed and the French stayed in control, later replaced by the Americans.

6 When the Tribune reported on Feb. 11, 1916, the shocking attempt by an anarchist to kill many of Chicago's most prominent figures, including Archbishop George Mundelein and Illinois Gov. Edward Dunne, by poisoning them with chicken soup, it wasn't the only toxic story on the front page. Also that day, readers learned of the tragic death in Lake Forest of a high school senior named Marion Lambert. The girl, whose boyfriend would be acquitted of trying to kill her with cyanide, would live on in local ghost stories about motorists driving Sheridan Road seeing "a girl in the snow."

7 In the National Football League, a free agent's team has the right to match another team's offer—if it can. But in 2006, the Minnesota Vikings found an ingenious—or underhanded— way to wrench Steve Hutchinson from the Seattle Seahawks. They offered Hutchinson $49 million with a poison-pill provision that guaranteed the full amount of the contract if he wasn't the highest paid offensive lineman on their team, knowing Seattle wouldn't make a matching counteroffer because it was already paying another lineman more. The Seahawks retaliated by offering Vikings wide receiver Nate Burleson a back-loaded $49 million contract that guaranteed the full amount if he played at least five games in the state of Minnesota, something the Vikings, who play eight games a year in Minneapolis, clearly wouldn't match. Such contract shenanigans are no longer allowed in the NFL.

8 A meteorite landed in Peru near Lake Titicaca in 2007, and fumes from the crater sickened dozens of villagers. Some speculated that the problem might be akin to the fictional Andromeda Strain, a toxic microbe from space. But ultimately, scientists concluded that heat from the meteorite activated arsenic in an underground water supply, creating a sickening steam.

9 Tillie Klimek was a serial husband poisoner not known for her subtlety. In 1922, when her fourth husband was hospitalized with a mysterious illness just a year after her third husband had died, Chicago officials got suspicious. During her trial for killing her third husband, neighbors testified that while he was sick she joked about the coffin she was going to get for him and what she would wear to his funeral. Though she was convicted of just the one murder, officials linked her to the arsenic deaths of husbands No. 1 and No. 2, a boyfriend and at least two cousins. She had taken life insurance policies out on all her husbands, including the fourth, who survived.

10 Amazon tribes made their arrows more deadly by bathing the tips in toxic secretions from frogs. Some tribes would pin down the poisonous frogs and rub arrows on the animals' skin. But the Choco people of Colombia instead roasted the frogs and caught the drippings in a bottle, allowing for easy dipping of their arrows.

10 THINGS YOU MIGHT NOT KNOW ABOUT
EXTREME WEATHER

1 A storm rolled through the Thomasville, Ala., area on the morning of June 28, 1957, and, boy, did it rain. It rained fish, and it rained frogs, and it rained crayfish. Thousands of them. Some believe the animals were sent airborne by a tornado that occurred 15 miles away.

2 For the record, hailstone sizes start at marble and continue to penny, nickel, quarter, half dollar, walnut, golf ball, hen egg, tennis ball, baseball, tea cup, grapefruit and softball,

Starting in the 1880s and lasting at least 50 years, U.S. government agencies were forbidden from forecasting tornadoes or even using the word.

according to the Storm Prediction Center. But that falls short of the largest hailstone ever confirmed: a monster nearly the size of a bowling ball that fell in Vivian, S.D., in 2010.

3 Emperor penguins famously huddle together to survive the bitter Antarctic cold, and the big ears of a jack rabbit help it stay cool in the desert heat. But the North American wood frog's answer to extreme winter weather goes to the extreme. It freezes. Despite its heart and breathing actually stopping and body temperature falling to 20 degrees, an antifreezelike blood high in sugar supports its cell structure so it can bounce back from multiple freeze-thaw cycles every season.

4 Starting in the 1880s and lasting at least 50 years, U.S. government agencies were forbidden from forecasting tornadoes or even using the word. Officials were leery of inaccurate predictions and panicking the public. The result was that hundreds of people were killed or injured even when forecasters had been confident a violent storm was imminent.

5 The top temperature recorded in Illinois was 117 degrees in East St. Louis on July 14, 1954. But East St. Louis wasn't even the hottest place that day in a 60-mile radius. Union, Mo., across the Mississippi River, was a degree hotter.

6 Isaac Cline, head of the U.S. Weather Bureau office for the Galveston, Texas, area, wrote in 1891 that it was "simply an absurd delusion" to think the Texas coast was vulnerable to tropical storms, and "it would be impossible for any cyclone to create a storm wave which could materially injure the city." Nine years later, a hurricane devastated Galveston, killing about 8,000.

7 North America appears to be the world's dustbin. Not only do millions of tons of Asian dust from massive Gobi Desert storms regularly cross the Pacific to dump all over us, but Saharan particles get blown over the Atlantic to the East Coast. Although few would welcome that much dirt, it creates vibrant sunsets and tamps down Atlantic hurricane activity.

8 Mark Twain probably never said, "The coldest winter I ever spent was a summer in San Francisco." That quote is often attributed to him, but scholars can't find any direct evidence he ever said or wrote it.

9 If you need to break some ice, you can't do much better than the Coast Guard's Polar Star, called upon in 2014 to rescue Russian and Chinese ships stuck in sea ice near Antarctica. The only U.S. heavy ice breaker can cruise at 3 knots through ice 6 feet thick. And if push comes to shove—or ramming—it can carve a path through ice more than 21 feet thick.

10 If somebody tells you it's 40 below zero, you don't need to ask if they're talking Fahrenheit or Celsius. At that temperature—and only at that temperature—the two are the same.

10 THINGS YOU MIGHT NOT KNOW ABOUT

ICE

1 Ice sheets and glaciers cover about 10 percent of the world's land. At its peak in the most recent ice age, ice covered nearly a third of the land, including nearly all of Illinois, Indiana and Iowa. Since the ice ages, Lake Michigan probably has never been completely frozen over, but in late February 1979, about 92 percent of it was covered by ice, and about 90 percent was covered in mid-February 1976.

2 When a piece of ice breaks off from a glacier, it is called calving. Depending on the size of that piece, it could be a growler (less than a meter above the surface), a bergy bit (1 to 5 meters above the surface) or an iceberg (everything bigger).

3 It's relatively common for football coaches to "ice the kicker," or call a timeout in hopes that the player will think too much and choke, but recent studies by The Wall Street Journal and ESPN show the tactic doesn't work and may even backfire.

4 Chicago was built on ice. The use of ice-cooled warehouses and refrigerator train cars allowed Chicago to become a meatpacking goliath and supply beef and pork to customers far away. Gustavus Swift pioneered the use of the cooled rail cars, knowing it would be cheaper to send dressed meat than live cows. But the railroads that feared losing a huge source of revenue refused to use his cars. Swift wouldn't give up and found a small railroad willing to take his business. Over time, competition forced the big railroads to accept the refrigerated cars.

5 You can start a fire with ice. How? Carve a chunk of ice into a lens so that it works as a sort of magnifying glass, concentrating sunlight on one spot. Outdoors experts can do this with special effort. The rest of us are better off starting our fires with a match.

6 A century ago, the Tribune ran headlines reading "Ice famine grips Gotham" and "Kenosha avoids ice famine." What the heck was an ice famine? Before home refrigerators were common, when people still relied on iceboxes to store their food, they needed real ice. Transportation problems or unusually warm weather sometimes disrupted shipments of ice from out of town, causing ice famines.

7 Contract riders for touring performers often contain unusual backstage demands, such as Van Halen's ban on brown M&M's and Metallica's insistence on a constant supply of bacon. Singer Janet Jackson's rider declared: "We will not tolerate the use of anything but fresh, clean, crushed or cubed ice. NO FISH ICE! If it had never happened, I wouldn't have to write this."

8 Frank Zamboni invented the Zamboni in the late 1940s to fix the surface at the Iceland Skating Rink in Paramount, Calif. His company later branched out, building or selling such products as the Astro Zamboni (to vacuum water from AstroTurf), the Grasshopper (to roll up artificial turf) and the Black Widow (to place dirt atop cemetery vaults).

9 The polar ice caps, glaciers and those wandering icebergs contain about 75 percent of the world's fresh water.

10 Red Grange, the Chicago Bears and University of Illinois legend, is famously the Gallopin' Ghost. But back home, he was the Wheaton Iceman because of the delivery job he took every summer during high school and college that he credited with keeping him football-fit. According to one biography, many housewives dressed up for the delivery by the already well-known, well-built young man.

10 THINGS YOU MIGHT NOT KNOW ABOUT
ZOOS

1 Dr. Seuss' 1950 book "If I Ran the Zoo" featured such animals as "a Nerkle, a Nerd and a Seersucker, too!" This is the likely origin of the slang term "nerd."

2 People visiting the Monkey House at the Bronx Zoo in September 1906 saw an orangutan and a parrot sharing a cage with Ota Benga. Born in Africa, Ota Benga was a Congolese Pygmy—a human being. The 23-year-old had been brought from Africa to the U.S. by an explorer, who took him to live at the zoo. African-Americans protested the exhibit, but The New York Times dismissed the complaints as "absurd" and said Ota Benga was "probably enjoying himself as well as he could anywhere in this country." Even so, Ota Benga was soon moved from the zoo to an orphanage and later worked at a tobacco factory. When his plans to take a ship back to Africa were thwarted by the outbreak of World War I, he killed himself.

3 Zoos have long been the object of April Fools' Day jokes, so much so that a few have succumbed and joined in the fun. The Como Park Zoo in St. Paul, Minn., set up special phone lines in spring 2015 for fools who were tricked into calling Ms. Ella Fint or Ms. Anna Conda. The phenomenon isn't a new one. In 1866, a jokester sold tickets for the public to see a full "procession of the animals" at a zoo in London. More than 300 people fell for it—and fell hard. When zoo officials told them that, of course, no such unsafe parade was forthcoming, it took a mass of policemen to avert a riot.

4 An Aldabra giant tortoise named Adwaitya died in 2006 in the Kolkata, India, zoo at the estimated age of 250, meaning that the tortoise was born when King George ruled the American colonies and died when George W. Bush was president.

5 Dubbed "Hairy Houdini" by the press, a zoo-born Bornean orangutan named Ken Allen befuddled his San Diego zookeepers in the summer of 1985 by leaving his enclosure seemingly at will. He never escaped when zoo employees were nearby, so they sent in a spy disguised like a tourist, complete with a camera, to discover his secret. Which was? The ingenious—immensely strong—ape would press his hands against an outside wall and his feet against a parallel dry moat wall and inch his way up. The zoo had to spend upward of $45,000 escape-proofing his enclosure. So how did Ken Allen enjoy his freedom? He sat on the wall and threw rocks at a neighboring orangutan named Otis, who was considered unfriendly but who lived with more females.

6 Actress Sharon Stone took her then-husband, San Francisco Chronicle Executive Editor Phil Bronstein, to the Los Angeles Zoo in 2001 as a Father's Day present. The highlight: an up-close visit with a Komodo dragon. But the 7-foot-long lizard attacked Bronstein's bare foot, severing tendons. Why was Bronstein barefoot? Because zoo officials had urged him to take off his white sneakers and white socks so the dragon wouldn't mistake them for white rats, its favorite food.

7 In Germany during World War I, zookeepers were more valuable than elephants. Zoo owner Carl Hagenbeck made a deal with the military to give them an Asian elephant named Jenny instead of conscripting more of his employees. Jenny felled trees and did a lot of grunt work and was returned safely to the zoo after the fighting abated.

8 Before Sylvester Stallone hit it big in the movies, he had a job cleaning the lions' cages at the Central Park Zoo in New York City.

9 Zoos have evolved from collections of exotic animals to champions of conservation, seeing success in saving the American black-footed ferret, bison, California condor and red wolf. American zoos also have engineered breakthroughs to help the Asian rhinoceros. In 2013, the frozen semen of an Asian rhinoceros named Jimmy was rushed from the Cincinnati Zoo to the Buffalo Zoo to inseminate Tashi, resulting in a successful birth—a significant event considering Jimmy had died nine years before without reproducing.

10 The Tower of London was a prison, a mint, a records office—and a zoo. In 1252, Henry III housed a polar bear, lions, leopards and a camel, as well as other exotic beasts. In 1254, King Louis IX of France gave his father-in-law an elephant. The animals were miserably kept, and at times some of the animals were made to fight wild dogs and bears. In the 18th century, the Tower zoo was opened to the public for three halfpence. If a London resident didn't have the money, a cat or dog to feed to the lions also sufficed.

ELEPHANTS

1 African and Asian elephants are different species. The African savanna elephant is taller and heavier, has bigger ears and a concave back. The Asian's trunk ends with just one lip, versus two on African elephants. The Asian has one fewer pair of ribs but more toenails. And Asian elephants are hairier, which makes sense, as they are more closely related to the extinct woolly mammoth than to their contemporaries in Africa.

2 Duchess, the first elephant at Chicago's Lincoln Park Zoo, once escaped. In October 1892, she ran through a pond before leaving the zoo grounds at about Clark Street and what is now Dickens Avenue. During her rampage she demolished a brewery door and wreaked havoc inside a bar. A horse also died in the fray. Chased by zoo keepers, residents and police, Duchess fled down Cleveland Avenue, "plunging through the board sidewalks at every step," the Tribune reported. Zookeepers finally slowed her down by getting ropes around her legs and tying her to trees.

3 A rare intersection of elephants and opera is Giuseppe Verdi's "Aida," which has often been staged with pachyderms. Before soprano Maria Callas lost weight, a critic quipped that "it was difficult to discern Callas' ankles from those of the elephant in the scene." Another mammoth insult was delivered by composer Gioachino Rossini to hefty contralto Marietta Alboni. He called her "the elephant that swallowed a nightingale."

4 While the word jumbo possibly didn't originate with the massive African elephant in the Barnum and Bailey Circus, he certainly popularized it. Jumbo was billed as the largest elephant in the world and was a huge draw in the U.S. He was killed in 1885 by a train in St. Thomas, Ontario. (Railway City Brewing Co. there makes a beer called Dead Elephant Ale.) Jumbo's stuffed body, which toured with the circus for four more years, was given to Tufts University, and became the school's mascot.

5 For both Asian and African elephants, pregnancy lasts about 22 months. Because of gestation and lactation time, a female elephant may have only six offspring her entire life.

6 Sexually mature male elephants go through periodic states known as musth, in which they produce high levels of testosterone, are dangerously aggressive and secrete a foul-smelling liquid from a gland behind their eyes.

For both Asian and African elephants, pregnancy lasts about **22 MONTHS.**

7 One of the most bizarre incidents in U.S. history—and a horrific example of animal cruelty—occurred in Erwin, Tenn., in 1916. A trainer with a traveling circus was killed by a five-ton elephant named Mary, and circus officials feared that surrounding towns would ban their show. So they took Mary to a rail yard and hanged her by the neck from a crane in front of 2,500 spectators, many of them children. The first attempt failed when the elephant's weight snapped a chain, causing her to fall and break her hip. A second try with a heavier chain succeeded. She was buried in a grave dug with a steam shovel.

8 Lincoln Park Zoo acquired Judy from Brookfield Zoo in 1943. But the 35-year-old elephant refused to ride in a flatbed truck, so she walked the 18 miles to her new home. Escorted by zoo staff and motorcycle cops, Judy set off at 7 p.m. and traversed the western suburbs and the West Side, resting for two hours in Garfield Park before reaching Lincoln Park at 2:15 a.m.

9 Walt Disney bought the rights to "Dumbo, the Flying Elephant" for $1,000 from Helen Aberson and Harold Pearl, a husband-and-wife team. Their original was published as a rare roll-a-book, a picture book on a scroll. The movie was released in 1941.

10 Ald. "Bathhouse John" Coughlin, one of Chicago's most corrupt and colorful politicians, bought a Lincoln Park Zoo elephant named Princess Alice for a reported $3,000 around 1905 and sent the elephant to his private zoo near Colorado Springs, Colo. The Chicago zoo was willing to give up the animal because its trunk was damaged when it got stuck in a door jamb.

EPIDEMICS

1 The 1918 pandemic was commonly known as the Spanish flu, but it did not start in Spain. (Many believe it began in Kansas.) The Spanish took the rap because their king, Alfonso XIII, got sick, and because their nation was neutral in World War I and allowed an uncensored press to report on the flu.

2 The word "quarantine" comes from the Italian word "quarantina," meaning a period of 40 days. During the Black Death, the city of Venice required ships suspected of carrying disease to sit at anchor for 40 days before they could land.

3 The 1918 flu reached far corners of the globe. In the Fiji islands, it killed 14 percent of the population in 16 days. In the remote eastern Canadian town of Okak, more than 200 of the 266 residents died. The virus struck Okak so quickly that citizens could not provide for their many dogs; the hungry animals invaded their homes, attacking both the living and the dead. One survivor, the Rev. Andrew Asboe, armed himself with a rifle and reportedly killed more than 100 dogs.

4 Mary Mallon was an Irish immigrant in New York City in the early 1900s. She was by all accounts a talented cook. But Mallon also was an asymptomatic carrier of typhoid. After she infected more than 20 people, with one dying, she was isolated in a hospital for nearly three years. Officials didn't know what to do with her, so she was given a second chance. Mallon, who likely never believed health officials who said she was infected, went back to cooking. Two more people died. This time, Typhoid Mary, as she became known, was given what amounted to a life sentence. She lived out her days—23 years—isolated in a one-room cottage on an island in the East River.

5 When the Black Death ravaged Europe in the 14th century, learned men believed it was caused by an Italian earthquake or an alignment of the planets Saturn, Jupiter and Mars.

No one knew the disease was spread by fleas and rodents. A leading French doctor warned that people could become infected simply by looking at someone who was sick.

6 During World War I, the U.S. government considered venereal disease to be a formidable enemy threatening troop readiness. Taking the offensive, authorities in the U.S. incarcerated about 30,000 suspected prostitutes and shut down red-light districts. That included New Orleans' famed Storyville, described by one official as "24 blocks given over to human degradation and lust." New Orleans Mayor Martin Behrman complained about the crackdown, saying, "You can make prostitution illegal in Louisiana, but you can't make it unpopular."

7 Nobody calls "Monty Python and the Holy Grail" a documentary, but the British comedy's "Bring out your dead" scene rings true. During the European plague, when the bodies were piling up, funeral services and processions were prohibited. Instead, corpse-removers gathered up the dead in carts to get rid of them quickly. If a house was quarantined, a relative had to throw the body into the cart from a second-floor window.

8 English sweating sickness, which caused profuse sweating and sometimes led to a rapid death, remains a mystery more than five centuries later. After raging for more than 60 years, the last major outbreak of the disease in England was recorded in 1551. Then the "English sweat" simply vanished, with its cause never established.

9 In the early years of the AIDS epidemic, Canadian flight attendant Gaetan Dugas was identified as "Patient Zero," who brought the virus to North American cities in the 1970s and early '80s. But some believe Dugas' role was exaggerated, and there is evidence that the virus was on this continent well before his travels. Tissue from a teenager who died in St. Louis in 1969 was preserved for study and was later found to contain the AIDS virus.

10 One of the last smallpox outbreaks in Europe struck Yugoslavia in 1972. Josip Tito's totalitarian regime declared martial law. He imposed a strict national quarantine that saw the army seal off entire villages. He ordered the entire population of 20 million vaccinated. More than 10,000 people who had come into contact with infected people were shut up in hospitals and hotels for weeks. In the end, 35 of the 174 infected died.

10 THINGS YOU MIGHT NOT KNOW ABOUT
HURRICANES

1 Hurricane, typhoon or cyclone? It isn't as simple as you might think, according to the Atlantic Oceanographic and Meteorological Laboratory. All are regional names for tropical cyclones. In the Atlantic, Caribbean and the eastern Pacific, call them hurricanes. But call them typhoons in the northwest Pacific, and cyclones in the southwest Pacific and the Indian Ocean.

2 After a hurricane battered Miami in 1926, a funeral was held for Thomas Gill, a worker on a dredge on Biscayne Bay. A minister was reading the 23rd Psalm when a man walked in and disrupted the service. It was Gill, who survived by swimming to shore from the vessel, where another body was misidentified as his.

3 A few days after Hurricane Katrina devastated New Orleans, TV's "The Price Is Right" broadcast a show offering a trip to New Orleans as a prize. The show was a rerun that was aired by mistake. The program apologized.

4 The naming of hurricanes has sometimes been controversial. In the '50s, lists were adopted with only female names, a practice that some people viewed as sexist. In 1979, male names were added. Further diversity has occurred with inclusion of Spanish and French names. But in 2003, Rep. Sheila Jackson Lee, D-Texas, complained about the lack of African-American names on the list.

5 An enduring story about Hurricane Camille in 1969 is that residents of the Richelieu Manor apartment building in Pass Christian, Miss., threw a "hurricane party," and that only one person survived. But that tale, told by survivor Mary Ann Gerlach, is in serious doubt. Other survivors have been identified, and one insisted that he and another person stayed not to party but to help a fellow resident. Contacted in 2011 by the Tribune, Gerlach stood by her story: "I don't care if anyone believes it or not. There was no reason for me to lie. I didn't get a penny out of it." Incidentally, when Gerlach was charged with killing her 11th husband (yes,

A hurricane's energy is the equivalent of a 10-megaton nuclear bomb exploding—every 20 minutes.

11th), years after Camille, her lawyer used an insanity defense, citing Gerlach's hurricane ordeal. That story didn't fly, and she did time in prison.

6 In December 1944, a U.S. Navy fleet under Adm. William "Bull" Halsey mistakenly steered straight into a typhoon in the Philippine Sea. Three destroyers sank and dozens of other ships were damaged. Nearly 900 people were killed. The aircraft carrier Monterey was badly damaged by fire. Among those who battled that blaze was Lt. Gerald Ford.

7 Generals and admirals had much to worry about during the bloody four years of the Civil War. What they didn't have to deal with was a hurricane. The longest hurricane-free period the continental United States has experienced in the last 160 years began in November 1861 and ended October 1865, roughly bracketing the War Between the States.

8 Beginning in the late 1950s, the U.S. Weather Service teamed up with the Navy on a research project to fight hurricanes. The plan was to bombard hurricanes with silver iodide in the hope it would collapse the storms' eyewall. Project Stormfury, as it was called, started meekly enough. Hurricane Daisy in 1958 shrugged off the attack. In 1961, Esther seemed to stagger—a segment of the eyewall did break down—but within two hours she returned to her original intensity. Other attempts showed some promise, but in the end were inconclusive. Stormfury died in 1983.

9 A hurricane's energy is the equivalent of a 10-megaton nuclear bomb exploding—every 20 minutes.

10 Chicago Bears fans' reputation for warmth and sensitivity took a hit after Hurricane Katrina. At the NFC championship game in January 2007, Soldier Field fans greeted the New Orleans Saints with signs such as "Bears Finishing What Katrina Started."

SPACE

1 Where does Earth's atmosphere end and outer space begin? NASA defines an astronaut as someone who has flown 50 miles above sea level. But some international groups prefer to define space as the area beyond the Karman Line, which is about 62 miles above sea level.

2 Living in space can cause subtle changes in the human body. For example, some astronauts find that their tastes in food change. "One of my favorite foods on the ground is shrimp, and up here I can't stand it," said International Space Station astronaut Peggy Whitson.

3 Speaking of food and space, South Korean researchers spent more than $1 million on kimchee that astronaut Yi So-yeon took to the International Space Station in 2008. Scientists had to develop a special version of the pickled cabbage dish to address fears that it would offend crew members from other countries with its smell or that it would start "bubbling out of control" in space conditions.

4 Neil Armstrong misspoke when he uttered the first words on his moonwalk in 1969. He was supposed to announce, "That's one small step for a man, one giant leap for mankind." But he left out the "a," producing a sentence that didn't really make sense. (Without the "a," "man" would mean the same thing as "mankind.") But, of course, everyone knew what he meant.

5 Sitting in the Centaurus constellation about 20 light years from Earth is star BPM 37093, also named Lucy. The white dwarf is one huge diamond, scientists say, that weighs in at 10 billion trillion trillion carats and is about the size of our moon.

6 In 1993, a meteoroid destroyed the European Space Agency's communication satellite Olympus. Don't think Hollywood explosion. Scientists suspect it was damaged by a few pebbles, and in trying to regain control, so much fuel was lost the satellite was rendered useless. While space shuttles, space stations and satellites have received minor damage from flying space rocks, the Olympus is the only satellite to be left unusable.

7 Before "The Big Bang Theory" was a TV show, it was an explanation for the development of the universe, and much of the credit (for the theory, not the TV show) goes to a former Chicagoan. Edwin Hubble set the Illinois high jump record while at Wheaton High School, won a Rhodes scholarship, and earned a doctorate at the University of Chicago. But the ultimate honor—the Nobel Prize—eluded him because some Nobel officials didn't think astronomy fit into the physics category.

8 The word "jovial" comes from Jove, another name for the god (and the planet) Jupiter. The god was considered jolly, so those who are similarly good-natured are jovial. But in space terms, a "jovian planet" is not at all jolly—it's a planet that, like Jupiter, is composed primarily of gases rather than solid matter.

9 When you point out the Big Dipper to your child, be careful not to call it a constellation. It's an asterism, or a collection of stars within a constellation or in multiple constellations that form another shape. Another famous asterism is Orion's Belt. There are 88 official constellations, including Orion, Gemini, the zodiac signs and Ursa Major, which includes the Big Dipper.

> The Big Dipper is an **ASTERISM**, not a constellation.

10 The ashes of more than 100 humans have been launched into space, including those of "Star Trek" creator Gene Roddenberry and hippie icon Timothy Leary. But the first human ashes to leave the solar system are expected to be those of Clyde Tombaugh. The remains of the astronomer who discovered Pluto are aboard the New Horizons spacecraft, which flew past Pluto in 2015 and is expected to reach interstellar space in about 2040.

10 THINGS YOU MIGHT NOT KNOW ABOUT
AIR TRAVEL

1 A cat flew across the Atlantic Ocean eight years before Charles Lindbergh. The cat, named Wopsie or Whoopsie, was a stowaway aboard the dirigible R34 when it traveled from

Scotland to New York in 1919. The cat wasn't the only creature who beat Lindy to a trans-Atlantic flight. More than 80 people also did. But Lindbergh was the first to fly solo.

2 Qantas, the Australian airline, is a former acronym for Queensland and Northern Territories Air Service. That name is strange, but others may be stranger. Airline pilot Patrick Smith, who wrote a column for salon.com, suggested that two of the worst airline names ever were Russia's Kras Air ("always just an H away from infamy," wrote Smith) and Taiwan's U-Land Airlines ("That's right. U-buy, U-fly and U-Land it yourself.").

3 In 1987, American Airlines removed one olive from each first-class salad for a savings of about $40,000 a year. In a more recent cost-cutting move, American announced in 2004 that it would get rid of pillows on its MD-80 planes for an annual windfall of about $300,000. The next year, Northwest Airlines ditched free pretzels in coach class on its domestic flights, saving $2 million a year.

4 Joseph of Cupertino, a 17th century Italian priest, is a Roman Catholic patron saint of pilots and air passengers. Known as the "flying friar" because of his reported ability to levitate, Joseph annoyed his fellow churchmen, who banned him from attending choir or visiting the refectory for 35 years.

5 National Airlines launched an ad campaign in the early 1970s featuring attractive young flight attendants—then known as stewardesses—and slogans such as "I'm Margie. Fly me." A group called Stewardesses for Women's Rights picketed the airline's offices and complained to the Federal Trade Commission about the ads. National was forced to tone down the campaign by including other airline workers. But somehow the idea of "flying" someone like, say, Ralph the baggage handler seemed a bit less alluring.

6 The producers of the 1980 comedy film "Airplane!" considered talk show host David Letterman and singer Barry Manilow for the lead role of washed-up pilot Ted Striker before settling on actor Robert Hays. The co-pilot played by basketball great Kareem Abdul-Jabbar was originally written for baseball star Pete Rose. According to the Internet Movie Database,

Rose was offered $30,000 but lost the part after asking for $35,000, which he wanted to spend on an Oriental rug.

7 Ten soldiers boarded a plane at California's Fort Hunter Liggett in the early 1960s, expecting a routine training mission. Instead, once they were airborne, the crew announced that an engine had stalled, the landing gear was inoperable and the plane would attempt to ditch in the ocean. Then the crew issued an odd demand: The soldiers would have to fill out insurance forms. After they dutifully did so, the plane landed, safely and routinely. The episode was an Army experiment to measure soldiers' performance under stress. Not surprisingly, a control group on the ground filled out the same insurance forms more accurately.

8 Passengers preparing to take off in 2008 on an Aeroflot jet from Moscow to New York revolted when the pilot appeared to slur his words over the loudspeaker. Officials of the Russian airline tried to calm them. According to the Moscow Times, an airline official said, "It's not such a big deal if the pilot is drunk. Really, all he has to do is press a button and the plane flies itself." But the passengers stood their ground, and the crew was replaced. The incident was another black eye for Aeroflot, remembered for a 1994 flight in which a pilot let his 15-year-old son take the controls. The boy accidentally disabled the autopilot, sending 75 people to their deaths.

9 When Amelia Earhart helped organize the New York, Philadelphia and Washington Airways in the early years of commercial aviation, the in-flight lunch consisted of hard-boiled eggs and saltine crackers, chosen because they seemed unlikely to contribute to airsickness.

10 A passenger boarded a Chicago-bound plane in Washington, D.C., in 2003 and handed a note to a flight attendant, asking her to take it to the pilot. The note read, "Fast. Neat. Average." The pilot had no idea what it meant and alerted authorities, who detained the passenger for questioning. The note was part of a well-known code at the Air Force Academy, based on cadets' answers on a dining-hall survey. If all had gone well, the passenger's note would have been returned with a note reading "Friendly. Good. Good," and the passenger would have been invited to visit the cockpit. But the pilot was not an Air Force grad, and the passenger missed his flight. As an Air Force spokesman noted, "Obviously, the world has changed since 2001."

CHAPTER 11
Kids & Education

10 THINGS YOU MIGHT NOT KNOW ABOUT
COLLEGE

1 Henry Ford II, grandson of the famous automaker, left Yale in 1940 after he was caught hiring someone to write a research paper for him. Visiting the college decades later to give a speech, he told the audience: "I didn't write this one either."

2 Why do so many people lie about their college credentials, and why don't employers always check? Yahoo CEO Scott Thompson quit in 2015 because he had falsely claimed a computer science degree from Stonehill College, which didn't even offer such a degree when he was a student there. Bogus college claims cost George O'Leary the Notre Dame football coaching job in 2001 and ousted Marilee Jones as dean of admissions at Massachusetts Institute of Technology in 2007. Perhaps more astounding are cases where the fabulist doesn't get fired. Bausch & Lomb CEO Ronald Zarrella lost a $1 million bonus but kept his job and $10 million in pay after it was revealed in 2002 that he didn't have a New York University master's as claimed. Bausch & Lomb's board said a firing would not be in the stockholders' interests.

3 Famous college roommates include director Wes Anderson and actor Owen Wilson (at the University of Texas at Austin), former Vice President Al Gore and actor Tommy Lee Jones (at Harvard), and actors Ving Rhames and Stanley Tucci (at State University of New York-Purchase).

4 Florida Polytechnic University in Lakeland may be one of the newest colleges in the country, boasting a striking Santiago Calatrava-designed science building and more than 500 students in its inaugural class. What it doesn't have are actual books in its library: It is all-digital.

5 The oldest continuously operating universities are in the Islamic world, and the longest-running of those is Karueein, or al-Qarawiyyin, founded in 859 in Fes, Morocco, and predating European higher education by more than 200 years. But some 16 centuries before that in what is now Pakistan, Takshashila was a thriving center of free higher education famous for many subjects, including physics and medicine.

6 Chicago has been the home of some very unorthodox colleges. There was Hobo College, founded in 1908 by Dr. Ben Reitman to give homeless people a place to gather and hear lectures on philosophy and literature. And there's the College of Complexes, a free-speech forum founded in 1951 and still going strong. (A recent topic: "Was Jesus a Proto-Communist?") And let's not forget the College of Coaches, an invention of Cubs owner P.K. Wrigley, in which the team had no manager in 1961 and '62 but was run by a group of coaches who took turns serving as head coach. Wrigley's idea flunked out, with 123 wins and 193 losses in those years.

7 Average tuition and fees at four-year public colleges skyrocketed about 375 percent in the last 40 years, from $2,600 in 1974-75 to $9,650 in 2016-17 (with both figures stated in 2016 dollars).

8 University of Michigan students refer to their undergraduate library as the UGLi.

9 A year before four students were killed at Kent State University in Ohio, a young man at North Carolina A&T State University in Greensboro was shot and killed on campus during civil rights protests at the historically black college. It was never determined who pulled the trigger to kill Willie Grimes in May 1969, but protesters insisted it was the police. What happened next, though, is undisputed. National Guard soldiers, backed up by a tank and several armored personnel carriers, invaded the campus in a pre-dawn assault. They enjoyed air superiority with a plane and helicopter dropping tear gas and "nausea gas" as they rounded up hundreds of students, most of whom were rousted from their beds after the locks on their dorm room doors were shot away.

10 The University of Chicago has boasted many distinguished graduates and must have thought it had another one when professor John Buettner-Janusch became chairman of New York University's anthropology department in 1973. But Buettner- Janusch was convicted of using his NYU lab to manufacture LSD and methaqualone. After Buettner-Janusch's parole, he sent poisoned Valentine's Day chocolates to the judge, whose wife ate the candy and fell ill but survived. The disgraced prof was convicted again and died in federal custody.

TESTS

1 A 15-year-old girl named Harlean Carpenter attended the Ferry Hall boarding school in Lake Forest, Ill., which is now part of Lake Forest Academy. But she was a mediocre student and lasted less than a year. By age 18 she was in Hollywood taking a screen test for the 1930 film "Hell's Angels." And she wasn't any better at that test than the ones at Ferry Hall. The screenwriter said, "My God, she has a shape like a dustpan." Director Howard Hughes agreed that "she's nix." But Hughes was ultimately talked into casting the young woman, who renamed herself Jean Harlow.

2 Max Verstappen became the youngest driver to start in a Formula One race when he took the wheel March 15, 2015, at the Australian Grand Prix. Then on March 29, he finished seventh in the Malaysian Grand Prix. But his big day came on Sept. 30 in Belgium, when he passed his driver's license test on his 18th birthday.

3 Applicants for Imperial China's civil service exam, which was first given in about the seventh century and continued into the 20th, not only had to know their stuff, they had to survive the test. The exam evolved over the centuries, partly to thwart cheaters, into an elaborate ordeal that required the test-takers to undergo invasive body searches before they took up their posts in one of thousands of cells in massive examination halls for a three-day, two-night marathon. The smart ones brought their own food—and toilets.

The No. 2 pencil can be traced back to a pencil factory run by writer Henry David Thoreau and his family.

4 The No. 2 pencil, a mainstay of America's testing culture, can be traced back to a pencil factory run by writer Henry David Thoreau and his family in Concord, Mass., in the 1840s. Thoreau pencils were available in four grades, with the number reflecting the hardness of the pencil graphite—also known as the "lead," even though it's not lead. And here's another piece of pencil trivia: The metal band that holds the eraser to the end of a pencil is called a ferrule.

5 When conducting tests on mass mailings, technicians may want to forgo the jokes. In the 1980s, a test message was accidentally included in Wells Fargo account statements, telling customers: "You owe your soul to the company store. Why not owe your home to Wells Fargo? An equity advantage loan can help you spend what would have been your children's inheritance." A similar gaffe occurred with a British Telecom marketing letter a few years later. An employee who was testing a program to personalize the letter forgot to delete a default phrase. That caused a few letters to start with "Dear Rich Bastard." Afterward, one person who didn't receive a letter complained, arguing that he was certainly prosperous enough to deserve a "rich bastard" letter.

6 Plenty of smart people have failed the bar exam but tried again and passed. They include California Govs. Pete Wilson and Jerry Brown, New York Mayor Ed Koch and Chicago Mayor Richard M. Daley. In 1973, Hillary Rodham Clinton failed the District of Columbia bar exam, and "she kept this news hidden for the next 30 years," according to biographer Carl Bernstein. (She passed the Arkansas version of the test.) And imagine the test pressure on John F. Kennedy Jr., who took three tries to pass. After one of his failures, the New York Post front page declared: THE HUNK FLUNKS.

7 In the Jim Crow era, Southern states used impossibly difficult literacy tests to keep blacks off the voter rolls. Reflecting the fact that discrimination against blacks was so ingrained in public life, President Dwight Eisenhower shared an anecdote about a white, talented Mississippi law student who failed the bar exam twice, prompting his father to visit the testers and see what was up. They showed him the test and he exclaimed, "For goodness' sake, you gave him the Negro examination!"

8 The multiple-choice test a) was first given on a mass scale to test the aptitude of World War I Army recruits in the United States, b) became popular in education in the early to mid-20th century because it helped schools handle a huge wave of immigrant students, c) was considered an objective test not for the way it assessed students but because it could be graded uniformly by teachers of varied experience, d) was later disavowed by its creator, Frederick J. Kelly, for failing to promote critical thinking, e) all of the above.

9 Ancient Egyptians developed a urine-based pregnancy test more than 3,200 years before it was invented by modern medicine in the 1920s. The woman was told to urinate on barley seeds and wheat seeds for several days. If the seeds germinated, she was pregnant. When the ancient method was tested in 1963, the seeds grew 70 percent of the time for pregnant women, but never for men and nonpregnant women.

> **ANCIENT EGYPTIANS** developed a urine-based pregnancy test more than 3,200 years before it was invented by modern medicine in the 1920s.

10 Six questions were thrown out on a statewide test for New York eighth-graders in 2012 after an uproar over a talking pineapple. The reading comprehension section included an essay in which the pineapple challenged a hare to a race, with other animals betting on the pineapple because they figured the fruit had a trick up its sleeve. In the end, the pineapple didn't move, the hare won, the pineapple was eaten and the moral of the story was that "pineapples don't have sleeves." Students were confused by the story and the follow-up questions, including why the animals ate the pineapple. After the New York Daily News publicized the test section, it was dropped. Which was a tough break for any young test-takers who nailed that section, truly understanding the social dynamics of talking pineapples.

10 THINGS YOU MIGHT NOT KNOW ABOUT
TOYS

1 Play-Doh was invented as a wallpaper cleaner.

2 When Milton Bradley bought the concept for a game called Pretzel, it changed the name to Twister. The game soared in popularity in 1966 after Johnny Carson played it with actress Eva Gabor on his television show.

3 The Chicago area has been a healthy playground for toymakers. The Radio Flyer red metal wagon was born in Chicago, and the headquarters remains here, though the metal wagons are now made in China. Tinkertoys were designed in Evanston by Charles Pajeau. Donald Duncan, a businessman from Oak Park, popularized the yo-yo, bringing joy to millions, but perhaps not making up for his nefarious promotion of another product, the dreaded parking meter.

4 The 1964 television special "Rudolph the Red-Nosed Reindeer" featured the Island of Misfit Toys, where unwanted playthings were exiled. The original program omitted the misfits in its happy ending—an oversight that brought viewer complaints. For the rebroadcast the next year, footage was added to show Santa delivering the misfits on Christmas Eve.

5 Gumby toys were ubiquitous in the 1960s as the television show gained popularity. The claymation character's name came from Michigan farm slang: Creator Art Clokey's father referred to a muddy clay road as a "gumbo."

6 You know her as Barbie. But her full name is Barbara Millicent Roberts. By various estimates, 10 percent to 25 percent of adults who collect Barbies are men—not that there's anything wrong with that.

7 When Hooters waitress Jodee Berry won a 2001 beer-sales contest at her Florida restaurant, she thought the prize was a Toyota. Instead, the restaurant gave her a "toy Yoda"—a "Star Wars" doll—in what her manager called an April Fool's joke. Berry laughed all the way to her lawyer's office. The case was settled, with Berry getting enough money to buy a car, the lawyer said.

8 Illinois-based RC2 Corp., maker of Thomas the Tank Engine, recalled more than 1 million of its wooden trains in 2007 because of lead paint from China. Then RC2 sent free boxcars to aggrieved customers as a goodwill gesture. Trouble was, some of those boxcars had lead paint too.

9 You know it's a bad, bizarre year for toys when a children's product is mentioned in the same sentence as "date-rape drug." In November 2007, 4 million craft kits called Aqua Dots were recalled because their beads were coated with a chemical that metabolizes into the drug GHB when swallowed. A Chinese company had substituted a cheaper—and toxic—chemical for the proper one. The Australian version of Aqua Dots, called Bindeez, had the same problem, and was coated in Bitrex, an extremely bitter "taste aversive" agent to discourage kids from putting it in their mouths.

10 In 2005, the Mujahedeen Brigades posted a grainy picture on a website, claiming it showed a U.S. soldier named John Adam who had been captured in Iraq and soon would be beheaded. But the U.S. military said no such soldier was missing. The hoax was exposed when a California toymaker reported that the soldier looked an awful lot like Cody, its foot-tall doll.

10 THINGS YOU MIGHT NOT KNOW ABOUT
TEACHERS

1 Pink Floyd's 1979 song "Another Brick in the Wall, Part II"—with lyrics such as "We don't need no education" and "Hey, teacher, leave them kids alone"—put an unwelcome spotlight on a maverick London high school instructor known for chain-smoking in class. Music teacher Alun Renshaw brought 23 students to a studio to record the song's chorus for Pink Floyd, but failed to secure his boss' permission. The school got lots of criticism, the music department got 1,000 pounds, and Renshaw got out of the country, moving to Australia.

2 When Americans are asked which occupations contribute the most to society's well-being, they answer teachers, second only to military personnel, according to a 2013 Pew Research survey. (Medical doctors were third and scientists were fourth.) That esteem for educators appears to be even higher among Generation Next, those born from 1981 to 1988, who are twice as likely as older generations to name a teacher or mentor when asked to list people they admire.

3 Teenage outlaw John Wesley Hardin, wanted for killing four men, hid from authorities for three months in the late 1860s by working as a teacher at his aunt's school in Texas. "John Wesley Hardin prayed before class every morning," a schoolgirl recalled.

4 Educators in 19 states, including Indiana and Missouri, can still discipline a student by paddling. While most of the states that allow corporal punishment are in the South, it is also legal in Idaho and Wyoming. New Mexico was the last state to ban the practice, back in 2011. At the time, Vernon Asbill, a Republican state senator and retired educator, argued, "The threat of it keeps many of our kids in line so they can learn." A 2010 bill in the U.S. House to ban corporal punishment in schools died in committee.

Educators in 19 states can still discipline a student by paddling.

5 When future president Lyndon Johnson taught speech at Sam Houston High School in Houston, he drove the debate team relentlessly, putting them through 50 practice competitions. The team charged through city and district competition but lost in the state finals, upsetting Johnson so badly that he ran to the bathroom and threw up.

6 Famed educator Maria Montessori left Italy and went into exile because of philosophical clashes with a former teacher—Italian dictator Benito Mussolini, whose students once nicknamed him il tiranno (the tyrant).

7 Teachers are heroes every day, but especially when violence erupts. Shannon Wright shielded a student and was fatally shot during a school massacre in Jonesboro, Ark., in 1998. Dave Sanders was killed while helping scores of students to safety at Columbine High School outside Denver in 1999. When a student started setting off pipe bombs at a school in San Mateo, Calif., in 2009, Kennet Santana tackled him. "I just thought to myself, 'If I'm wrong, I'll apologize to his parents later,'" he explained.

8 Some guidebooks for teachers encourage them to use euphemisms to avoid offending students and parents. A student is not described as lazy—instead, he's "a reluctant scholar." A student isn't spoiled—instead, she "only responds positively to very firm handling." Those dice in math class aren't really dice—they're called "probability cubes" to avoid upsetting parents opposed to gambling.

9 Kiss bassist Gene Simmons, the rocker known for his heavy makeup and long tongue, was once a teacher. "I used to be a sixth-grade teacher in Spanish Harlem," he said. "I did it for six months, and I wanted to kill every single kid." But in a separate interview, he said: "Children need to learn to be selfish, to put themselves first and not care what other people think."

10 Female instructors in Chicago became more active in the women's suffrage movement in the 1890s after school board member William Rainey Harper (also president of the University of Chicago) rejected the idea of raises for teachers, noting that they already made more money than his wife's maid. He also suggested a compromise: raises for male teachers only.

10 THINGS YOU MIGHT NOT KNOW ABOUT
TWINS

1 Many of us started out as twins, whether we know it or not. An estimated one in eight natural pregnancies begins that way. In the quite common "vanishing twin syndrome," one of the twins is reabsorbed by the mother during the first trimester while the other remains viable.

2 One in 80 deliveries in the United States results in twins, but the rate is much higher among the Yoruba ethnic group in Nigeria: One in 11 people is a twin. In ancient times, the Yoruba viewed twins with suspicion, and sometimes sacrificed them. But now twins are considered lucky. In contrast to the Western view, the firstborn twin is considered the younger of the two. The Yoruba believe that the "senior" twin sent the younger one out first to scout the world.

3 Peggy Lynn of Danville, Pa., delivered fraternal twins Eric and Hanna 84 days apart—one in November 1995, one in February 1996.

4 Fraternal twins can be the result of two acts of sexual intercourse that occur days apart. For that reason, it is possible for fraternal twins to have different fathers, as demonstrated in an 1810 case in the U.S. in which one child was white and the other was what people then called mulatto, mixed black and white.

5 Of particular interest to psychologists are lifelong "twinless twins," people whose twin died at or near birth. According to psychologist Peter Whitmer, such surviving twins go to great lengths to assert their uniqueness, yet often feel as if they're living for two people. Perhaps the most famous was Elvis Presley, whose identical twin brother, Jesse, was stillborn. Others include painter Diego Rivera, pianist Liberace and writers Thornton Wilder and Philip K. Dick.

6 Actresses Scarlett Johansson and Parker Posey are twins. No, not with each other. Each of them has a twin brother.

7 Frederick and Susan Machell were a happily married couple in Australia in the 1980s. They both knew they had been adopted and thought it was an amusing coincidence that they had been born in the same hospital on the same day. But after 20 years of marriage, they investigated further because their child had a genetically related illness. Yes, they were twins. But they stayed married anyhow.

8 Identical twins can vary markedly in certain skills. Jose Canseco had 7,057 at-bats in the major leagues and hit 462 home runs. His identical twin brother, Ozzie, had 65 at-bats with no homers. You might guess that Jose's edge was steroid use, but Ozzie was exposed in the steroid scandal too.

9 Painter Ivan Albright's meticulously detailed work is displayed at the Art Institute of Chicago and featured in the 1945 film "The Picture of Dorian Gray." But Ivan was only half of his own story. He had a twin named Malvin. The two attended the School of the Art Institute, flipping a coin to determine which of them would study painting and which would learn sculpture. Though the coin flip put Ivan in the painting classes, Malvin eventually embraced that medium as well, but less successfully. Malvin signed his paintings "Zsissly," so that when the twins' work was displayed together, the catalog would have Albrights at the beginning and the end.

10 Other famous twins: Diplomat Kofi Annan (sister), journalist Seymour Hersh (fraternal brother), model Gisele Bundchen (fraternal sister), actor Montgomery Clift (sister), actor Vin Diesel (fraternal brother), actor Ashton Kutcher (fraternal brother), singer-songwriter Alanis Morissette (brother), writer Sarah Vowell (fraternal sister) and actor Billy Dee Williams (sister).

CHAPTER 12
Money & Finance

10 THINGS YOU MIGHT NOT KNOW ABOUT
MONEY

1 Hyperinflation was so bad in Zimbabwe a few years ago that the government printed $100 trillion bank notes. But don't be impressed: At one point in 2009, that was less than the price of a bus ticket. The troubled African nation abandoned its currency, but a Zimbabwean $100 trillion bill still has some value today, with an asking price of about $25 to $40 on eBay.

> The **COWRIE SHELL** was likely the first universal currency.

2 The cowrie shell was likely the first universal currency, circulating in parts of Africa, Europe, North America, Oceania and Asia as early as the 13th century B.C. and continuing for hundreds of years. The little shell was a perfect natural coin. It was uniform in size so it could be accurately traded by volume, weight or by counting. It was durable, resistant to rot or vermin and, of course, waterproof. It was pleasing to the eye and touch, and easier to handle and pick up than a coin. Possibly most important, it was nearly impossible to counterfeit.

3 Slang terms for money include the captain, coconuts, shiners, greenery, cabbage, stack, flash roll, glue and scram. A dollar is sometimes called a "simoleon," but there's no certainty about the origin. In the 1700s, a British sixpence was called a "simon," and in the 1800s, French gold coins were called Napoleons, so perhaps the two terms were combined.

4 Money doesn't grow on trees—except when it does. The Mayans and the Aztecs recognized the full value of chocolate and used cocoa beans as their currency. Three beans bought a turkey egg, but a buyer needed 100 beans to bring home the actual turkey hen or a slave.

5 The U.S. Treasury hasn't persuaded Americans to accept a dollar coin, but Canadians have embraced the "loonie," so named because it features the image of a common loon. The loonie almost didn't happen, though. When Canada went to dollar coins in the 1980s, it planned to use the image of a voyageur canoe. But the master dies for the coin disappeared mysteriously in transit, and the Canadian mint dumped the canoe for the loon to prevent counterfeiting. It later admitted that it had transported the dies through a local courier rather than an armored car service because it wanted to save $43.50.

6 The dollar sign with its capital S and two vertical lines predates the U.S. dollar. While there is debate to its origin, the symbol is certainly not the overlap of the U and S from the United States. Why not? The symbol was used to designate the peso before the U.S. dollar was even adopted in 1785.

7 Police in Manchester, England, released a photo in January 2015 of a 20-pound note that was an astonishingly bad counterfeit, featuring two color photocopies placed back-to-back and stapled together in all four corners. Even more astonishing was the fact that the note was accepted by a business, which the police declined to name "to avoid embarrassment."

8 For most of American history, no president's face appeared on a circulating U.S. coin. The first came in 1909 when Abraham Lincoln went on the penny.

For most of American history, no president's face appeared on a circulating U.S. coin.

9 Career criminal Willie Sutton was asked why he robbed banks and was famous for the reply: "Because that's where the money is." But the quote itself may be a crime against journalism—Sutton insisted he never said it. "The credit belongs to some enterprising reporter who apparently felt a need to fill out his copy," wrote Sutton, who disclosed that his real reason for robbing banks was "because I enjoyed it."

10 Filthy lucre is filthy. A 2014 New York University study scrubbed a dollar bill and found 3,000 types of bacteria, the most common of which was one that causes acne.

THE LOTTERY

1 A Powerball drawing in 2005 produced more than 110 second-place winners—far more than normal—and organizers worried that fraud was afoot. That is, until winners began explaining that they got the numbers from fortune cookies. A mass-produced slip of paper with five of the six winning numbers was traced to a fortune cookie factory in New York.

2 Lotteries come and lotteries go, and many states outlawed them after Congress authorized a Grand National Lottery in 1823 to help pay to beautify Washington, D.C. But the private agent organizing the contest absconded with the receipts, and the winner had to take his claim all the way to the Supreme Court to get his $100,000. (That would be worth nearly $2 million today.)

3 Shirley Jackson's short story "The Lottery" deals with an annual drawing in a small town in which (spoiler alert!) the "winner" is stoned to death by fellow citizens. Though the story is a classic today, its publication in 1948 disturbed many, including the author's mother. "Dad and I did not care at all for your story in The New Yorker," Jackson's mom wrote, adding that "it does seem, dear, that this gloomy kind of story is what all you young people think about these days. Why don't you write something to cheer people up?"

4 A low point in the lofty career of George Washington came in 1769 when he helped organize a lottery in which 55 slaves were raffled off in parcels that separated parents from children.

5 A stripped-down version of the lottery—drawing straws—made winners of all jazz lovers in 1934. That's when young Ella Fitzgerald drew straws with two girlfriends to decide which one would enter an amateur contest at the Apollo Theater in Harlem. Fitzgerald drew the short straw and intended to enter the dance contest. But she thought the competition was too stiff among the dancers, so she switched to the singing contest and won, launching a brilliant career.

6 Carl Atwood, 73, of Elwood, Ind., was one of the fortunate lottery players capturing a spot on a televised "Hoosier Millionaire" competition in 2004. He did well on the show, amassing $57,000, with the opportunity to go for a $1 million prize later. "I must admit I never expected to be leaving the show with this amount of money," he said. "Now I can purchase a very nice car." But Atwood's luck ended there. A few hours later, he was hit by a truck and killed.

7 Nobody wanted to win the lottery held Dec. 1, 1969. Ordered by President Richard Nixon to rectify the inequities in the Vietnam draft, it drew national TV coverage as a man pulled little balls out of a deep glass bowl to determine who was going to war. Except it wasn't so random. Late-year birthdays averaged much lower numbers, meaning young men born in November and December were more likely to be called to fight. What happened? According to a New York Times story a month later, the organizers packed the capsules, month by month, into a box, which was shaken several times. The capsules were poured into the bowl, but nobody stirred them. Why? Officials remembered that for a 1940 draft, some capsules broke open after they were mixed.

> Men born in November and December were more likely to be called to fight in the 1969 draft.

8 Thank Louisiana for the fact that you can't buy a lottery ticket through the U.S. mail. After the Civil War, the Southern states were desperate for cash. Louisiana's lottery, called the Serpent, was hugely successful and notoriously corrupt, slithering into every state of the union—and a whole lot of pockets in the Louisiana legislature. By one account, almost 50 percent of all mail coming into New Orleans was connected to the lottery. Pressured by other states, Congress in 1890 forbid using the Postal Service to peddle lotteries. The law stands today.

9 Winning the big jackpot may actually be worse than not winning it. Stories abound of newly made millionaires mismanaging their windfall and ending up destitute and alone. Jeffrey Dampier Jr. seemed to be handling the $20 million he won in Illinois in 1996 relatively well. He moved to Florida, took care of his family and bought a business. But in July 2005, he was kidnapped and killed by his sister-in-law and her boyfriend. Despite Dampier's apparent generosity, the motive was still greed, prosecutors said.

10 Everybody knows the chances of winning that huge Powerball jackpot are small, but it's impossible for most people to get their minds around what 1 in 175 million really means. Stanford University mathematician Keith Devlin offered this translation: "Imagine a standard NFL football field. Somewhere in the field, a student has placed a single, small, common variety of ant that she has marked with a spot of yellow paint. You walk onto the field blindfolded, and push a pin into the ground. If your pin pierces the marked ant, you win. Otherwise you lose. Want to give it a go?"

10 THINGS YOU MIGHT NOT KNOW ABOUT
DEBT

1 The rapidly rising national debt has us longing for the financial dependability of the Founding Fathers. But not all of them. Thomas Jefferson spent so recklessly that his heirs couldn't afford to live in Monticello. Robert Morris was hailed as the "Financier of the American Revolution" but fell on hard times afterward, landing in debtors prison for about three years. And then there was fellow Declaration of Independence signer James Wilson, who served on the U.S. Supreme Court at the same time he was in jail for nonpayment of bills.

2 There's a slang term in the United Kingdom for someone who is able to pay off only the interest on a payday loan but never reduce the principal. That person is a "zombie debtor."

3 The United States had no national debt for a brief time around January 1835, under President Andrew Jackson. But since then it's dug a $20 trillion hole.

The United States had no national debt for a brief time around January 1835.

4 When you measure countries' debt as a percentage of their gross domestic product, the United States is far from the worst, though it worsened considerably since the Great Recession. According to 2016 figures, the U.S. debt was 104 percent of GDP, lower than those of Japan (235%), Greece (182%) and Italy (133%), on par with Spain (100%) and Canada (99%), but higher than France (97%), United Kingdom (92%), Germany (69%), Mexico (50%) and Russia (14%).

5 The U.S. national debt is at an all-time high in raw numbers—but not as a percentage of GDP. "The Greatest Generation" had the greatest percentage of debt, peaking at 122 percent in 1946 because of World War II costs.

6 There's no doubt that the word "debt" is spelled funny. The Middle English word was spelled and pronounced "dette," but after an etymological respelling—a craze during the Renaissance perpetrated by scholars who wanted to appear smarter—it gained the "b" as a nod to its Latin root debitum.

7 Canadian naturalist Ernest Thompson Seton, a father figure in the development of the Boy Scouts, had a difficult relationship with his own dad. When Seton turned 21, his father handed him an itemized bill for everything spent on him up to that point, including the doctor's fee for his birth. The total came to $537.50, and his father set the interest rate at 6 percent. Seton reportedly paid the debt.

8 In George Pullman's famous company town near Chicago, workers ended up in debt simply by showing up. In 1893, after wages were slashed but rent went unchanged, some families were left with pennies on payday.

9 Before 1759 in New York City, there was no prison dedicated to debtors, so a deadbeat was held in the City Hall's attic—unless it got too crowded and he was tossed into the subbasement with the condemned criminals. But as "gaols will pay no debts," smarter creditors could force a bad debtor into indentured servitude for as long as seven years.

10 The 18th-century slang term "maneuvering the apostles" was a new way of saying you were "robbing Peter to pay Paul."

10 THINGS YOU MIGHT NOT KNOW ABOUT
TRAFFIC TICKETS

1 President Ulysses S. Grant got a ticket for speeding in his one-horse carriage. When the Washington police officer realized who his suspect was, he offered to forget about it, but Grant insisted on paying the fine.

2 The radar gun was invented by John Barker Sr. and first used by a police department in Glastonbury, Conn., in 1947, though that first model was hardly hand-held. To use it, Barker had to park on the side of the road and open his trunk so the equipment faced the traffic.

3 On Sunday, Aug. 16, 1903, Evanston, Ill., police set up multiple speed traps, the first in the morning at Ridge Avenue and Noyes Street, and collared 17 "autoists." Long before the age of radar guns—this was just about a month after Henry Ford sold his first Model A, after all—the trap worked like this: A plainclothes patrolman waved his handkerchief in front of his face when a car passed him, and colleagues an eighth of a mile down the road stopped any motorists who reached their spot too quickly. It was a rich haul, nabbing not only the police chief of Riverside but also Samuel Insull, Chicago Edison president. How fast were they going? Police said all were moving along at a healthy clip—at least 12 mph—well over the speed limit of 8 mph.

4 Babe Ruth got two speeding tickets in New York City in 1921, for driving 27 mph and 26 mph. After the second violation, a magistrate threw him in jail for a few hours. He was released 30 minutes after the start of the Yankees game against the Cleveland Indians and drove his maroon Packard 9 miles in 19 minutes—speeding again—to the Polo Grounds. Only then did he walk—to lead off the sixth inning.

5 Some of America's most notorious criminals were captured during traffic stops. Oklahoma City bomber Timothy McVeigh was pulled over for a missing license plate. Polygamist sect leader Warren Jeffs was stopped because his temporary car tag was partially illegible.

Serial killer Ted Bundy was arrested after a police car pulled up behind him and put on bright lights to read his license plate, prompting Bundy to speed away and run stop signs before he was caught. The police were less lucky with three Sept. 11 terrorists ticketed just months before the attack—Hani Hanjour and Ziad Samir Jarrah for speeding and Mohamed Atta for not having a valid driver's license. Atta ignored his ticket, and a bench warrant was issued. But when an officer later stopped Atta for speeding, he was unaware of the warrant and let Atta go with a warning.

Some of America's most notorious criminals were captured during traffic stops.

6 A not-so-simmering feud between Democratic presidential candidate Bobby Kennedy and Los Angeles Mayor Sam Yorty boiled over on May 29, 1968, when Kennedy's motorcade was hopscotching across Los Angeles campaigning for the California primary. City police slapped the motorcade with 23 tickets, mainly for running red lights and blowing stop signs, after Kennedy was denied a police escort.

7 During the huge bicycle craze in the late 1890s, when the problem of speeding cyclists called "scorchers" was particularly bad, one mounted policeman on Chicago's North Side who was tired of chasing offenders took to throwing a cobblestone attached to a rope into a speeder's wheels to bring him crashing down.

8 American segregationists used every weapon imaginable in battling the civil rights movement, from outright murder to dogs to traffic tickets. During the 1955-56 Montgomery, Ala., bus boycott—sparked by Rosa Parks' refusal to relinquish her seat to a white man—African-American motorists who carpooled were pulled over repeatedly and ticketed for speeding, running stop signs and other trumped-up charges.

9 Did a south suburb rename itself because of the notoriety of its infamous speed traps? According to a Tribune article, Specialville changed its name to Dixmoor in 1929 because publicity over speed traps ordered up by Mayor Charles Special "became so hot." The speed traps continued. But Special was convicted in 1938 of cheating motorists and was ordered to pay a $2,000 fine and serve a year in prison.

10 Soul singer James Brown's wife Adrienne hired a very creative lawyer when she contested speeding and other charges in 1988. Noting that the singer had been praised as "America's No. 1 ambassador," the lawyer claimed diplomatic immunity for Brown and his wife. It didn't fly.

10 THINGS YOU MIGHT NOT KNOW ABOUT
TIPPING

1 The nation's best tippers dine in Boston, leaving an average gratuity of 20 percent, according to Zagat's 2016 State of American Dining survey. Americans overall tip at an 18.9 percent rate, down a smidge from 19.2 percent in 2012. Chicago's rate is on the high side at 19.6. The stingiest? San Antonio at 17.1 percent.

2 Some people believe tipping is aristocratic, undemocratic and un-American—that it promotes the idea of a servant class. In 1910, U.S. labor leader Samuel Gompers complained that tipping in Europe "borders on blackmail," and that many American travelers there suffered "mosquito bites"—demands for tips—almost hourly. Yet a century later, Americans are among the globe's premier tippers, sometimes criticized abroad for throwing supply-and-demand out of whack by being too generous.

3 A travel tip: Don't leave a gratuity in Japan. It would be considered an insult.

4 More than 100 Chicago waiters were arrested in 1918 amid accusations that restaurant workers were plotting to slip "Mickey Finn" drugs into the food and drink of bad tippers.

5 John D. Rockefeller gave away an estimated 20,000 to 30,000 coins in his lifetime. The tipping tycoon doled out dimes to adults and nickels to children, using the coins as icebreakers for conversations and as rewards for fellow golfers, amusing storytellers and others he met. When something was spilled on the floor, Rockefeller would cast dimes atop the stains to reward the person who cleaned up the mess. But he would sometimes play tricks, giving people horse chestnuts instead of coins, explaining that the chestnuts would ease their rheumatism. A dime in Rockefeller's day was the equivalent of $1.36 today.

6 "Autograt" is slang for an automatic gratuity—the built-in tip that restaurants may charge in certain cases, such as for large tables.

7 "Canadian" is a restaurant slang term for a presumably bad tipper, i.e. "Jodie just sat six Canadians in your section, dude." The term is not necessarily a slur against actual Canadians; some believe it is a racist code word aimed at blacks or other minorities.

"CANADIAN" is a restaurant slang term for a presumably bad tipper.

8 Marwan al-Shehhi was not only a terrorist but a lousy tipper. After the September 11 attacks, an exotic dancer named Samantha remembered the hijacker being cheap as he patronized the Olympic Garden Topless Cabaret in Las Vegas. "I'm glad he's dead with the rest of them, and I don't like feeling something like that," Samantha told the San Francisco Chronicle. "But he wasn't just a bad tipper—he killed people."

9 Among the nicknames for a tip is baksheesh, from a Persian word for gift.

10 In June 2000, a British tourist in Chicago visiting the Leg Room appreciated his waitress so much he left a $10,000 tip for a $9 drink. The bar's manager didn't believe it—it was 3 a.m., after all—and photocopied the man's passport and had him sign a statement confirming his generous intentions. The credit card transaction was initially approved, but the British bank later rejected the charge. In the cold, sober light of day, the man decided he wouldn't pay the tip. "I don't recall the details," he told a British newspaper. "I had had a few drinks." But some stories do end well: The bar's owners made good on the tip.

10 THINGS YOU MIGHT NOT KNOW ABOUT

TAXES

1 Did 7 million American children suddenly disappear in 1987? On paper, it seemed so. That's the year the IRS began requiring Social Security numbers for dependent children, and the number dropped dramatically.

2 Before there was Al Capone, there was a South Carolina bootlegger named Manny Sullivan. In the 1927 ruling United States vs. Sullivan, the U.S. Supreme Court declared that income derived from illegal means was taxable. Sullivan argued that reporting his ill-gotten gains would violate his 5th Amendment rights against self-incrimination. The court unanimously disagreed. That set the table for Capone's conviction in October 1931, and for today's requirement in some states that marijuana dealers buy tax stamps.

3 There might be no such thing as Busch Stadium if Fred Saigh hadn't cheated on his taxes. Saigh, owner of the St. Louis Cardinals baseball team in the early 1950s, was forced to sell the team after being sentenced to 15 months in prison for tax evasion. The Busch family bought the team and owned it for four decades.

4 What did actress Sophia Loren have in common with Chicago Mayor Harold Washington, Illinois Gov. Otto Kerner, rock 'n' roller Chuck Berry, hotel magnate Leona Helmsley, comedian Richard Pryor, lobbyist Jack Abramoff and evangelist Sun Myung Moon? They all did jail time on tax charges.

In 1697, England taxed homeowners based on the number of windows in their houses.

5 In 1697, England taxed homeowners based on the number of windows in their houses. Glass was expensive, so a tax on windows was a somewhat fair gauge of wealth. Nevertheless, some citizens viewed the tax as the ultimate daylight robbery. When today's tourists see bricked-up windows on old English buildings, it's often a testament to their owners' efforts to avoid the tax, which was repealed in 1851.

Actress Sophia Loren, Chicago Mayor Harold Washington, Illinois Gov. Otto Kerner, rock 'n' roller Chuck Berry, hotel magnate Leona Helmsley, comedian Richard Pryor, lobbyist Jack Abramoff and evangelist Sun Myung Moon all did jail time on tax charges.

6 Nearly 129 million federal taxpayers used e-file in 2015, meaning more than 90 percent of all federal returns were paperless. In 2001, just 31 percent were e-filed.

7 The man who once helped formulate tax policy for the world's largest economy messed up his own taxes by filing through the TurboTax software program. But former Treasury Secretary Timothy Geithner blamed himself, not TurboTax, for failing to report more than $34,000 in International Monetary Fund income, a stumble that complicated but did not derail his Senate confirmation.

8 The Stamp Act of 1765, the first direct tax on American colonists, is familiar to students of the Revolutionary War. But less understood is how pervasive the tax was. Nearly every commercial, legal and government document had to be written on special paper carrying an embossed stamp. That included marriage licenses, wills, college diplomas, calendars, almanacs and newspapers. That's not all: The act taxed playing cards and even dice.

9 Here's a little-known American hero: Donald Alexander, the Internal Revenue Service commissioner from 1973 to 1977 who found that President Richard Nixon was using a secret cadre of IRS investigators to attack people on his "enemies list." Alexander disbanded the unit, and later wrote: "The evening of the same day, President Nixon made his first effort to fire me." But Alexander outlasted his boss. He died in 2009, honored for withstanding political pressure and simply doing his job.

10 Another former IRS boss, Joseph Nunan Jr., is less fondly remembered. In 1952, Nunan was convicted of tax evasion for failing to report at least $86,000 in income, including his winnings when he bet that President Harry Truman would be elected in 1948. Nunan wagered $200 on Truman with 9-to-1 odds, earning $1,800—and a five-year prison sentence.

CHAPTER 13
Arts & Culture

10 THINGS YOU MIGHT NOT KNOW ABOUT
SOCIAL MEDIA

1 In 2011, an Israeli couple, Lior and Vardit Adler, named their daughter Like, after the Facebook feature.

2 Credit a good old Chicago snowstorm for giving social media an early boost. Chicagoan Ward Christensen couldn't get to work Jan. 27, 1978, after 12 inches of snow blanketed the region, so he called his friend Randy Suess and began working on the first Bulletin Board System, or BBS, which allowed early users to post messages or share computer code—via modem, of course.

3 The stairway to heaven is on the internet. Lineforheaven.com gives visitors a "spiritual journey in a fun, light-hearted, nonhostile environment." In effect, you try to earn your way into heaven by collecting "karma points." All participants share a message with other contestants about why they are worthy. They earn karma points in several ways, such as judging the worthiness of others and confessing their own sins. There's even the modern version of indulgences—buying their way into heaven. A dollar is worth 10 points, and "Your donation helps keep your favorite Heaven website alive."

4 About 35 percent of recently married American couples met online. That's according to research led by University of Chicago professor John Cacioppo using a Harris Poll of nearly 20,000 Americans who got married in 2005-2012. But another conclusion of the study— that these online couples are less likely to separate or divorce—has inspired some skepticism, in part because the study was funded by the eHarmony online dating site. But Cacioppo stands by his research, published in Proceedings of the National Academy of Sciences. In 2016, Pew Research reported that just 5 percent of Americans in marriages or committed relationships said they met online.

5 Crowd funding is a new term for a very old idea—asking people to make small contributions toward a larger cause. That's how churches got built, how Chicago's Hull House was

"What hath God wrought?"

—SAMUEL MORSE

operated and how the pedestal of the Statue of Liberty was financed. But internet sites like Kickstarter, Crowdtilt and Indiegogo are giving the idea new reach and power. Many projects are uplifting, such as the Crowdtilt campaign to replace David Henneberry's boat, which was damaged by gunfire when Boston bombing suspect Dzhokhar Tsarnaev hid inside. But other efforts seem ridiculous, including personal appeals to fund a new smartphone or a Vegas bachelor party. There was even a website devoted to women's requests for help paying for breast implants.

6 The first telegraph message, transmitted on May 24, 1844, by Samuel Morse, was "What hath God wrought?" The first words spoken by phone, on March 10, 1876, by Alexander Graham Bell, were, "Mr. Watson—come here—I want to see you." And the first Twitter message, tweeted by co-founder Jack Dorsey on March 21, 2006, was, "Just setting up my twttr."

7 Twitter co-founder Dorsey's first tweet referred to "twttr" because that's what it was originally called—sans vowels. Dorsey's group soon realized that it needed to add an I and an E, and it acquired the twitter.com domain name from a bird lover. Facebook (previously called The Facebook) didn't originally own the fb.com domain name. It was the property of the American Farm Bureau Federation, which sold it to Facebook for $8.5 million.

8 The power of social media to mobilize the public behind a common cause is already legendary, possibly most notably as part of the Arab Spring revolt in Egypt in 2011. But sometimes the cause is more pedestrian, like a girl's Sweet 16. In Hamburg, Germany, a teen mistakenly posted an invitation to her birthday bash to the public. More than 1,500 crashed the June 2011 event. Before it was over, the poor girl reportedly had to flee from her own house, more than 100 cops had been called to disperse the mob and 11 people were arrested for assault and property damage.

9 You know that feeling you get reading your old high school girlfriend's Facebook page or seeing what your neighbor does when he isn't home? It has a name: ambient intimacy. Coined by Leisa Reichelt, a social media expert based in London, it means, "a level of regularity and intimacy that you wouldn't usually have access to." Knowing what somebody ate for breakfast, what irked them reading the newspaper, who they're having drinks with tonight, all creates intimacy, Reichelt wrote on her blog in 2007. "It's not so much about meaning, it's just about being in touch."

10 If you join a MMORPG, you might lose your FOMO and eventually meet someone FTF who will say BTWITILY. Or, in other words, if you join a massively multiplayer online role-playing game, you might lose your fear of missing out and eventually meet someone face-to-face who will say, "By the way, I think I love you."

10 THINGS YOU MIGHT NOT KNOW ABOUT
RACY MOVIES

1 Marlon Brando was so bad at memorizing lines during the filming of "Last Tango in Paris" that he asked the director if he could write some of his lines on co-star Maria Schneider's rear end.

2 Police official M.L.C. Funkhouser was Chicago's official movie censor in the 1910s, banning pictures for "making a travesty on marriage and women's virtue." For some films, he removed certain scenes. For others, he issued adults-only "pink permits." He reportedly cut scenes in a Charlie Chaplin movie because the comedian was "bumping a woman's back." Funkhouser's aides were especially on the lookout for "Wisconsin copies"—films shipped from Wisconsin that did not include the cuts ordered especially for Chicago.

3 What's racy? Movies in the U.S. are rated by the Motion Picture Association of America, or more specifically, by a group of about a dozen anonymous parents whose children must be ages 5-15. They rate movies based on what they think most U.S. parents would find suitable. In Sweden, films are reviewed by professionals in the behavioral sciences who gauge them on whether scenes and images are deemed harmful to children, either psychologically or behaviorally.

4 The differences between U.S. and Swedish movie ratings can be startling. "Still Alice," a movie starring Julianne Moore about a woman coming to grips with early onset Alzheimer's disease, earned a PG-13 rating in the U.S. for "mature thematic material, and brief language including a sexual reference." Swedish reviewers said it "contains nothing that could be detrimental to the welfare of children in any age."

5 The sizzling sexuality of Dorothy Dandridge in the 1954 film "Carmen Jones" made some people uneasy. Dandridge had to be persuaded to take the "bad girl" role, worried that it would hurt the image of African-Americans. Author James Baldwin accused the film of "a sterile and distressing eroticism," noting that Dandridge's co-star, Harry Belafonte, was not allowed to be nearly as sexy because "the Negro male is still too loaded a quantity for them to know quite how to handle." Dandridge was the first black woman to get a best actress Oscar nomination, but her career went downhill after "Carmen Jones." About a decade later, she was dead of a drug overdose, with $2.14 in her bank account.

6 Under the Hays Code that regulated movies in the mid-20th century, close-ups of the milking of cows were banned as vulgar, according to author Aubrey Malone, who noted: "It was recommended for one film that the action of an electric milking machine be suggested rather than shown."

Under the Hays Code, close-ups of the milking of cows were banned as vulgar.

7 "Risky Business," the 1983 teen classic that catapulted Tom Cruise to stardom, earned its R rating with multiple scenes of female nudity, but for some moviegoers it was young Cruise's lip-sync dance to Bob Seger's "Old Time Rock and Roll" that got hearts racing. The script simply stated, "(He) dances in underwear through the house." So that's what Cruise did. "Most of that was ad-lib," he said. "Yeah. All of that was ad-lib."

8 Director Billy Wilder clashed with studio censors many times, including over a comedic scene in which two male prisoners of war dance in the 1953 film "Stalag 17." A censor said there should be no "snuggling," nor should one call the other "darling." He warned: "If there is any inference in the finished scene of a flavor of sex perversion, we will not be able to approve it under the code." But Wilder left the scene as planned, and it got through.

9 Chicago censors hated one 1916 movie not just because it "portrays the life of a prostitute and tends to condone her life of immorality," but even because the title—"The Courtesan"—was deemed "objectionable."

10 In the 1932 film "Red-Headed Woman," Jean Harlow plays a husband-stealing harlot and appears topless onscreen ever so briefly. Though the movie was banned in Great Britain, King George V kept a personal copy at Buckingham Palace.

10 THINGS YOU MIGHT NOT KNOW ABOUT
TV ADS

1 The first legal television commercial was pretty simple: A picture of a clock on a U.S. map, with a voice-over saying, "America runs on Bulova time." The 10-second spot on July 1, 1941, aired on the New York NBC station and cost the watch company $9.

2 Your favorite hourlong, prime-time broadcast show is closer to 45 minutes, once you subtract commercials and network promotions. From 1991 to 2013, the total time viewers spent not watching the show jumped to 14 minutes, 15 seconds from about 13 minutes per prime-time hour. Many countries regulate the amount of advertising per hour, but a similar industry agreement in the U.S. was ruled illegal in the 1980s.

3 As of December 2011, a law now requires a TV ad to be aired at the same volume as the program it's running in. The two-page bill took two years to pass.

The longest-running TV commercial appears to be for Discount Tire, and **FIRST AIRED IN 1975**.

4 The longest-running TV commercial appears to be for Discount Tire. The 10-second spot, which first aired in 1975, shows an old lady throwing a tire through a store window as the announcer says, "If you're not satisfied with one of our tires, please feel free to bring it back." But that's no granny tossing a tire. The woman hired to play the disgruntled customer wasn't strong enough, so a man on the production crew named John Staub

The "I'd like to buy the world a Coke" commercial in the early 1970s was so popular that people called local TV stations to request it.

stood in for the stunt. "I'm an old lady with a mustache in the window reflection, but you can't really see it because it edits so fast," he said.

5 Sometimes the commercials bleed into the shows. In 1959, the script for a "Playhouse 90" about the Nuremberg war crimes trials included the word "gas" in reference to the Nazi death chambers. But that word was edited out of the script at the insistence of the show's sponsor, a natural gas industry group. Despite that, some references to "gas ovens" made it through, so they were removed during the live broadcast. Actors' lips moved, but viewers heard "(silence) ovens."

6 According to a 2016 ORC International survey, 76 percent say they skip TV ads. As recently as 2011, Nielsen reported that 45 percent of all recorded TV commercials were still viewed.

7 Public service announcements were first created by the Ad Council during World War II to get Rosie to work and to tighten loose lips. In 1971, on the second Earth Day, the world met "the crying Indian," played by Iron Eyes Cody. The famous anti-pollution ad, which showed Cody paddling a canoe and watching motorists litter, effectively gave the new ecology movement a huge boost. As it turns out, Cody was of Italian descent (real name Espera De-Corti), but he appeared in hundreds of movies and TV shows as a Native American and denied his European ancestry until his death in 1999.

8 The "I'd like to buy the world a Coke" commercial in the early 1970s was so popular that people called local TV stations to request it. It was reprised with the original singers and their children for a 1990 Super Bowl ad.

9 In 1989, Pepsi ran a TV commercial that advertised a TV commercial. An ad during the Grammy Awards revealed that a Pepsi commercial featuring Madonna and her hit, "Like a Prayer," would debut a week and a half later. Indeed it did, but the impact was ruined amid the outrage over the song's racy video.

10 For a time, "The Flintstones" was sponsored by Winston cigarettes, and commercials showed prehistoric puffing by Fred, Barney and Wilma.

10 THINGS YOU MIGHT NOT KNOW ABOUT
TV TECHNOLOGY

1 Philo Farnsworth was a 14-year-old Idaho farm boy when he came up with a brainstorm that eventually led to the first practical electronic television. Working with a horse-drawn harrow to harvest potatoes one row after another, it occurred to him that an electronic image could be scanned and reproduced line by line—one row after another.

2 Why is there no Channel 1 on American TV? Because in the 1940s, TV and radio shared some frequencies, raising the prospect of interference. Channel 1 was used only by low-watt TV stations, so the industry was willing to surrender the frequency to radio. TV could have reordered its remaining channels to start with 1, but it chose not to.

3 The late 1940s and early '50s were a freewheeling time in Chicago TV. When NBC-owned WNBQ used a special effect to split one image into dozens, network execs in New York asked about this new "image multiplier." The Chicagoans refused to explain. The New York bosses insisted. Finally, the Chicagoans shipped them the cutting-edge technology: a common glass building block that they had held in front of the lens.

4 The yokels got cable TV first. We think of cable as a means to deliver 200-plus channels, but its first customers had no choices at all—people in remote areas whose TV reception was terrible. "Community antennas" were built on high ground in Arkansas, Oregon and Pennsylvania in 1948. Then cables carried the signals to individual homes.

5 The wireless TV remote control was born in the Chicago area in 1955. Zenith engineer Eugene Polley created the Flash-Matic, which sent a light signal to the television. Trouble was, sunlight could cause confusion. A year later, Zenith's Robert Adler devised a remote called the Space Command that used ultrasound and was state of the art for decades. Eventually, infra-red signaling took over. When Adler died in 2007, some admirers called for a sitting ovation.

6 Japanese manufacturer Ikegami Tsushinki invented a hand-held TV camera that it called a "handy-looky," mimicking the slang term "walkie-talkie." The product caught on. The nickname did not.

7 Because history is written by the victors, few people have heard of the DuMont Television Network, which went out of business in 1955. Founder Allen DuMont pioneered development of cathode ray tubes and launched his own TV manufacturing company and broadcast network. He lacked the clout of rival companies that had been involved in radio for decades, though many believe his studio equipment and home sets were technologically superior. And he didn't lack for marketing pluck. A 1946 print ad quoted actress Betty Hutton as saying: "I'll be practically in your lap—on DuMont television!"

8 In a technological feat that some saw as pointless, CNN unveiled "hologram" reporting on Election Night 2008. Correspondent Jessica Yellin was sent to Chicago's Grant Park, and her three-dimensional image was beamed back to the studio, as if she had never left. CNN exec Jon Klein explained: "The hologram allowed us to pull people figuratively out of a very noisy environment in Grant Park and actually have a conversation with them. One day all TV news will be done that way." Or not. Holography experts noted that CNN wasn't really using holograms, since the 3-D images weren't projected in space, but only on screen. Technically, that meant they were tomograms, not holograms.

9 Early TV cameras sometimes were thrown off by certain colors. After Soviet broadcaster Olga Vysotskaya gave a gymnastics demonstration while wearing a certain hue in 1938, she got letters from viewers asking her why she had appeared in the nude.

10 In 2007, Hitachi researched a "brain-machine interface" in which the TV would sense that you wanted to change channels, and would do so instantly. In 2017, Netflix engineers repurposed a Muse headband, which reportedly senses brainwaves and helps train people to meditate, to browse their TV app without a remote control. All the more reason to make friends with your technology, before your spouse does.

10 THINGS YOU MIGHT NOT KNOW ABOUT
FILM CRITICS

1 Pauline Kael—the hugely influential, acerbic critic for The New Yorker from 1968 to 1991 (except for a short stint about 1980 when she tried to work in the film industry)—got her start in San Francisco in 1953 when a magazine editor overheard her and a friend debating Charlie Chaplin's film "Limelight" at a coffeehouse and asked them each to write a review. Only Kael turned one in. She called the movie "Slimelight."

2 David Manning was born in 2000 and made an impact as a film reviewer almost immediately. That's because Manning was invented by a Sony Pictures Entertainment marketer. The fake critic praised Rob Schneider's "The Animal" as "another winner" but was soon exposed—prompting an exec associated with the film, Joe Roth, to tell Newsweek: "If he doesn't exist, he should at least have given us a better quote." Sony later settled a lawsuit, allowing filmgoers to file $5-per-ticket claims if Manning's praise of "The Animal" or other films had misled them into attending.

3 Tribune film critic Michael Phillips told the website Rotten Tomatoes that a formative moviegoing experience occurred at age 9 when he watched "It's a Mad, Mad, Mad, Mad World," expecting to like it but instead hating it. ". . . Being sent into a low-grade funk by that alleged 'comedy to end all comedies' probably had something to do with me becoming a critic. I wanted to figure out why it didn't click, at least for me."

4 Reviewers write a fine line in telling enough without revealing too much. Rarely was that more crucial than for "The Crying Game." The 1992 film's plot turned on the fact that a female character was really a man, a twist so important that the film's producers pleaded with the media and moviegoers to keep it a secret. That didn't sway the Tribune's Gene Siskel, who gave it away on a special Oscars edition of "Siskel and Ebert." The revelation infuriated Ebert, who called the move "arrogant" and said Siskel should have discussed it beforehand. The flip side was The New York Times' Janet Maslin, who managed with the artful avoidance of pronouns to keep the secret throughout a 1,350-word profile of the androgynously named actor Jaye Davidson.

5 For decades, Tribune movie reviewers wrote under a fake byline as Mae Tinee (Get it? "Matinee"). Among the writers using the byline were Frances Peck Kerner, Anna Nangle and Maurine Dallas Watkins, who wrote the play that was adapted into the award-winning musical "Chicago."

6 Everyone loved "Gone With the Wind" when it came out, right? Wrong. African-American critic Melvin B. Tolson, writing in the Washington Tribune, objected to the film's depiction of well-treated slaves and its sympathy toward slaveholders. He said the takeaway for white moviegoers was that "Dixie was a heaven on Earth until the damned Yankees and carpetbaggers came."

7 When we think about Carl Sandburg, we might recall his poem describing Chicago as the "city of the big shoulders," or his six-volume biography of Abraham Lincoln. It's less likely that Sandburg's review of the silent film "Nanook of the North" will come to mind. But, in fact, Sandburg wrote more than 2,000 articles about the movies for the Chicago Daily News, according to author Arnie Bernstein.

8 Los Angeles Times critic Kenneth Turan repeatedly lambasted 1997's "Titanic," calling it "a witless counterfeit of Hollywood's Golden Age." Director James Cameron was furious and demanded Turan's firing, arguing that the film's popularity showed that the critic was out of touch. "Forget about Clinton—how do we impeach Kenneth Turan?" Cameron wrote.

9 The porn film "Deep Throat," which was caught up in 1970s censorship battles, was reviewed by upper-crust critics who ordinarily wouldn't write about such fare. Ellen Willis of the New York Review of Books called it "about as erotic as a tonsillectomy." But Arthur Knight of the Saturday Review testified at a New York obscenity trial that the film deserved praise "for expanding the audience's sexual horizons and producing healthier attitudes towards sex." The judge didn't buy it, leading to a movie theater marquee in Times Square reading: "Judge Cuts Throat, World Mourns."

10 Critics may be at their best reviewing bad films. Ebert in 2000: "'Battlefield Earth' is like taking a bus trip with someone who has needed a bath for a long time." Phillips on "Did You Hear About the Morgans?" in 2009: "It's not just the sound of crickets you hear watching this movie. It's the sound of dead crickets." But perhaps the most withering review was also the shortest. Leonard Maltin's complete review of the 1948 film "Isn't It Romantic?": "No."

> *"It's not just the sound of crickets you hear watching ['Did You Hear About the Morgans?'].*
> *It's the sound of dead crickets."* —MICHAEL PHILLIPS

10 THINGS YOU MIGHT NOT KNOW ABOUT
CLASSICAL MUSIC

1 Paul Wittgenstein, brother of philosopher Ludwig Wittgenstein, lost his right arm while serving in the Austrian army during World War I. But he performed as a professional pianist anyway, commissioning left-handed compositions from Maurice Ravel, Richard Strauss and Sergei Prokofiev.

2 "Couac" is a French word for a bad note from a defective or mishandled reed instrument, so named because it sounds like a duck's quack.

3 Felix Mendelssohn, a prodigy often compared to Mozart, may not have been the most talented musician in his family. When his older sister Fanny was just 12, she played from memory 24 preludes from J.S. Bach's "Well-Tempered Clavier." Later, Felix would publish some of Fanny's work under his own name, partly because of societal mores against her doing so. One of them, "Italien," became very popular, so much so that in 1842 when Felix met Queen Victoria of England, she sang the piece to him. Reportedly, Felix admitted it was his sister's composition.

4 An early version of the trombone was called a sackbut.

5 John Cage's most famous composition, "4'33"," requires a musician to make no sound for four minutes and 33 seconds. In 2010, more than half a century after Cage's work debuted, his British admirers silently recorded a version called "Cage Against the Machine" and campaigned to make it the No. 1 United Kingdom single for Christmas week. But their effort to turn Dec. 25 into "a silent night" ended up No. 21 on the charts.

6 Composer Giacomo Puccini and conductor Arturo Toscanini were friends who sometimes feuded. One Christmas, Puccini sent Toscanini a traditional holiday gift—an Italian sweet bread called a panettone. Then Puccini remembered that he and Toscanini were on bad terms, and he followed up with a telegram reading: PANETTONE SENT BY MISTAKE. PUCCINI. He got a telegram back: PANETTONE EATEN BY MISTAKE. TOSCANINI.

7 British composer Gerald Hugh Tyrwhitt-Wilson, also known as Lord Berners, was an odd bird. He organized meals based on color schemes—for example, matching beet soup with lobster, tomatoes and strawberries. When serving such a meal, he also would dye the pigeons and doves outside his home a matching hue. In addition, Berners constructed a tower at his estate west of London and posted a sign: "Members of the public committing suicide from this tower do so at their own risk."

8 In the 19th century, a singer who was on tour would bring along a "suitcase aria," a favorite piece of music to be inserted into whatever opera was being performed, whether it made any dramatic sense or not.

9 When a composer wants to push the boundary of what an instrument can do, he might require extended techniques. Henry Cowell's "Sinister Resonance" about 1930 required the pianist to pluck, strum and scrape the strings *inside* the piano.

10 Who knew the baton was a safety device? Before batons were used, conductors used a longer staff to keep time, sometimes to dangerous effect. While conducting a performance in the 1600s, French composer Jean-Baptiste Lully hit his foot with the staff. The injury turned gangrenous and killed him.

10 THINGS YOU MIGHT NOT KNOW ABOUT

MODERN ART

1 There were plenty of people in early 20th century Paris who thought they were doing Amedeo Modigliani a favor. They accepted the charming but poverty-stricken artist's work in exchange for food. But they didn't realize what they had. A restaurateur stored Modigliani's paintings in his basement, where rats chewed them up. The operator of a potato stall used Modigliani's drawings to wrap her fried chips. In 2006, more than eight decades after Modigliani's death, one of his works sold for $30 million.

"I hate flowers—I paint them because they're cheaper than models and they don't move."

—GEORGIA O'KEEFFE

2 Georgia O'Keeffe's flower paintings have fascinated many people, but the fuss over them annoyed the artist. She once told art critic Emily Genauer: "I hate flowers—I paint them because they're cheaper than models and they don't move."

3 When the Picasso sculpture was installed in Chicago's Daley Plaza in 1967, then-Ald. John Hoellen (47th) called on the city to "deport" the artwork to

France and replace it with a statue of Cubs slugger Ernie Banks. (Pop quiz: What's the title of the sculpture? Answer: It doesn't have one.)

4 Robert Rauschenberg produced a 1953 work titled "Erased de Kooning Drawing" by using rubber erasers to rub out a drawing that artist Willem de Kooning had given him for that purpose.

5 Chicago painter Ivan Albright was so meticulous that during a typical five-hour workday, he would paint about a half of a square inch.

6 You've heard of op art and pop art—but "plop art"? It's a term for public art that bears no relation to its environment, as if it was plopped down in its location without any thought.

7 Andy Warhol's paintings of Campbell's soup cans were the ultimate pop art. But not everyone was impressed. When Warhol's first soup-can exhibit opened in New York City in 1962, a competing gallery put actual Campbell's cans in its windows with a sign reading, "Buy them cheaper here—sixty cents for three cans."

8 Edward Hopper's wife, Jo, once bit his hand to the bone.

9 Max Ernst's embrace of surrealism seems more understandable when you understand that his father, an amateur weekend painter, had a problem with plain old reality. The senior Ernst, painting a picture of his garden but struggling with how to depict a tree in the scene, solved the problem by grabbing an ax and chopping down the tree.

10 Chris Burden, a California performance artist in the '70s, stuffed himself into a school locker for five days, nailed himself to the roof of a Volkswagen Beetle in a mock crucifixion, arranged for an assistant to shoot him in the arm and fired a gunshot at a plane passing overhead. If he did any of those things today, he'd get his own reality TV show.

MUSIC FESTIVALS

1 Creedence Clearwater Revival was the first big-name band lined up for Woodstock. The group's signing encouraged others to appear at the 1969 event, but Creedence ended up with a lousy time slot: about 1:30 a.m., after the Grateful Dead. Said Creedence frontman John Fogerty: "Wow, we got to follow the band that put a half a million people to sleep."

2 The name of the Bonnaroo festival in Manchester, Tenn., came from Dr. John's album "Desitively Bonnaroo," a title based on New Orleans slang. "Desitively" is a combination of "definitely" and "positively"; "bonnaroo" is an amalgam of two French words, "bon" and "rue," meaning the best on the streets.

3 The end of the Franco-Prussian War was celebrated with a music fest in Boston, of all places. Composer Johann Strauss conducted about 17,000 singers and an orchestra of 1,500 at the World's Peace Jubilee and International Musical Festival of 1872.

4 Kris Kristofferson's 1969 appearance at the Newport Folk Festival, one of his first breaks as a performer, was arranged by the late country legend Johnny Cash. Kristofferson made an impression on Cash by landing a helicopter on his lawn and handing him a demo tape.

5 Live Aid begat Farm Aid. Bob Dylan was performing at the Philadelphia portion of the huge 1985 festival, which was intended to benefit the starving peoples of Ethiopia, when he said he hoped some of the money could go to help the American farmer. Live Aid organizer Bob Geldof said Dylan's plea "was crass, stupid and nationalistic." Two months later, the first Farm Aid concert took place in Champaign.

6 U2's legendary performance at Live Aid is widely credited with launching the Irish band to superstardom. But at the time, it was a disaster. After Bono left the stage to dance with fans for more than two minutes during an unplanned 13-minute rendition of "Bad," U2 didn't

> *"Wow, we got to follow the band that put a half a million people to sleep."*
>
> —JOHN FOGERTY ON FOLLOWING THE GRATEFUL DEAD AT WOODSTOCK

have time to play their third song. The rest of the band was so angry they asked Bono to quit. "I thought I'd made a big mistake," Bono said. "I went out and drove for days. . . . And when I got back, I found people were saying the bit they remembered was U2."

7 Supermodel Kate Moss booted up the popularity of Hunter Wellies when she sported the rugged footwear at the muddy Glastonbury music festival in Britain in 2005. Fashionistas interviewed by Canada's Globe and Mail said the 2011 fest faves included feathers, scarves and floppy hats.

8 Our nomination for best fest name: Blistered Fingers, a bluegrass event in Maine. Possibly the worst-named: a Kansas festival called Kanrocksas.

9 Milwaukee's Summerfest was nearly silenced on opening day in 2006. An electrocuted falcon caused a three-hour power failure, rendering numerous electric guitars useless. That didn't stop the University of Wisconsin-Madison marching band, which required no artificial amplification. The students played an impromptu show that included "Roll Out the Barrel."

10 Jessica Pardoe, who was hailed as Britain's tallest teen girl and described by the Sunday Mirror as "6 foot 9 inches in bare feet," told the newspaper in 2011: "I love going to music festivals, and it's great to be able to see over everyone's heads."

CHAPTER 14
Sports

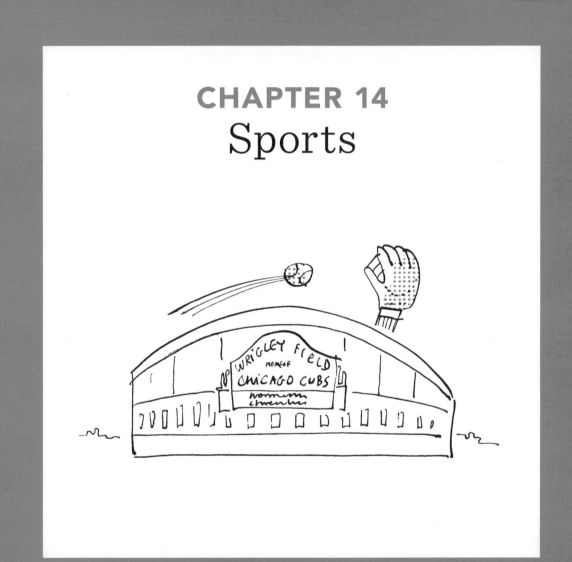

10 THINGS YOU MIGHT NOT KNOW ABOUT
FOOTBALL COACHES

1 Curly Lambeau's Green Bay Packers trailed 16-14 after the first half of the 1938 championship game against the New York Giants at the Polo Grounds. But Lambeau's halftime was even more difficult. The coach got lost walking to the locker room, went through a door leading outside the stadium and didn't realize his mistake until the door had locked behind him. It took him precious minutes to convince stadium staff that he was really the Packers' coach and should be let back in. Green Bay lost 23-17.

2 At every game, Louisiana State University coach Les Miles performs a ritual "that lets me know that I'm a part of the field and part of the game." What is it? He eats the grass. But Miles downplays his routine: "I chew one blade of grass. It's not a casserole. One blade. Not a meal."

3 Long before National Football League head coaches developed brain trusts and held film sessions, they put their bodies on the line with the rest of the team. During a game in 1927, Bears player-coach George Halas rushed to deliver a blindside hit on the New York Giants' passer, but future Hall of Famer Joe Guyon got rid of the ball and, in a flash, turned to meet Halas with his knee. The Bears' defensive end went down with several broken ribs. "Come on, Halas," said Guyon, who was Native American. "You should know better than to try to sneak up on an Indian."

4 Legendary NFL coaches Paul Brown and Weeb Ewbank had a "Tuesday rule," meaning players could not have sex after Tuesday if they were playing that weekend.

5 When Rice University recruited quarterback J.T. Granato from a nearby Houston high school in 2014, assistant coach Billy Lynch wrote a letter to Granato's cat: "I know you'd like to keep him close so he can feed you and change the litter box. Please help us to get him to choose us. Paw me if you have any questions." The letter worked—Granato committed to Rice.

"Immediately after it happened, I knew I had gone too far."
—DALE CHRISTENSEN

6 Dale Christensen, Libertyville High School's football coach, tried to fire up his team for the playoffs in 1993 by staging a shooting during a motivational speech. He arranged for a student to fire a starter's pistol at him and then fell down and smeared ketchup on his shoulder. Students scrambled for cover and called the police. "Immediately after it happened, I knew I had gone too far," said the coach. He lost his job.

7 DePaul announced in 1938 that it was dropping intercollegiate football, but the school's gridiron past lives on at the College Football Hall of Fame, where a former coach is an inductee. Dr. Eddie Anderson coached football at DePaul at the same time he was playing professionally for the Chicago Cardinals and attending Loyola Medical School. He went on to greater glory at Holy Cross and Iowa. While at Iowa, he would perform medical duties at the university hospital in the morning before shifting to coaching duties in the afternoon.

8 Fritz Pollard became the first African-American head coach in the NFL in 1924 when he led the Hammond Pros. The Chicago native had a remarkable life, growing up at the turn of the last century in predominantly white Rogers Park, where he became best friends with Charles "Chick" Evans, the future golf legend. On the gridiron, Pollard recruited and coached Paul Robeson, the stage, screen and singing star, and he also finagled to play against Red Grange during the University of Illinois star's barnstorming tour in 1925. And in 1911, as a three-sport star at Lane Tech High School, he was one game away from playing for the city's indoor baseball title against a Crane Tech High School team that starred . . . George Halas.

9 The NFL waited 65 years before hiring its second African-American head coach: Los Angeles Raiders owner Al Davis hired Art Shell in 1989.

10 Before coach Jackie Sherrill's Mississippi State team faced Texas in 1992, its preparation included the players witnessing the castration of a bull on the practice field. Sherrill defended the demonstration as both motivational and educational but later apologized "if this incident was in any way not perceived as proper." (His team won the game.)

10 THINGS YOU MIGHT NOT KNOW ABOUT
COLLEGE FOOTBALL

1 The first college football game west of the Allegheny Mountains took place in 1879 at the Chicago White Stockings' baseball park in what is now Millennium Park. The University of Michigan defeated Racine (Wis.) College.

2 The first all-America quarterback, chosen in 1889, was Princeton's Edgar Allan Poe, grandnephew of the famed writer of the same name. (No, he wasn't drafted by the Ravens.) Two literary giants who played college football were poet Archibald MacLeish of Yale and novelist F. Scott Fitzgerald of Princeton.

3 In 1916, Georgia Tech led Cumberland College at halftime 126-0. Even so, Tech coach John Heisman (the guy they named the trophy after) wasn't satisfied. "Men, don't let up," he exhorted in his halftime speech. "You never know what those Cumberland players have up their sleeves." Not much, as it turned out. Tech won 222-0.

4 A 1920s football player at the University of Southern California named Marion Morrison lost his athletic scholarship because of an injury and dropped out of school. He went into the movie business and became known by another name: John Wayne. Other notables who played college football include former Detroit Mayor Kwame Kilpatrick (Florida A&M), comic actor Kevin James (State University of New York at Cortland) and Hillary Clinton's father, Hugh Rodham (Penn State).

5 The Rose Bowl is held in Pasadena, Calif., right? Except in 1942, when fears of a Japanese attack on the West Coast forced a move. Chicago's Soldier Field offered to stage the game, but it was shifted to Durham, N.C., where Duke welcomed Oregon State and lost 20-16.

6 Soldier Field has hosted such famous tilts as the 1926 Army-Navy game in front of 110,000 fans. Less famous as a college football venue is Wrigley Field, where DePaul played before dumping football as a varsity sport in the late 1930s. (DePaul's team nickname, Blue Demons, came from the fact that athletes were known as "D-men" because they wore sweaters with D's on them.)

7 Once glorious, now defunct: The Oil Bowl in Houston, the Refrigerator Bowl in Evansville, Ind., and the Salad Bowl in Phoenix, Ariz.

8 Before the 2004 Rose Bowl game against Michigan, USC coach Pete Carroll invited comedian Will Ferrell to practice with the team. Ferrell, a USC alumnus who was a kicker in high school, showed up in full uniform, with his last name on his jersey, and caught a pass for a gain of about 40 yards. Other celebrities who have visited USC practices: George Lucas, Kirsten Dunst, Jessica Simpson, Snoop Dogg, Spike Lee, Alyssa Milano, Anthony Kiedis, Wilmer Valderrama, Jake Gyllenhaal and Andre 3000.

9 As part of a Cuban sports festival in 1937, two American football teams, Auburn and Villanova, were invited to play in the Bacardi Bowl in Havana. But Cuban military dictator Fulgencio Batista flew into a rage because his photo was omitted from the game program. Only a quick trip to the printer averted the game's cancellation.

10 In the Texas-Texas A&M game in 2004, Texas scored a touchdown, but its point-after kick was blocked, and an A&M defender picked up the ball. If he had managed to run all the way down the field, it would have been worth 2 points for A&M. But instead he fumbled backward into the end zone where Texas had just scored its touchdown, and another A&M player jumped on the ball. It was ruled a "1-point safety," giving Texas its extra point in a very strange way.

10 THINGS YOU MIGHT NOT KNOW ABOUT
BICYCLES

1 In the book "The 100 Greatest Inventions of All Time" by Tom Philbin, the wheel comes in No. 1, while the bicycle is No. 95, just behind the oven and ahead of the tape recorder.

2 President George W. Bush made headlines at the G-8 summit in Scotland in 2005 by losing control of his bicycle and slamming into a constable. The president suffered only abrasions; the lawman was treated at a hospital. The incident was foreshadowed six years earlier by the pilot episode of "The West Wing," in which a bicycling president runs into a tree. When chief of staff Leo McGarry is asked, "Is anything broken?" he answers: "A $4,000 Lynex Titanium touring bike that I swore I'd never lend anyone."

3 Susan B. Anthony, the civil rights leader, considered the bicycle a great tool for the women's rights movement. During the huge cycling craze in the 1890s, which was enjoyed by both genders and which saw women straddling the bike in bloomers instead of riding sidesaddle in dresses like on a horse, Anthony said, "Let me tell you what I think of bicycling. I think it has done more to emancipate women than anything else in the world. I stand and rejoice every time I see a woman ride by on a wheel."

4 It didn't take long for the Tour de France to descend into scandal. In 1904, just the second year of the bicycle race, the top four finishers were disqualified for blatant cheating, which included taking the train and hopping rides on cars. Race founder Henri Desgrange was so discouraged afterward that he said, "The Tour de France is finished, and I'm afraid its second edition has been the last."

5 Bike technology has influenced plenty of other technologies. Pneumatic tires, essential for auto travel, were first mass-produced for bikes. The development of the bicycle also led to advancements in ball bearings, which were later used in roller-skating, fly-fishing and aviation. And speaking of aviation, let's not forget two stellar bike mechanics named Orville and Wilbur Wright.

6 Author Ray Bradbury, an avid bicyclist, never got a driver's license.

7 The bicycle is such a logical idea that it's an amazing fact that the invention is only a century-and-a-half old. An early 19th-century forerunner was called the "draisine" or "dandy horse" or "velocipede," a two-wheeled vehicle powered by the rider pushing along the ground with his feet and coasting down hills. In the 1860s came an improved contraption with pedals that was called a bicycle.

8 Marcel Duchamp's "Bicycle Wheel"—a bike wheel attached to a stool—is an icon of modern art. But the version at the Museum of Modern Art in New York is not the 1913 original, which is considered "lost." (That means if you find an old bike wheel on a stool in your garage, it might be worth millions.) The later MoMA version, created by Duchamp in 1951, went missing, too, in a little-publicized incident in 1995. A mystery man picked it up, carried it out of the museum and escaped in a cab. A day later, it reappeared—tossed over MoMA's garden wall, with no explanation.

9 Chicago's annual Bike the Drive, which closes down Lake Shore Drive's eight lanes to auto traffic for four hours on a Sunday morning, attracts more than 20,000 riders. But the one-day-a-year event pales in scope to Ciclovia in Bogota, Colombia, which shuts down nearly 100 miles of streets once a week from 7 a.m. to 2 p.m. Begun in the late 1970s, the Ciclovia idea—and similar programs like Open Streets and Free Sundays—has spread to dozens of cities around the world, including Tokyo, Los Angeles, San Francisco, Minneapolis, Ann Arbor, Mich., and Evanston, Ill. But you can have too much of a good thing. After the early success of Bike the Drive, when activists began pushing for a more frequent event, then-Mayor Richard M. Daley put the kibosh on the idea: "You can't. Let's get common sense."

10 An innovative alternative to bike helmets has been developed in Sweden. The Hovding air bag is worn like a fashionable neck wrap by a bike rider and inflates to protect the rider's head when a sensor detects a bike accident is occurring.

10 THINGS YOU MIGHT NOT KNOW ABOUT
WRIGLEY FIELD

1 The ballpark you know as Wrigley Field, home of the Cubs, used to be Weeghman Park, home of a Federal League team known variously as the Feds, ChiFeds, Tinx, Buns and Whales. "Tinx" was a reference to manager Joe Tinker. "Buns" was a nod to owner Charles Weeghman's quick-lunch eateries. The inspiration for "Whales" is unclear—perhaps it suggested that the team was a big deal. In any case, the Whales went belly up after 1915, and the Cubs moved in.

2 The Wrigley Field scoreboard was originally reddish-brown but was repainted green a few years after its installation in 1937. Likewise, the iconic marquee at Clark and Addison wasn't always red—it was once fern green.

3 For a ballpark that's considered traditional, Wrigley has been the scene of much innovation. The tradition of letting fans keep foul balls started there, as did the permanent ballpark concession stand. Two experiments that didn't work: rows of Chinese elms planted on either side of the scoreboard (they were damaged by high winds and removed in the early 1940s) and a "speedwalk" moving walkway in the grandstand (it was plagued by maintenance problems and pulled out around 1960).

4 Fans are close to the action at Wrigley, but they used to be even closer. During high-turnout games before 1937, fans stood on the field ringing the outfield. Balls that went into the crowd were counted as ground-rule doubles.

5 Perhaps the most legendary event at Wrigley Field was Babe Ruth's "called shot" during the 1932 World Series. Or it's the alleged called shot because it's disputed whether the Yankees slugger was pointing to center field or just waving his fingers around before he hit his home run. In attendance were at least 15 future Baseball Hall of Famers*, sportswriters Grantland Rice and Westbrook Pegler, tap-dancer Bill "Bojangles" Robinson, Chicago Mayor Anton Cermak and New York Gov. Franklin Roosevelt, who was just a month away from being elected president. Two not-yet-famous people said they were there, too: John Paul Stevens, then age 12 and later a U.S. Supreme Court justice, and Ray Kroc, then a 30-year-old paper cup salesman and later head of McDonald's.

6 Some describe Wrigley as the world's largest beer garden, but the first suds weren't served there until 1933—19 years after the park opened. (Prohibition was in force for most, but not all, of that time.)

7 Wrigley Field hosted a ski-jumping contest in January 1944, with a ramp set up in the upper deck and jumpers landing around second base.

8 Soldier Field is the longtime home of the Bears, but Wrigley Field was their home field longer, from 1921 to 1970. Soldier Field will take over the honors in 2021, if the Bears stay there.

9 Wrigley looked ridiculously lopsided during the 1927 season. The upper deck already had been constructed along the third-base line, but it wasn't built along the first-base line until after the season.

10 In 1951, a mighty hitter smashed a ball that bounced off the Wrigley center field score-board. Then he hit another ball that flew over it. He was Sam Snead, using a 4-iron, a 2-iron and two golf balls.

* The Hall of Famers at Wrigley on Oct. 1, 1932, included the Yankees' Babe Ruth, Lou Gehrig, Lefty Gomez, Red Ruffing, Bill Dickey, Earle Combs, Tony Lazzeri, Herb Pennock, Joe Sewell and manager Joe McCarthy; the Cubs' Gabby Hartnett, Burleigh Grimes, Billy Herman and Kiki Cuyler; and umpire Bill Klem.

10 THINGS YOU MIGHT NOT KNOW ABOUT
SPORTS GAMBLING

1 The University of Chicago boasts about its connection to 25 winners of the Nobel Prize in economics, but little is heard about a U. of C. graduate named Charles McNeil who helped transform the economics of gambling. McNeil was an early proponent of the point spread and indeed may have invented the concept, in which the margin of victory is the key number. As one bookie put it: "The point spread was the greatest invention since the zipper."

2 A bookmaker's commission on a bet is called juice, or vigorish, or simply vig. Vigorish is Yiddish slang, from the Russian vyigrysh, meaning winnings.

3 History's most famous sports gambling scandal occurred when the Chicago White Sox threw the 1919 World Series to the Cincinnati Reds. Eight so-called Black Sox, including star outfielder "Shoeless" Joe Jackson, were banned from baseball for life. Eliot Asinof's book about the plot was called "Eight Men Out," but there was a ninth man out. St. Louis Browns second baseman Joe Gedeon, who didn't play in the series but heard about the fix from his Sox friends, was banned because he didn't tell authorities.

4 In soccer, an "own goal" occurs when a player accidentally knocks the ball into his own goal, giving the opposition a point. Colombia defender Andres Escobar did that in the 1994 World Cup against the United States, costing his team the game. When he returned to Medellin, he was shot to death. The motive has never been firmly established, but many observers believe disgruntled gamblers ordered his murder.

5 In the history of bookmaking, one particular incident is known as Black Sunday. Before Super Bowl XIII in 1979, Pittsburgh started out as a 2½-point favorite over the Cowboys. When most bettors picked Pittsburgh, the bookmakers moved their line to 4½ to attract balancing wagers on Dallas. But when Pittsburgh ended up winning by 4 points, the bookies were "middled"—they had to pay off the early bets on Pittsburgh and the late bets on Dallas.

6 In 1993, "The Wiz Kid" sold NFL predictions to bettors for $25 per phone call. Only later did the service's proprietor, David James, reveal that his 4-year-old son made the picks.

7 "Proposition bets," involving aspects of the game other than the final score, are wildly popular for Super Bowl bettors. When hockey star Wayne Gretzky's wife, Janet Jones, got caught up in a gambling scandal in 2006, it was reported that she bet $5,000 on the Super Bowl coin flip. People also wager on the length of the game's first punt, the number of penalties and which player will score the first touchdown. Bears star Devin Hester's touchdown on the opening kickoff of the 2007 Super Bowl earned bettors a ridiculous 25-1 payoff.

8 Some Super Bowl "prop bets" don't even involve the game. In 2007, wagers were taken on whether Billy Joel's national anthem would be longer or shorter than 1 minute and 44 seconds (it was shorter). One sports book gave 50-1 odds that Carmen Electra would make an unscheduled appearance with Prince at halftime (she didn't) and 2-1 odds that Prince would have a wardrobe malfunction (he didn't).

9 British bookmaking firm William Hill offers bets on sports but also features wacky non-sports bets, such as who will be the first celebrity to be arrested in a given year. Singer Amy Winehouse was the co-favorite for 2008, along with rocker Pete Doherty. Before the last Harry Potter novel came out, William Hill set odds on whether the saga would end with Harry's death (it didn't).

10 Las Vegas wastes no time. Sports books released odds on the 2009 Super Bowl before the 2008 Super Bowl had even been played. The Las Vegas Hilton listed the New England Patriots as a strong favorite. For the record, the Pittsburgh Steelers defeated the Arizona Cardinals, 27-23, and the Pats didn't even make the playoffs.

10 THINGS YOU MIGHT NOT KNOW ABOUT
THE OLYMPICS

1 Olympic sites are chosen by secret ballot, so we're not sure how London beat Paris for the 2012 Summer Olympics. Some blame French President Jacques Chirac, who insulted Britain before the vote by saying, "After Finland, it's the country with the worst food." France's bid wasn't getting British support anyway, but Finland had two IOC members, and some speculate that they were swing votes in the 54-50 outcome.

2 Tug-o-war made its last appearance as an Olympic sport in 1920.

3 Pierre de Coubertin, founder of the International Olympic Committee, decreed in his will that his heart be sent to the site of ancient Olympia in Greece, where it is kept in a monument. The rest of him was buried in Lausanne, Switzerland.

4 Chicago was supposed to host the 1904 Olympics, but St. Louis stole it away. The Games were a fiasco. Only 14 of 32 participants finished the marathon, which was held in 90-degree heat with a single water well at the 12-mile mark. Cuban marathoner Felix Carvajal, who lost his money in a craps game in New Orleans, hitchhiked to St. Louis and ran the race in street shoes. He stopped to chat with spectators and to steal apples from an orchard but still finished fourth. American Fred Lorz dropped out after nine miles, rode in a car for 11, then rejoined the race and crossed the finish line first, quickly admitting his hoax. The prize went to American Thomas Hicks, whose supporters gave him strychnine (a stimulant in low doses) and brandy—the first known use of performance-enhancing drugs in the Olympics.

5 French athletes bent the rules at the 1932 Los Angeles Olympics: Despite Prohibition, they were allowed wine with their meals.

6 George Patton, who would later become a famous U.S. general, competed in the 1912 Stockholm Olympics pentathlon, an event combining pistol shooting, swimming, fencing, cross country and steeplechase. Patton performed poorly in his best event—pistols—but shined in fencing, defeating the French army champion. Old Blood and Guts finished fifth overall, the only non-Swede to make the top seven.

7 The greatest star of the 1936 Berlin Olympics was the 10th child born to an Alabama sharecropper family named Owens. But he was not born with the name Jesse. He was called James Cleveland Owens, and as a child moved to his namesake city—Cleveland. A teacher asked his name, and he said "J.C." The teacher thought he said "Jesse," and the boy was too polite to disagree. (Former Mayor Richard M. Daley often cited Owens in pushing Chicago's failed bid, and indeed Owens was a Chicagoan, but only late in life. A dozen years after the Olympics, Owens settled in Chicago, and he is buried in Oak Woods Cemetery on the South Side.)

8 Another great Olympian with Chicago ties was Johnny Weissmuller, the winner of five gold medals in swimming who later starred as Tarzan in the movies. Weissmuller swam brilliantly in the 1924 and '28 Olympics—and also in the waters off Chicago's North Avenue Beach on a stormy day in July 1927. Weissmuller was training on the lakefront with his brother Peter when a sudden storm swamped the pleasure boat Favorite. The disaster killed 27 of the 71 people aboard—mostly women and children—but the Weissmuller brothers rescued 11 people.

9 No boxing was held at the 1912 Stockholm Olympics because the sport was illegal in Sweden.

10 A study of the 2004 Athens Olympics found that athletes who wore red while competing in "combat sports" such as wrestling scored higher than opponents wearing blue.

10 THINGS YOU MIGHT NOT KNOW ABOUT
OLYMPIANS

1 For two Olympians who were the first-ever representative of their countries, dreams turned to "duhs." In 1960, Wym Essajas, from the South American nation of Suriname, was misinformed on when his 800-meter heat was scheduled and slept through it. In 1988, Eduard Paululum, a boxer from the Pacific nation of Vanuatu, woke up early enough to eat a big breakfast, then showed up a pound over the weight limit and was disqualified.

2 Margaret Abbott was a pretty good golfer, having won contests at the Chicago Golf Club. She just happened to be in Paris in October 1900, so she decided to enter a local golf tournament. She won the event, becoming the first American woman Olympic gold medalist. It's not clear whether she even knew she was competing in the Olympics; the Games were so new and poorly organized that some participants didn't realize the special nature of the events. Abbott also achieved bragging rights in her own family: Her mother placed eighth in the event.

3 Russia's military shooting team arrived in London for the 1908 Games nearly two weeks after its event, having followed the Julian calendar while London was on the Gregorian calendar.

4 Some Olympians seem born to the task. Jeff Float was a gold-medal swimmer in 1984, David Fall was a silver-medal diver in 1924, Ernst Fast was a bronze-medal marathoner in 1900, Shane Gould was a three-time gold medalist in 1972 and Carl "Luz" Long was a silver-medal long jumper in 1936.

5 An Australian sculler named Henry Pearce was easily winning his 1928 quarterfinal heat in Amsterdam when, alerted by alarmed spectators, he stopped rowing to let a family of ducks pass safely. His competition caught up and gained a five-length lead. Pearce not only came back to win by 20 lengths, he broke the course record by three seconds. He went on to win the gold and the hearts of the Dutch.

6 Czechoslovakian runner Emil Zatopek shocked the world in 1952 when he won gold not only in the 5,000- and 10,000-meter races but also in the marathon. By all accounts, he was an affable, friendly guy, but he was known as the Beast of Prague because he contorted his face and upper body when he ran.

7 Korean downhill skier Kyung Soon Yim trained on grass. At Squaw Valley in 1960, he finished last in nearly every race and was a crowd favorite.

8 Chicagoan Johnny Weissmuller's road from Olympian to Tarzan is well-known. Ditto with Buster Crabbe. But the Olympics-Tarzan connection goes deeper. Shot-putter Herman Brix medaled in 1928 and was playing Tarzan on-screen seven years later, and 1936 decathlete gold medalist Glenn Morris donned a loincloth in "Tarzan's Revenge." But 1960 pole-vault champ Donald Bragg took the cake when he let out a jungle yell from the medal podium. Bragg's vine-swinging dreams were dashed four years later, however, when the Tarzan movie he was about to film was ordered halted for copyright infringement.

9 The 1936 Berlin Olympics are best remembered for black American Jesse Owens' repudiation of Adolf Hitler's Aryan superiority claims, but another ethnic statement was made by Korean marathoner Sohn Kee-chung. Korea was occupied by Japanese forces at the time, forcing Sohn to compete with the Japan team. When he won, the Korean newspaper Dong-a Ilbo published a photo of him on the victory stand, but it covered up the Japanese flag on his sweatshirt. Because of that rebellious retouching, Japanese officials shut down the newspaper for nine months.

10 A 16-year-old Chicago-area girl named Betty Robinson was the world's first female gold medalist in the 100 meters. But three years after the Riverdale girl won in the 1928 Games, she suffered a broken leg in the crash of a small plane. Doctors said her days of competition were over. Indeed, she couldn't take the proper sprinter's crouch because of her injury, but she was able to run the third leg of the 4x100-meter relay at the 1936 Olympics, and captured another gold.

10 THINGS YOU MIGHT NOT KNOW ABOUT
THE OLYMPIC TORCH

1 The Nazis invented the Olympic torch relay. Fire was an Olympic symbol in ancient Greece, and torch relays were conducted apart from the Olympics. But the Nazis first combined those elements to create pageantry and propaganda before the 1936 Berlin Games. On its way to Germany, the torch went through Greece, Bulgaria, Yugoslavia, Hungary, Austria and Czechoslovakia. Within six years, Nazi Germany had annexed or occupied all of those countries.

2 The torch has been transported by canoe, steamboat, parachute, camel and Concorde. Before the 1976 Montreal Games, it traveled by satellite, sort of. A sensor in Greece detected the "ionized particles" of the torch and transmitted coded impulses by satellite to Canada, where they activated a laser beam that "re-created" the Olympic flame.

3 Before the 1956 Melbourne Games, a group of Australian students pulled off the greatest hoax in torch relay history. They fashioned a torch out of a plum pudding can, part of a chair leg and a pair of underpants set aflame. Then one of them joined the relay route, presented the contraption to the mayor of Sydney and slipped into the crowd before anyone realized he was an impostor.

4 The torch was transported under water at the Great Barrier Reef before the 2000 Sydney Games. The specially designed solid-fuel torch operated like a distress flare.

5 The identity of the final torch bearer, who lights the caldron, is kept secret until the opening ceremonies. At the Los Angeles Olympics in 1984, many thought Romanian gymnast Nadia Comaneci would be chosen because her nation was the only East Bloc member that didn't boycott the event. But U.S. Olympic hero Rafer Johnson won out. Far less attention was paid to the man who later doused the flame. Gas company worker Marv Wig, 59, put it this way: "There are two switches that both essentially cut the fuel to the flame. I haven't decided which one I'll flip. One needs to build a little suspense."

6 Critics complained that the red-and-yellow caldron at the 1996 Atlanta Games resembled the french-fry containers used by McDonald's, an Olympic sponsor.

7 Antonio Rebollo, a disabled archer who shot a flaming arrow to light the caldron at the 1992 Barcelona Games, complained days later that he wasn't given tickets to any competitions, not even archery. A local Olympic committee spokesman responded that Rebollo had been sent a thank-you letter and, "I can only assume he hasn't gotten the letter yet."

8 Olympic officials always keep an extra "pure" flame on standby in case a torch goes out. During the 1976 Montreal Olympics, a downpour doused the flame, and an official relit it with a cigarette lighter. Olympic purists were appalled. They extinguished the unclean flame and relit it the proper way.

9 Yoshinori Sakai, the torch relay runner who lit the caldron for the 1964 Tokyo Games, was born near Hiroshima two hours after the atomic bomb was dropped there.

10 As Chinese philosopher Lao-tzu said, "A journey of 1,000 miles must begin with a single step." For the 2008 Summer Games in Beijing, the journey created one heck of a carbon footprint. According to calculations by wired.com, the Air China A330 jet transporting the Olympic torch burned 462,400 gallons of jet fuel, emitting 11 million pounds of carbon dioxide. Let the Games begin, if only for the sake of the environment.

10 THINGS YOU MIGHT NOT KNOW ABOUT
RUNNING

1 The verb "run" has 645 meanings, more than any other word in the Oxford English Dictionary. In addition to putting one foot in front of the other rapidly, there's "running an idea up the flagpole," "the days running into weeks," "running the numbers," "running a fever," "running with the wrong crowd" and "running your mouth." When early 20th century Australians said they were "running the rabbit," that meant they were bringing home liquor.

The verb "run" has 645 meanings, more than any other word in the Oxford English Dictionary.

2 A cheetah runs faster than a sand gazelle, which is speedier than a zebra, which is faster than a kangaroo, which outruns a human, which can outleg a rhino. (This is based on estimated maximum running speeds; do not try at your local zoo.)

3 Dr. Gabe Mirkin, author of "The Sports Medicine Book," asked more than 100 elite runners if they would be willing to take a magic pill that would make them an Olympic champion but would kill them within a year. More than half said yes.

4 The Chicago marathon was called the Mayor Daley Marathon in its first two years. Its first running in 1977 got off to a rocky start: Three people were sent to the hospital with powder burns when the starter's cannon misfired.

5 "Freak races" were a favorite form of entertainment in 17th and 18th century England. In one race witnessed by the king, two runners were evenly matched: Each had a wooden leg. In another race, a man on stilts faced off against an accomplished runner on foot. In yet another contest, a man was given an hour to run seven miles while carrying 56 pounds of fish on his head.

6 Haitian runner Dieudonne Lamothe was 78th—the final finisher—in the 1984 Los Angeles Olympics marathon. And it's a good thing for Lamothe that he finished. He later revealed that dictator "Baby Doc" Duvalier's henchman had threatened to kill him if he did not complete the race.

7 Until 1950, a major league baseball player who was on base could be replaced by a "courtesy runner" without having to leave the lineup. In modern times, a pinch runner is allowed, but the player being replaced is out of the game for good. Perhaps the most unusual pinch runner was Oakland's Herb Washington, who played in 105 games over two seasons in the 1970s and never came to bat or played the field. A track star, Washington was strictly a pinch-runner.

8 Two great American runners overcame potentially crippling illnesses. Sprinter Gail Devers suffered from Graves' disease, and doctors were close to amputating her feet before her condition improved and she went on to win Olympic gold in 1992. Decades earlier, sprinter Wilma Rudolph became the first American woman to win three track-and-field gold medals in a single Olympics—a glorious fate for a woman who was sickly as a child and wore a leg brace. "My doctor told me I would never walk again. My mother told me I would," said Rudolph. "I believed my mother."

9 Ron Paul, the former 12-term congressman and frequent presidential candidate, likes to run. He has run for political office for most of the last four decades, and as a high school junior in Pennsylvania, he raced to a state title in the 220-yard dash.

10 University of Oregon track coach Bill Bowerman was trying to develop a new athletic shoe, and one day in 1971 he used the family's waffle iron to meld urethane into a wafflelike tread pattern. The idea caught on for the company he started with Phil Knight. First known as Blue Ribbon Sports, it was renamed Nike. Today, a life-size statue of Bowerman at the university stands on a base of waffle irons.

SOURCES

CHAPTER 1: Oddities & Oddballs

Conspiracy Theories "Conspiracy Films" by Barna William Donovan; "Religion of Fear" by Jason C. Bivins; "New York Knicks: The Complete Illustrated History" by Alan Hahn; "Dead and Alive: Beliefs in Contradictory Conspiracy Theories" by Michael J. Wood, Karen M. Douglas and Robbie M. Sutton; Texas Monthly; New York magazine; Gallup News Service; USA Today; rogerebert.com; insider.espn.go.com; news.discovery.com; westword.com; worldcat.org; dawn.com; The Washington Post; The Telegraph.

Cheaters "Frontier Gambling" by G.R. Williamson; "52 Ways to Cheat at Poker" by Allan Zola Kronzek; "Grafters and Goo Goos: Corruption and Reform in Chicago" by James L. Merriner; The Associated Press; thetimes.co.uk; "Cassell's Dictionary of Slang" by Jonathon Green; "Robert Kennedy: His Life" by Evan Thomas; "The Echoing Green" by Joshua Prager; "A Moment in Time: An American Story of Baseball, Heartbreak, and Grace" by Ralph Branca and David Ritz; Pew Research Center; Josephson Institute, Character Counts.org; Chicago Tribune; Palm Beach Post; paralympic.org; Tribune archives.

Losers "The New Dickson Baseball Dictionary" by Paul Dickson; "Encyclopedia of the Ancient World" by Shona Grimbly; "Cassell's Dictionary of Slang" by Jonathon Green; The Wall Street Journal; Las Vegas Review-Journal; Spy magazine; snopes.com; people.com; Tribune archives.

Stunts "Dictionary of Greek and Roman Biography and Mythology" edited by William Smith; "Profiles in Folly: History's Worst Decisions and Why They Went Wrong" by Alan Axelrod; "Stunt: The Story of the Great Movie Stunt Men" by John Baxter; "Hero of the Air: Glenn Curtiss and the Birth of Naval Aviation" by William Trimble; "The Tour de France" by Christopher S. Thompson; "The Katy Railroad and the Last Frontier" by V.V. Masterson; Chicago Tribune; The New York Times; Wisconsin State Journal; New York Daily News; Cowboys & Indians magazine; cnn.com; snopes.com; imdb.com; nationalaviation.org.

Selfies "The Self-Portrait: A Cultural History" by James Hall; theguardian.com; New York magazine; believermag.com; smarthistory.khanacademy.org; "The Ongoing Moment" by Geoff Dyer; NPR's Robert Krulwich; PLOS ONE; Library of Congress; usatoday.com; time.com; newyork.cbslocal.com; psycnet.apa.org; HTC One Selfie Phenomenon survey.

Predictions "The History and Power of Writing" by Henri-Jean Martin; "Paper: Paging Through History" by Mark Kurlansky; "The Guns of August" by Barbara W. Tuchman; "The Secession Movement in North Carolina" by J.C. Sitterson; "The Fall of the House of Dixie" by Bruce C. Levine; "Eurekas and Euphorias: The Oxford Book of Scientific Anecdotes" by Walter Gratzer; "Fleet Fire: Thomas Edison and the Pioneers of the Electric Revolution" by L.J. Davis; "With the Beatles" by Alistair Taylor; "Superforecasting: The Art and Science of Prediction" by Philip E. Tetlock and Dan Gardner; prb.org; pbs.org; hbr.org; Healthland.time.com; politico.com; billboard.com; Agence France-Presse; Tribune archives.

Mascots "Blumenfeld's Dictionary of Musical Theater" by Robert Blumenfeld; deseretnews.com; tvacres.com; theatlantic.com; sportsillustrated.cnn.com; The Associated Press; Los Angeles Times; Random House Dictionary; drewfriedman.blogspot.com; sfgate.com; Chicago Tribune; The New York Times.

Doomsday "The End: 50 Apocalyptic Visions From Pop Culture That You Should Know About . . . Before It's Too Late" by Laura Barcella; "The End-Of-The-World Delusion: How Doomsayers Endanger Society" by Justin Deering; "The Official Underground 2012 Doomsday Survival Handbook" by W.H. Mumfrey; "When Time Shall Be No More: Prophecy Belief in Modern American Culture" by Paul S. Boyer; "Expecting Armageddon: Essential Reading in Failed Prophecy" by Jon R. Stone; "Apocalypses" by Eugen Weber; "Palm Sunday" by Kurt Vonnegut Jr.; Ipsos Global Research; Smithsonian magazine; Chicago Tribune; National Geographic; amherst.edu; nasa.gov; stamfordhistory.org.

Sweaters "The KGB's Poison Factory" by Boris Volodarsky; "Bad Fads" by Mark A. Long; Chicago Tribune; The Sunday Times; "Golf: Four Decades of Sports Illustrated's Finest Writing on the Game of Golf"; New York magazine; Foreign Policy.

Desperadoes "In Search of Butch Cassidy" by Larry Pointer; "Digging Up Butch and Sundance" by Anne Meadows; "Dillinger: The Untold Story" by G. Russell Girardin and William J. Helmer; "To Serve and Collect" by Richard C. Lindberg; "To Inherit the Earth" by Angus Wright and Wendy Wolford; "Encyclopedia of Chess Wisdom" by Eric Schiller; "The Arkansas Journey" by Trey Berry; Time magazine; Americas magazine; The Spokesman-Review in Spokane, Wash.; Toronto Sun; New Zealand Herald; drinksmixer.com, britannica.com; news.bbc.co.uk; pbs.org; dictionary.reference.com; imdb.com.

Stanleys "Somebody: The Reckless Life and Remarkable Career of Marlon Brando" by Stefan Kanfer; snopes.com; nhl.com; Tribune archives.

Underwear "How Underwear Got Under There: A Brief History" by Kathy Shaskan; "Unmentionables: A Brief History of Underwear" by Elaine Benson and John Esten; "Origins of the Specious: Myths and Misconceptions of the English Language" by Patricia T. O'Conner and Stewart Kellerman; "The Book of Answers" by Barbara Berliner with Melinda Corey and George Ochoa; "Underwear: A Fashion History" by Alison Carter; fashionencyclopedia.com; vintageadsandstuff.com; snopes.com; Los Angeles Times; The New York Times; The Dallas Morning News; New York Post; Tribune archives.

Atheists "Atheists, Agnostics, and Deists in America" by Peter M. Rinaldo; The New York Sun; cnn.com; Tribune archives and news services.

April Fools' Day museumofhoaxes.com; snopes.com;infoplease.com; The Independent; St. Paul Pioneer Press; babyblues.com; WXRT-FM 93.1; Tribune news services.

CHAPTER 2: The Human Condition

Blame "The Blame Game" by Ben Dattner with Darren Dahl; "Scapegoat: A History of Blaming Other People" by Charlie Campbell; Encyclopedia of Chicago; greatchicagofire.org; "The Great Chicago Fire and the Myth of Mrs. O'Leary's Cow" by Richard F. Bales; The Wall Street Journal; Tribune archives; jewishencyclopedia.com.

Distractions "Red Herrings & White Elephants—The Origins of the Phrases We Use Every Day" by Albert Jack; "New Literacies Around the Globe: Policy and Pedagogy" edited by Cathy Burnett, Julia Davies, Guy Merchant and Jennifer Rowsell; National Transportation Safety Board; Harvard University's Center on the Developing Child; Daniel Engber at slate.com; Sam Anderson at nymag.com: Annie Murphy Paul at pbs.org; The New York Times; New York magazine; skinema.com.

Lies "The Liar in Your Life" by Robert Feldman; "They Never Said It" by Paul F. Boller Jr. and John George; "How We Know What Isn't So" by Thomas Gilovich; "Why We Lie" by David Livingstone Smith; "The Divided Berlin 1945-1990" by Oliver Boyn; "Closed Borders: The Contemporary Assault on Freedom of Movement" by Alan Dowty; "The Second Arab Awakening" by Adeed Dawisha; "Euphemania" by Ralph Keyes; "Dictionary of Euphemisms" by R.W. Holder; "Cassell's Dictionary of Slang" by Jonathon Green; "Dictionary of Contemporary Slang" by Tony Thorne; Boston Herald; Los Angeles Times; nytimes.com; theguardian.com; english.al-akhbar.com.

Gaffes "Football Hall of Shame 2" by Bruce Nash; Chicago Tribune; The Washington Post; The New York Times; San Francisco Chronicle; Agence France-Presse; The Guardian; Detroit Free Press; usnews.com; poynter.org; jimromenesko.com; ibnlive.in.com; snopes.com.

Fear "Fear: A Cultural History" by Joanna Bourke; Playboy interview with Ray Bradbury; "Isaac Asimov: The Foundations of Science Fiction" by James Gunn; "Buried Alive: The Terrifying History of Our Most Primal Fear" by Jan Bondeson; "The Word Lover's Delight" by the Editors of the Captivate Network; "Safire's Political Dictionary" by William Safire; "Nothing to Fear: FDR's Inner Circle and the Hundred Days that Created Modern America" by Adam Seth Cohen; "FDR and Fear Itself: The First Inaugural Address" by Davis W. Houck; "Alfred Hitchcock: Interviews" edited by Sidney Gottlieb; Tribune archives; Popular Science; Nature.com; Boingboing.net; thesmokinggun.com.

Sweat "Lifestyle Medicine," 2nd edition, edited by James M. Rippe; "Preventive Dermatology" edited by Robert A. Norman; "Fitness and Health" by Brian J. Sharkey and Steven E. Gaskill; "Disgusting Things: A Miscellany" by Don Voorhees; "Letters to a Young Gymnast" by Nadia Comaneci; "The Quote Verifier" by Ralph Keyes; "Greek Athletics and the Genesis of Sport" by David Sansone; "The Hardest Working Man: How James Brown Saved the Soul of America" by James Sullivan; "Flash of the Spirit: African & Afro-American Art & Philosophy" by Robert Farris Thompson; NBC News; twitter.com; yahoo.com; miamiherald.com; cleveland.com.

Apologies "The Politics of Official Apologies" by Melissa Nobles; "Lives of the Popes" by Richard P. McBrien; "The Church in History" by B.K. Kuipe; "Mea Culpa: A Sociology of Apology and Reconciliation" by Nicholas Tavuchis; "Cash: The Autobiography" by Johnny Cash; "The Art of the Public Grovel" by Susan Wise Bauer; "The Role of Apology in International Law" by Richard B. Bilder; americanrhetoric.com; upenn.com; wsj.com; metronews.ca; pinstripealley.com; nj.com; usmagazine.com; Chicago Tribune; BBC News; Los Angeles Times.

Tattoos "American Sideshow: An Encyclopedia of History's Most Wondrous and Curiously Strange Performers" by Marc Hartzman; "Maori Tattooing" by H.G. Robley; "Bodies of Inscription: A Cultural History of the Modern Tattoo Community" by Margo DeMello; Chicago Tribune; The New York Times; The Guardian; Business Wire; Japan Economic Newswire; The Telegraph; Harris Poll; reason.com.

Blonds "Strike the Baby and Kill the Blonde: An Insider's Guide to Film Slang" by Dave Knox; "Encyclopedia of Hair: A Cultural History" by Victoria Sherrow; "Encyclopedia of Prostitution and Sex Work, Vol. 1" by Melissa Hope

Ditmore; "On Blondes" by Joanna Pitman; "Peekaboo: The Story of Veronica Lake" by Jeff Lenburg; "Alfred Hitchcock: A Life in Darkness and Light" by Patrick McGilligan; "Punk: The Definitive Record of a Revolution" by Stephen Colegrave and Chris Sullivan; "Heavier Than Heaven: A Biography of Kurt Cobain" by Charles R. Cross; "The Rolling Stone Film Reader" article by Chris Mundy; Life magazine; Boston Herald.

Height   "Facts about the Presidents" by Joseph Kane; "Tallest in the World: Native Americans of the Great Plains in the Nineteenth Century" by Richard H. Steckel and Joseph M. Prince; "Grande Expectations: A Year in the Life of Starbucks' Stock" by Karen Blumenthal; "The Tall Book" by Arianne Cohen; "Empire: A Tale of Obsession, Betrayal, and the Battle for an American Icon" By Mitchell Pacelle; "The Rat Pack" by Lawrence J. Quirk and William Schoell; "Great Mythconceptions: The Science Behind the Myths" by Karl Kruszelnicki and Adam Yazxhi; "The 'Visual Cliff'" by Eleanor J. Gibson and Richard D. Welk; npr.org; World Book Encyclopedia; New York Daily News; The Associated Press; San Francisco Chronicle; Orange County Register; The New Yorker; Anchorage Daily News; Vancouver Sun; The Star-Ledger in Newark, N.J.; Toronto Star; Houston Chronicle; politico.com; thehill.com

Skin Color   "Skin: The Bare Facts" by Lori Bergamotto; "Beautiful Skin of Color" by Jeanine Downie and Fran Cook-Bolden, with Barbara Nevins Taylor; "The Simpsons: An Uncensored, Unauthorized History" by John Ortved; "Was Superman a Spy?: And Other Comic Book Legends Revealed" by Brian Cronin; "Leaving Springfield: The Simpsons and the Possibility of Oppositional Culture" by John Alberti; "The Complete Stories" by Zora Neale Hurston; "Encyclopedia of Family Health" by David B. Jacoby and R.M. Youngson; "Strapless: John Singer Sargent and the Fall of Madame X" by Deborah Davis; "Don't Mind If I Do" by George Hamilton and William Stadiem; "Yellow: Race in America Beyond Black and White" by Frank H. Wu; "Savage Perils: Racial Frontiers and Nuclear Apocalypse in American Culture" by Patrick B. Sharp; "The Discourse of Race in Modern China" by Frank Dikotter; Texas Monthly; New York magazine; crayola.com; artble.com; webmd.com; mayoclinic.com; encyclopedia.com.

Beards   "One Thousand Beards: A Cultural History of Facial Hair" by Allan Peterkin; "Encyclopedia of Hair: A Cultural History" by Victoria Sherrow; "Sir Thomas More" by William Holden Hutton; "Holy People of the World, Vol. 1" by Phyllis G. Jestice; "Cassell's Dictionary of Slang" by Jonathon Green; "Almost History: Close Calls, Plan B's and Twists of Fate in America's Past" by Roger Bruns; "Lincoln President-elect" by Harold Holzer; "The Very Best Men: Four Who Dared: The Early Years of the CIA" by Evan Thomas; "The Untold Civil War: Exploring the Human Side of War" by James Robertson; "Who's Who in Gay and Lesbian History" edited by Robert Aldrich and Garry Wotherspoon; Lincoln Lore journal; The Advocate; byu.edu; newadvent.org; catholic.org; cnn.com; www.phrases.org.uk; Tribune news services.

CHAPTER 3: Controversies & Ideas

Guns   "Hemingway's Boat: Everything He Loved in Life, and Lost, 1934-1961" by Paul Hendrickson; "The Limits of Dissent: Clement L. Vallandigham & the Civil War" by Frank L. Klement; "A Life of Clement L. Vallandigham" by James Laird Vallandigham; "Guns in American Society" by Gregg Lee Carter; "The Civil War" by Shelby Foote; "Historical Dictionary of the U.S. Army" edited by Jerold E. Brown; "From My Cold, Dead Hands: Charlton Heston and American Politics" by Emilie Raymond; "Mr. Gatling's Terrible Marvel" by Julia Keller; "The Gun That Changed the World" by Mikhail Kalashnikov with Elena Joly; The Sydney Morning Herald; The New York Times; gallup.com; popularmechanics.com; espn.com; news.com.au.

Immigration "The American Revelation: Ten Ideals That Shaped Our Country from the Puritans to the Cold War" by Neil Baldwin; "The American Kaleidoscope: Race, Ethnicity, and the Civic Culture" by Lawrence H. Fuchs; "Communion of Immigrants: A History of Catholics in America" by James T. Fisher; "Beyond Ethnicity" by Werner Sollors; "Closing the Gate: Race, Politics, and the Chinese Exclusion Act" by Andrew Gyory; "Coming to America" by Roger Daniels; "On Sunset Boulevard: The Life and Times of Billy Wilder" by Ed Sikov; Encyclopedia of Chicago; Migration Policy Institute; Gallup; Chicago Tribune; The Wall Street Journal; slate.com; census.gov; foreignpolicy.com; time.com.

Marijuana "Marihuana, The First Twelve Thousand Years" by Ernest L. Abel; "Marijuana: Opposing Viewpoints" edited by Jamuna Carroll; Encyclopedia Britannica; High Times; Tribune news services.

Censorship "Censoring Hollywood" by Aubrey Malone; "Tawdry Knickers and Other Unfortunate Ways to Be Remembered" by Alex Novak; "Richard Wright: The Life and Times" by Hazel Rowley; "Banned in Boston" by Neil Miller; "Forbidden Animation" by Karl F. Cohen; "The Yale Book of Quotations" edited by Fred R. Shapiro; "A Concise Dictionary of Greek and Roman Antiquities" edited by Sir William Smith and Francis Warre Cornish; "A Concise Survey of Western Civilization" by Brian A. Pavlac; "Banned Books: Censorship in Eighteenth-Century England" by Anastasia Castillo; "Curiosities of Literature" by Isaac Disraeli; foreignpolicy.com; Los Angeles Times.

Juries "We, the Jury" by Jeffrey B. Abramson; "Encyclopedia of Crime and Punishment" edited by David Levinson; "Terrorism on American Soil" by Joseph T. McCann; "Clarence Darrow: Attorney for the Damned" by John Aloysius Farrell; "The Trial of Socrates" by I.F. Stone; "Wrigley Field: The Unauthorized Biography" by Stuart Shea; "The Judge Who Hated Red Nail Polish" by Ilona M. Bray, Richard Stim and the editors of Nolo; "Courageous Judicial Decisions in Alabama" by Dr. Jack Kushner; The Woman Citizen magazine; ABA Journal; "Jim Crow Laws" by Leslie V. Tischauser; U.S. Supreme Court; Chicago Tribune archives; Chattanooga Times Free Press; enr.construction.com.

1968 "1968: The Year That Rocked the World" by Mark Kurlansky; "Movies in American History: An Encyclopedia" edited by Philip C. DiMare; "Pictures at a Revolution: Five Movies and the Birth of the New Hollywood" by Mark Harris; "The Complete Idiot's Guide to African American History" by Melba Duncan; FBI Uniform Crime Reports; Chicago Tribune; The New York Times; modernhistorian.blogspot.com; npr.org.

Flags "The United States Flag: Federal Law Relating to Display and Associated Questions" by the Congressional Research Service; "Irish Brigade in the Civil War" by Joseph G. Bilby; "Immortal Images: A Personal History of Two Photographers and the Flag-raising on Iwo Jima" by Tedd Thomey; "Burning the Flag: The Great 1989-1990 American Flag Desecration Controversy" by Robert Justin Goldstein; "The Spirit of the Laws in Mozambique" by Juan Obarrio; The Washington Post; Tallahassee Democrat; Chicago Tribune; chicagomag.com; time.com; hoaxes.org; famouspictures.org; rmg.co.uk; govtrack.us; britannica.com.

Unions "There Is Power in a Union: The Epic Story of Labor in America" by Philip Dray; "The Imperfect Union: A History of Corruption in America's Trade Unions" by John Hutchinson; "A. Philip Randolph: A Biographical Portrait" by Jervis Anderson; "A. Philip Randolph and the Struggle for Civil Rights" by Cornelius L. Bynum; "It Happened in West Virginia" by Rick Steelhammer; "Workers in America: A Historical Encyclopedia" by Robert E. Weir; "Sweat and Blood: A History of U.S. Labor Unions" by Gloria Skurzynski; "On the Ground: Labor Struggle in the American Airline Industry" by Liesl Miller Orenic; "Outlaws of the Atlantic: Sailors, Pirates, and Motley Crews in the Age of Sail" by

Marcus Rediker; "Handbook to Life in Ancient Egypt" by Ann Rosalie David; Organisation for Economic Cooperation and Development; Bureau of Labor Statistics; Congressional Research Office; ufw.org; wvgazette.com; pawv.org; Stan Hochman in the Philadelphia Daily News; The Washington Post; Chicago Tribune.

Defective Products "Forgotten Fads and Fabulous Flops" by Paul Kirchner; "Modern Tort Law" by V.H. Harpwood; "The Business of Civil War" by Mark R. Wilson; "Textiles, and the Origin of Their Names" by Robert H. Megraw; "Why the Earth Quakes" by Matthys Levy; "Dictionary of Word Origins" by Jordan Almond; Scottish Council of Law Reporting; Consumer Product Safety Commission; nrc.gov; International Business Times; Chicago Tribune; msn. com; time.com.

Security Measures "U.S. Homeland Security: A Reference Handbook" by Howard Ball; "A Heart, A Cross, and a Flag: America Today" by Peggy Noonan; "Red Horizons: The True Story of Nicolae and Elena Ceausescus' Crimes, Lifestyle and Corruption" by Ion Mihai Pacepa; "Sonia Gandhi: An Extraordinary Life, an Indian Destiny" by Rani Singh; "In the President's Secret Service" by Ronald Kessler; "The Art of the Funnies: An Aesthetic History" by Robert C. Harvey; "The Medieval Fortress: Castles, Forts and Walled Cities of the Middle Ages" by J. E. Kaufmann, H. W. Kaufmann and Robert M. Jurga; The Globe and Mail; CBC News; The Washington Post; The Guardian; The Independent; Wired magazine; nature.com; probarrier.com; cwc.gov; dhs.gov.

Prison "Cash: The Autobiography" by Johnny Cash with Patrick Carr; "Gandhi: A Political and Spiritual Life" by Kathryn Tidrick; "History's Greatest Lies: The Startling Truths Behind World Events Our History Books Got Wrong" by William Weir; The New York Times; The Washington Post; bop.gov; chicagohs.org; bbcnews.com; snopes.com; prisonstudies.org; justicepolicy.org.

Fox News "The Fox Film Corporation, 1915-1935: A History and Filmography" by Aubrey Solomon; "My Turn at the Bully Pulpit" by Greta Van Susteren and Elaine Lafferty; The New York Times; The Washington Post; CNN; The Telegraph; Los Angeles Times; New York Daily News; npr.org; nbc.com; pewresearch.org; politifact.com; observer.com.

CHAPTER 4: Food & Drink

Extreme Eating "Clipping the Clouds: How Air Travel Changed the World" by Marc Dierikx; "Beyond Bizarre" by Varla Ventura; "Eating to Excess" by Susan E. Hill; "A Theory About Sin" by Orby Shipley; "The Oxford Companion to American Food and Drink" edited by Andrew F. Smith; "Revolution at the Table: The Transformation of the American Diet" by Harvey Levenstein; National Geographic; Aquatic Biology; Fort Worth Star-Telegram; South Florida Sun Sentinel; Los Angeles Times; The Telegraph.

Hamburgers "Casell's Dictionary of Slang" edited by Jonathan Green; "Hash House Lingo" by Jack Smiley; "Grinding It Out: The Making of McDonald's" by Ray Kroc with Robert Anderson; "The Hamburger: A History" by Josh Ozersky; "Encyclopedia of Junk Food and Fast Food" by Andrew F. Smith; "Hamburger America" by George Motz; "Selling 'Em by the Sack: White Castle and the Creation of American Food" by David Gerard Hogan; "The Snowball: Warren Buffett and the Business of Life" by Alice Schroeder; Time; Los Angeles Times; The Washington Post; Tribune archives; Center for Investigative Reporting; snopes.com.

Wine "Beethoven: The Last Decade, 1817-1827" by Martin Cooper; "Drink This: Wine Made Simple" by Dara Moskowitz Grumdahl; "The Wine Lover's Guide to Auctions" by Ursula Hermacinski; "A Benjamin Franklin Reader" by Walter Isaacson; "The Billionaire's Vinegar" by Benjamin Wallace; The New York Times; People; The Independent; The Guardian; Proceedings of the National Academy of Sciences; njmonthly.com; eatmedaily.com.

Beer "The Big Book O' Beer" by Duane Swierczynski; "From Beer to Eternity" by Will Anderson; "Beer: A History of Brewing in Chicago" by Bob Skilnik; snopes.com; samueladams.com; realbeer.com.

Drunkenness "Alcohol: The World's Favorite Drug" by Griffith Edwards; "Perfect I'm Not" by David Wells with Chris Kreski; "White Man's Wicked Water" by William E. Unrau; "Dean and Me" by Jerry Lewis and James Kaplan; "The Lonely Hunter" by Virginia Spencer Carr; Urban Dictionary; Moderndrunkardmagazine.com; doubletongued. org; Reason magazine; Newsweek; The Patriot-News in Harrisburg, Pa.; Tribune news services.

Candy "The Emperors of Chocolate" by Joel Glenn Brenner; "Candy: The Sweet History" by Beth Kimmerle; "Sweets: A History of Candy" by Tim Richardson; candyusa.org; snopes.com.

Ice Cream International Dairy Foods Association; Tribune reporter Hugh Dellios; "The Great Clowns of American Television" by Karin Adir; "Slavery in the United States" by Jenny B. Wahl of Carleton College on eh.net; "Ice: Great Moments in the History of Hard, Cold Water" by Karal Ann Marling; "Famous Wisconsin Inventors & Entrepreneurs" by Marv Balousek; "The Scoop" by Lori Longbotham; "Chocolate, Strawberry and Vanilla" by Anne Cooper Funderburg; "The Audacity of Hope" by Barack Obama; evinrude.com; San Francisco Chronicle; Tribune news services.

Salt "Salt: A World History" by Mark Kurlansky; "Salted: A Manifesto on the World's Most Essential Mineral" by Mark Bitterman; "Cassell's Dictionary of Slang" by Jonathon Green; "Dictionary of Word Origins" by Jordan Almond; "Thomas Jefferson and the New Nation" by Merrill D. Peterson; "The Road to Monticello" by Kevin J. Hayes; "The Story Behind Salt" by Heidi Moore; International Council for the Control of Iodine Deficiency Disorders; mortonarb. org; mortonsalt.com; detroitsalt.com; wadeburleson.org; The Detroit News.

Tomatoes "In Praise of Tomatoes" by Ronni Lundy with John Stehling; "Pure Ketchup" by Andrew F. Smith; Federal News Service; "Long Walk to Freedom" by Nelson Mandela; "Part of My Soul Went With Him" by Winnie Mandela; "Red Horizons: The True Story of Nicolae and Elena Ceausescus' Crimes, Lifestyle, and Corruption" by Ion Mihai Pacepa; "The Great Tomato Book" by Gary Ibsen with Joan Nielsen; U.S. Supreme Court's "Nix v. Hedden"; "The Galapagos" by Robert I. Bowman; "Ecology and Evolution: Islands of Change" by Richard Benz; "Galapagos: A Natural History" by John C. Kricher; "Eat Your Food! Gastronomical Glory From Garden to Gut" by Aaron Brachfeld and Mary Choate; National Gardening Association; Journal of Laboratory and Clinical Medicine; Latomatina.org; Tribune archives.

Turkey "Hunting Tough Turkeys" by Brian Lovett; "Hunting the First State: A Guide to Delaware Hunting" by Steven Kendus; "Howard Hughes: The Hidden Years" by James Phelan; "The Private Correspondence of Benjamin Franklin, Vol. 1"; National Wildlife Turkey Federation; "The Gourmet Cookbook" edited by Ruth Reichl; "The Wicked Waltz and Other Scandalous Dances" by Mark Knowles; "General Patton: A Soldier's Life" by Stanley Hirshson; heritageturkeyfoundation.org; snopes.com; baseball-reference.com; engelfoundation.com; The New York Times; Tribune archives.

Mexican-Americans "My Turn at Bat: The Story of My Life" by Ted Williams and John Underwood; "Latinos in U.S. Sport" by Jorge Iber, Samuel O. Regalado, Jose M. Alamillo and Arnoldo De Leon; "Mexico's Most Wanted" by Boze Hadleigh; "American Ethnicity" by Howard M. Bahr, Bruce A. Chadwick and Joseph H. Stauss; "Studies in Symbolic Interaction" by Norman K. Denzin; "Meeting the Enemy: American Exceptionalism and International Law" by Natsu Taylor Saito; "Latino Education in the United States" by Victoria-Maria MacDonald; mexonline.com; Hispanic Engineer & Information Technology magazine; psywarrior.com; imdb.com; The Washington Post; The Texas Tribune; U.S. Army; npr.com; Hispanically Speaking News.

Cuba "The Real Fidel Castro" by Leycester Coltman; "Wildlife of the Caribbean" by Herbert A. Raffaele and James W. Wiley; "What They Didn't Teach You in American History Class" by Mike Henry; "Che's Afterlife: The Legacy of an Image" by Michael J. Casey; "Companero: The Life and Death of Che Guevara" by Jorge G. Castaneda; "Cuba Open from the Inside" by Chris Messner; "In Black and White: The Life of Sammy Davis, Jr." by Wil Haygood; American Photo magazine; Evan Thomas in Washington Monthly; Brian McKenna on sabr.org; wildlifeextra.com; time.com; globalsecurity.org; slate.com; cia.gov; cnn.com; forward.com; The Daily Beast.

North Korea U.S. State Department; The Wall Street Journal; Irish Daily Mirror; Esquire; The Strait Times in Singapore; news.bbc.co.uk; golf.com; washingtonpost.com; nytimes.com; time.com; Yonhap news agency; World Health Organization; Agence France-Presse; independent.co.uk.

Chinese Leaders "This Is China: The First 5,000 Years" by Haiwang Yuan; "China Condensed: 5000 Years of History & Culture" by Siew Chey Ong; "The Analects of Confucius" translated by James Legge; "From the Shadows: The Ultimate Insider's Story of Five Presidents and How They Won the Cold War" by Robert M. Gates; "Death Ritual in Late Imperial and Modern China" by James L. Watson; "Heaven Cracks, Earth Shakes: The Tangshan Earthquake and the Death of Mao's China" by James Palmer; "Mao Zedong's China" by Kathlyn Gay; "The Early Civilization of China" by Yong Yap and Arthur Cotterell; "China: The Land and the People" by Keith Buchanan, Charles P. FitzGerald and Colin A. Ronan; "The Revolution in Geology From the Renaissance to the Enlightenment" by Gary D. Rosenberg; The Washington Post; The Associated Press.

Syria "Commanding Syria: Bashar al-Asad and the First Years in Power" by Eyal Zisser; "A New Old Damascus: Authenticity and Distinction in Urban Syria" by Christa Salamandra; "Extreme War" by Terrence Poulos; "Steve Jobs: The Man Who Thought Different" by Karen Blumenthal; "Women in the Middle East: Past and Present" by Nikki R. Keddie; "Jerry Seinfeld: The Entire Domain" by Kathleen Tracy; cia.gov; owni.eu; transparency.org; The New York Times; The Guardian; Ebony; The Hill; The Associated Press.

Russia snopes.com; geology.com; CIA Factbook; "Encyclopedia of World Geography" edited by Peter Haggett; "Encyclopedia of Ecology"; "World Book Encyclopedia"; "Encyclopedia of Literary Translation Into English" edited by Olive Classe; "A New Dictionary of Eponyms" edited by Morton S. Freeman; "What Caesar Did for My Salad" by Albert Jack; "Russia and the United States" by Nikolai V. Sivachev and Nikolai N. Yakovlev; "Russia's Life-saver: Lend-lease Aid to the U.S.S.R. in World War II" by Albert Loren Weeks; "Magicians on Ice: The Story of the Single Greatest Hockey Dynasty of All Time" by Timothy J. Thompson; The New York Times; Chicago Tribune; The Sunday Times.

The Irish "The American Irish" by William V. Shannon; "Saint Patrick" by David N. Dumville; "A Skeleton Key to Finnegans Wake" by Joseph Campbell and Henry Morton Robinson; "Bono: His Life, Music, and Passions" by Laura Jackson; "Bono" by Bono and Michka Assayas; "The Greatest Brigade" by Thomas J. Craughwell; "Encyclopedia of the American Civil War" edited by David Stephen Heidler, Jeanne T. Heidler and David J. Coles; "Notre Dame Fighting Irish: Colorful Tales of the Blue and Gold" by Eric Hansen; "Shake Down the Thunder: The Creation of Notre Dame Football" by Murray Sperber; "My Father, Marconi" by Degna Marconi; "Wherever Green Is Worn: The Story of the Irish Diaspora" by Tim Pat Coogan; "Lola Montez: A Life" by Bruce Seymour; "'No Irish Need Apply': A Myth of Victimization" by Richard Jensen in Journal of Social History; Chicago Tribune.

Ohio Tribune news services; Ohio Historical Society; The Plain Dealer; Detroit Free Press; New York magazine; snopes.com.

Texas "Finding Anything About Everything in Texas" by Edward Walters; "Texas Curiosities" by John Kelso; "The Civil War" by Shelby Foote; pokerpages.com; Tribune news services; "Texas Death Row" edited by Bill Crawford.

Wisconsin National Center for Education Statistics; "Cassell's Dictionary of Slang" by Jonathon Green; "The New Partridge Dictionary of Slang and Unconventional English" by Eric Partridge; "The Complete Idiot's Guide to Cheeses of the World" by Steve Ehlers and Jeanette Hurt; "Famous Wisconsin Inventors & Entrepreneurs" by Marv Balousek; "Firestorm at Peshtigo" by Denise Gess and William Lutz; "Wisconsin Biographical Dictionary" by Caryn Hannan; dot.wisconsin.gov; Wisconsin State Journal; Milwaukee Journal Sentinel; The Associated Press; wisconsinhistory.org; usgs.gov; imdb.com; snopes.com; channel3000.com; politifact.com; congress.gov.

Iowa "Conversations with Flannery O'Connor" edited by Rosemary M. Magee; "The Iowa Precinct Caucuses: The Making of a Media Event" by Hugh Winebrenner; "Ashton Kutcher" by Marc Shapiro; "Amazing Iowa" by Janice Beck Stock; Encyclopedia Britannica; Des Moines Register; Quad-City Times; Newsweek; WDBQ-AM; Feld Entertainment; Historical Society of Pottawattamie County; iowahawkeyes.net; imdb.com; Tribune archives and news services.

Small Towns "Place Names of Illinois" by Edward Callary; miketheheadlesschicken.org; tvacres.com; U.S. Census Bureau; Chicago Tribune; Orlando Sentinel; The New York Times; The Washington Post; The Associated Press; phillyvoice.com.

CHAPTER 6: Politics

Clout "Safire's Political Dictionary" by William Safire; "The Oxford Dictionary of American Political Slang" edited by Grant Barrett; "NYPD: A City and Its Police" by James Lardner and Thomas Reppetto; "The Greatest Menace: Organized Crime in Cold War America" by Lee Bernstein; "The Master of the Senate" by Robert A. Caro; "The Use and Abuse of Power: Multiple Perspectives on the Causes of Corruption" edited by Annette Y. Lee-Chai and John A. Bargh; "The Kid Stays in the Picture" by Robert Evans; The Telegraph; Chicago Tribune; The New York Times; Los Angeles Times.

Dirty Politics "How to Get Elected" by Jack Mitchell; "Dirty Politics" by Bruce L. Felknor; "American Pharaoh" by Adam Cohen and Elizabeth Taylor; "Going Dirty" by David Mark; Newsweek; Time; doubletongued.org; Washington Monthly; Tribune news services.

Campaign Slogans "Gaming the Vote" by William Poundstone; "Governor Richard Ogilvie: In the Interest of the State" by Taylor Pensoneau; "Presidents" by Neil A. Hamilton; "Elections in Dangerous Places" edited by David Gillies; "Posters, Propaganda, and Persuasion in Election Campaigns Around the World" by Steven A. Seidman; "Encyclopedia of American Political Parties and Elections" by Larry J. Sabato and Howard R. Ernst; "Presidential Campaigns" by Paul F. Boller Jr.; "Presidential Campaigns, Slogans, Issues, and Platforms" by Robert North Roberts, Scott John Hammond and Valerie A. Sulfaro.

Political Ads "Chicago Divided: The Making of a Black Mayor" by Paul Kleppner; "Troublemaker: Let's Do What It Takes to Make America Great Again" by Christine O'Donnell; "Mudslingers: The Twenty-Five Dirtiest Political Campaigns of All Time" by Kerwin Swint; "Presidential Campaigns" by Paul Boller Jr.; "Selling the President, 1920" by John A. Morello; conelrad.blogspot.com; Los Angeles Times; Newsweek; youtube.com; livingroomcandidate.org.

Presidential Also-rans "Almost President: The Men Who Lost the Race But Changed the Nation" by Scott Farris; "Legendary Locals of Louisville" by Kris Applegate; "Ben Hardin: His Times and Contemporaries, with Selections from His Speeches" by Lucius P. Little; "Notorious Victoria: The Life of Victoria Woodhull, Uncensored" by Mary Gabriel; "There's a Riot Going On: Revolutionaries, Rock Stars, and the Rise and Fall of '60s Counterculture" by Peter Dogget; "Chicago '68" by David Farber; "American Dreamer: The Life and Times of Henry A. Wallace" by John C. Culver and John Hyde; "Martin Van Buren: The American Presidents Series: The 8th President, 1837-1841" by Edward L. Widme; The New York Times; mentalfloss.com; Heritage Auctions; npr.org; biography.com.

House Speakers "Speaker: Lessons From Forty Years in Coaching and Politics" by Dennis Hastert; "Know Your Power: A Message to America's Daughters" by Nancy Pelosi; "Galusha A. Grow: The People's Candidate" by Robert D. Ilisevich; "Galusha A. Grow: Father of the Homestead Law" by James T. DuBois, Gertrude S. Mathews; "Polk: The Man Who Transformed the Presidency and America" by Walter R. Borneman; "Master of the Senate" by Robert A. Caro; "The Heroic and the Notorious: U.S. Senators From Illinois" by David Kenney and Robert E. Hartley; history.house. gov; history.com; opensecrets.org; chsmedia.org; Chicago Tribune.

Patriots "Herstory: A Woman's View of American History" by June Sochen; "American Patriots: The Story of Blacks in the Military From the Revolution to Desert Storm" by Gail Buckley; "Peekskill's African American History" by John J. Curran; "The Deportations Delirium of Nineteen-Twenty" by Louis F. Post; "Thurgood Marshall: American Revolutionary" by Juan Williams; "The My Lai Massacre in American History and Memory" by Kendrick Oliver; "My Lai: An American Atrocity in the Vietnam War" by William Thomas Allison; Southern Poverty Law Center; The New York Times; euromaidanpress.com; theguardian.com; masshist.org.

Third Parties Presidency Project at University of California-Santa Barbara; National Heritage Museum; "Citizen Perot" by Gerald Posner; "The Bull Moose Years: Theodore Roosevelt and the Progressive Party" by John Allen Gable; "Encyclopedia of U.S. Campaigns, Elections, and Electoral Behavior, Vol. 1" by Kenneth F. Warren; "Democracy's Prisoner: Eugene V. Debs, the Great War, and the Right to Dissent" by Ernest Freeberg; "Run the Other Way: Fixing the Two-Party System, One Campaign at a Time" by Bill Hillsman; "Victoria Woodhull's Sexual Revolution" by Amanda

Frisken; Seattle Post-Intelligencer; Los Angeles Times; Reuters; Rockford Register Star; The Washington Post; snopes.com; u-s-history.com; uselectionatlas.org; akip.org.

The U.S. Supreme Court "American Original: The Life and Constitution of Supreme Court Justice Antonin Scalia" by Joan Biskupic; "The Supreme Court: the Personalities and Rivalries that Defined America" by Jeffrey Rosen; "Hugo Black and the Judicial Revolution" by Gerald T. Dunne; "Supreme Court for Dummies" by Lisa Paddock; "More Than Petticoats: Remarkable Illinois Women" by Lyndee Jobe Henderson; The New York Times; The Christian Science Monitor; Milwaukee Journal Sentinel; Washington City Paper; supremecourt.gov; slate.com; cnn.com.

CHAPTER 7: Language & Letters

Insults "Cassell's Dictionary of Slang" by Jonathon Green; "The Dozens: A History of Rap's Mama" by Elijah Wald; "Encyclopedia of African-American Popular Culture" by Jessie Carney Smith; "Gentlemen's Blood" by Barbara Holland; "It Happened in New Orleans" by Bonnye E. Stuart; "Dueling in the Old South" by Jack K. Williams; "Some Like It Wilder: The Life and Controversial Films of Billy Wilder" by Gene Phillips; "Contemporary Portraits" by Frank Harris; rogerebert.com; politicsdaily.com; cnn.com; palmbeachpost.com; Chicago Tribune; The New York Times; The Washington Post.

Profanities "An Encyclopedia of Swearing" by Geoffrey Hughes; "A Cursing Brain? The Histories of Tourette Syndrome" by Howard I. Kushner; "Alphabet Kids from ADD to Zellweger Syndrome" by Robbie Woliver; "Thing-amajigs and Whatchamacallits: Unfamiliar Terms for Familiar Things" by Rod L. Evans; "Kenneth Tynan: A Life" by Dr. Dominic Shellard; "How to Swear Around the World" by Jason Sacher; "Hunters, Herders, and Hamburgers" by Richard W. Bulliet; "Saturday Night: A Backstage History of Saturday Night Live" by Doug Hill and Jeff Weingrad; "Who's Swearing Now?" by Kristy Beers Fagersten; dictionary.com; politico.com; gwpapers.virginia.edu; 10news.com.

Misspellings "Sergey Brin, Larry Page, Eric Schmidt, and Google" by Corona Brezina; "Law of the Internet" by George B. Delta and Jeffrey H. Matsuura; "Icons of Rock" by Scott Schinder and Andy Schwartz; "Monopoly: The World's Most Famous Game—and How It Got That Way" by Philip E. Orbanes; "Crimes of the Century" by Gilbert Geis and Leigh B. Bienen; "U Cn Spl Btr" by Laurie E. Rozakis; "A Life in Letters" by F. Scott Fitzgerald, edited by Matthew J. Bruccoli; "Ernest Hemingway, Selected Letters, 1917-1961" by Ernest Hemingway, edited by Carlos Baker; "Dear Papa, Dear Hotch: The Correspondence of Ernest Hemingway and A.E. Hotchner" by Ernest Hemingway, edited by Albert J. DeFazio III; slate.com; cnn.com; The New York Times; Chicago Tribune archives; miaminewtimes.com; ksl.com; wistv.com.

Obscure Words "Predicting New Words" by Allan Metcalf; The Merriam-Webster New Book of Word Histories; waywordradio.org; wordspy.com; new-statesman.com; theguardian.com; merriam-webster.com; kokogiak.com /logolepsy; wordsmith.org; science-mag.org; dictionary.reference.com; nationalgeographic.com; phrontistery.info.

Signatures "Shakespeare: A Life" by Park Honan; "Hitler" by John Toland; "The Bridge: The Life and Rise of Barack Obama" by David Remnick; "The Last Days of Hitler" by Hugh Trevor-Roper; "Casell's Dictionary of Slang" by Jonathon Green; "Legends, Lies & Cherished Myths of American History" by Richard Shenkman; "The Quote Verifier" by Ralph Keyes; "Chicago's Nelson Algren" by Art Shay; "Great Forgers and Famous Fakes" by Charles Hamilton; "History in Your Hand: Fifty Years of the Manuscript Society" by John M. Taylor; manuscript.org; Heritage

Historical Manuscripts Auction #6019; Journal of Accountancy; Internal Revenue Service; The Guardian; The Associated Press; snopes.com.

Lists "Of Sneetches and Whos and the Good Dr. Seuss" by Thomas Fensch; Edmund Morris essay in "People of the Century" by CBS News; "From Rags to Bitches" by Richard Blackwell; "Seven Dirty Words: The Life and Crimes of George Carlin" by James Sullivan; "Writing Systems: A Linguistic Introduction" by Geoffrey Sampson; vvmf.org; pbs.org/newshour; Bar Ilan University (biu.ac.il); Exodus 32 (New International Version of the Bible); Los Angeles Times; Tribune archives.

Victory Speeches "Brinkley's Beat: People, Places, and Events That Shaped My Time" by David Brinkley; Chicago Tribune; New York Daily News; The Dallas Morning News; The New York Times; San Francisco Chronicle; The Washington Post; The East Hampton Star in East Hampton, N.Y.; Sports Illustrated; Australian Open TV; cbsnews.com; washington.cbslocal.com; nixonlibrary.gov; history.com; mentalfloss.com; cnn.com.

Literary Enigmas "Safire's Political Dictionary" by William Safire; "Author Unknown: On the Trail of Anonymous" by Don Foster; "Dr. Seuss and Mr. Geisel: A Biography" by Judith Morgan and Neil Morgan; "James Tiptree Jr.: The Double Life of Alice B. Sheldon" by Julie Phillips; "William Faulkner: His Life and Work" edited by David Minter; "Faulkner: A Biography" by Joseph Blotner; "The Life & Letters of Mary Wollstonecraft Shelley"; "Virtuous Vice: Homoeroticism and the Public Sphere" by Eric O. Clarke; "The Encyclopedia of Cremation" edited by Douglas J. Davies and Lewis H. Mates; Frank Rich in the New York Times; Daniel Schorr on National Public Radio; New York magazine; The New York Times; poemuseum.org; quoteinvestigator.com; snopes.com; crimelibrary.com; cbsnews.com; agathachristie.com; sethkaller.com; Newsweek.

Fictional Mothers "Marmee & Louisa: The Untold Story of Louisa May Alcott and Her Mother" by Eve LaPlante; "How to Be Like Walt: Capturing the Disney Magic Every Day of Your Life" by Pat Williams with James Denney; "Walt Disney: The Triumph of the American Imagination" by Neal Gabler; "A Rose for Mrs. Miniver: The Life of Greer Garson" by Michael Troyan; "Life Is Not a Stage" by Florence Henderson; "Harriet Beecher Stowe: A Life" by Joan D. Hedrick; "Stepmonster: A New Look at Why Real Stepmothers Think, Feel, and Act the Way We Do" by Wednesday Martin; "Ancient Stepmothers: Myth, Misogyny and Reality" by Patricia A. Watson; Rick Manzella, One Stop Comics; The New York Times; Houston Chronicle; E! News transcripts; marvel.com; imdb.com; dinnerpartydownload.org; spinof.comicbookresources.com.

Fictional Fathers "My Losing Season: A Memoir" by Pat Conroy; "Glued to the Set: The 60 Television Shows and Events that Made Us Who We are Today" by Steven D. Stark; "Gregory Peck: A Biography" by Gary Fishgall; "Television Characters" by Vincent Terrace; "Encyclopedia of Television" by Horace Newcomb; Paley Center for Media; "Out in All Directions: A Treasury of Gay and Lesbian America" by Eric Marcus; out.com; timesonline.co.uk; imdb.com; Tribune archives.

Acronyms wordspy.com; doubletongued.org; langmaker.com; reference.com; globalsecurity.org; Computer Weekly; The News & Observer in Raleigh, N.C.

Double Talk "A Dictionary of Euphemisms & Other Doubletalk" by Hugh Rawson; "How Not to Say What You Mean: A Dictionary of Euphemisms" by R.W. Holder; "Propaganda and the Ethics of Persuasion" by Randal Marlin; wordspy.com, buzzwhack.com; globalsecurity.org; euphemismlist.com; networkworld.com; pbs.com; bnet.com;

businessweek.com; bobsutton.typepad.com; The Guardian; Imperial War Museum; Universal Press Syndicate; Tribune news services.

Punctuation "The Civil War: A Narrative" by Shelby Foote; "Memoirs of Nikita Khrushchev: Statesman, 1953-64" by Nikita Khrushchev, Sergei Khrushchev, George Shriver and Stephen Shenfield; "Encyclopedia of Emotion" by Gretchen Reevy, Yvette Malamud Ozer and Yuri Ito; "A Rhetoric of Irony" by Wayne C. Booth; "Eats, Shoots & Leaves" by Lynne Truss; "Has modern life killed the semicolon?" by Paul Collins in slate.com; editorandpublisher.com; The Author; Tribune news services.

Made-Up Words wharton.universia.net; urbandictionary.com; dictionary.reference.com; doubletongued.org; wordspy.com; "American Government and Politics Today: The Essentials" by Barbara A. Bardes, Mack C. Shelley and Steffen W. Schmidt.

CHAPTER 8: Rich & Famous

Donald Trump "No Such Thing as Over-Exposure: Inside the Life and Celebrity of Donald Trump" by Robert Slater; "Trump: The Art of the Deal" by Donald J. Trump with Tony Schwartz; "The Trumps: Three Generations That Built an Empire" by Gwenda Blair; The New York Times; The Wall Street Journal; People magazine; Chicago Tribune; New York Daily News; trump.com; nytimes.com; npr.com; chicagomag.com; leagle.com; usmagazine.com; time.com.

Elvis Presley "All Shook Up: Elvis Day by Day, 1954-1977" by Lee Cotton; "The Inner Elvis" by Peter Whitmer; "The Life and Cuisine of Elvis Presley" by David Adler; "The Death of Elvis: What Really Happened" by Charles C. Thompson II and James P. Cole; "Baby Names Now" by Linda Rosenkrantz and Pamela Redmond Satran; The Commercial Appeal in Memphis, Tenn.; Tribune news services.

Oprah Winfrey oprah.com; Chicago magazine; Tribune news services; International Directory of Business Biographies; "Oprah: The Real Story" by George Mair; "Roger Ebert's Movie Yearbook" by Roger Ebert.

Abraham Lincoln "Lincoln Legends: Myths, Hoaxes, and Confabulations Associated with Our Greatest President" by Edward Steers Jr.; "The Civil War Day by Day" by E.B. Long with Barbara Long; "The Origin of Certain Place Names in the United States" by Henry Gannett; "Birds of the Great Basin: A Natural History" by Fred A. Ryser; "Abraham Lincoln: The Prairie Years and the War Years" by Carl Sandburg; "Abraham Lincoln and the Forge of National Memory" by Barry Schwartz; "Abraham Lincoln & the Colony on Ile-a-Vache" by Robert Bray of Illinois Wesleyan University; Chicago Tribune archives; American Heritage magazine; legendsrevealed.com; thebirdist.com; civilwar.org; museumofhoaxes.com; presidency.ucsb.edu.

Royal Mothers "The Emperors of Modern Japan" edited by Ben-Ami Shillony; "Cuisine and Culture: A History of Food and People" by Linda Civitello; "Nero Caesar Augustus: Emperor of Rome" by David Shotter; "Walt's People: Talking Disney With the Artists Who Knew Him" by Didier Ghez; "Historical Dictionary of Women in Sub-Saharan Africa" by Kathleen Sheldon; "Women Rulers Throughout the Ages" by Guida Myrl Jackson-Laufer; "Victoria's Daughters" by Jerrold M. Packard; "Queen Victoria" by Elizabeth Longford; "Rose Kennedy: The Life and Times of a Political Matriarch" by Barbara A. Perry; "Memoirs of Her Late Majesty Caroline, Queen of Great Britain" by Robert Huish; disney.com; britannica.com; smithsonianmag.com.

Founding Fathers (And Mothers) "Politics: Observations & Arguments; 1966-2004" by Hendrik Hertzberg; "For You They Signed" by Marilyn Boyer; "Flag: An American Biography" by Marc Leepson; "Signing Their Lives Away: The Fame and Misfortune of the Men Who Signed the Declaration of Independence" by Denise Kiernan and Joseph D'Agnese; "Stupid History" by Leland Gregory; "Washington: A Life" by Ron Chernow; "Molly Pitcher: Heroine of the War for Independence" by Rachel A. Koestler-Grack; Gleaves Whitney of the Hauenstein Center for Presidential Studies at gvsu.edu; poetryfoundation.org; betsyrosshouse.org; snopes.com; britannica.com; The San Diego Union-Tribune.

Dick Cheney "Now It's My Turn" by Mary Cheney; Tribune archives and news services.

The Dalai Lama "Kundun" by Mary Craig; Shambhala Sun; Tribune archives and news services.

The Kennedys "The Kennedy White House: Family Life and Pictures, 1961-1963" by Carl Sferrazza Anthony; "John F. Kennedy on Leadership: The Lessons and Legacy of a President" by John A. Barnes; "Grace and Power: The Private World of the Kennedy White House" by Sally Bedell Smith; "Joseph McCarthy: Re-examining the Life and Legacy of America's Most Hated Senator" by Arthur Herman; "John F. Kennedy: A biography" by Michael O'Brien; "Football: The Ivy League Origins of an American Obsession" by Mark F. Bernstein; jfklibrary.org; The New York Times; Tribune archives.

Michael Moore Tribune news services; "Michael Moore" by Emily Schultz; The New Yorker; Rolling Stone.

Sarah Palin "Trailblazer: An Intimate Biography of Sarah Palin" by Lorenzo Benet; "Sarah" by Kaylene Johnson; "Going Rogue" by Sarah Palin; wickedlocal.com; Tribune news services.

CHAPTER 9: Military & War

Terrorism "Terrorism As Crime: From Oklahoma City to Al-Qaeda and Beyond" by Mark S. Hamm; "The Ku Klux Klan: A Guide to an American Subculture" by Marty Gitlin; "Defence Against Terrorism" by Adil Duyan and Mustafa Kibaroglu; "Remember, Remember: A Cultural History of Guy Fawkes" by J.A. Sharpe; "Terrorism on American Soil" by Joseph T. McCann; "Lucy Parsons: American Revolutionary" by Carolyn Ashbaugh; "Anthrax Attacks Around the World" by Tahara Hasan; historytoday.com; slate.com; ktvu.com; telegraph.co.uk; The Associated Press; Chicago Sun-Times; The New York Sun; New York Daily News; Time; The Wrap; Tribune archives.

War Heroes "Soldier Stories: True Tales of Courage, Honor, and Sacrifice from the Frontlines" by Joe Wheeler; "500 Little-Known Facts in U.S. History" by George W. Givens; "A Shower of Stars: The Medal of Honor and the 27th Maine" by John J. Pullen; "Medal of Honor: Historical Facts & Figures" by Ronald J. Owens; Los Angeles Times; Tampa Bay Times; Richmond Times-Dispatch; nmajmh.org; army.mil; robertsmalls.com; commondreams.org; si.edu; guardianofvalor.com.

The Afghan War "My Life With the Taliban" by Abdul Salam Zaeef, Alex Strick Van Linschoten and Felix Kuehn; "Brookings Afghanistan Index" by Ian S. Livingston and Michael O'Hanlon; "In Afghanistan" by David Loyn; "Where Men Win Glory: The Odyssey of Pat Tillman" by Jon Krakauer; "The Wars of Afghanistan" by Peter Tomsen; The Washington Post; The Telegraph; urbandictionary.com; defense-update.com; U.S. Bureau of Prisons; The New York Times; The Herald; BBC News.

Obscure Wars "Dictionary of Wars" by George Childs Kohn; "Britannia's Glories: The Walpole Ministry and the 1739 War With Spain" by Philip Woodfine; "Michigan's Early Military Forces" by Le Roy Barnett and Roger Rosentreter; "Stupid History: Tales of Stupidity, Strangeness, and Mythconceptions Throughout the Ages" by Leland Gregory; "Military Honour and the Conduct of War: From Ancient Greece to Iraq" by Paul Robinson; "The New Concise History of the Crusades" by Thomas F. Madden; "Encyclopedia of the United Nations and International Agreements: A to F" by Edmund Jan Osmanczyk and Anthony Mango; "Navy: An Illustrated History" by Chester G. Hearn; Chicago Tribune; daviesscountyhistoricalsociety.com; texasescapes.com; lib.unc.edu; tshaonline.org; warmuseum.ca; history.state.gov.

Military Speak "The Second World War: A Military History" by Gordon Corrigan; "FUBAR: Soldier Slang of World War II" by Gordon L. Rottman; "War Slang" by Paul Dickson; "Churchill by Himself" by Winston Churchill; "Military Comedy Films" by Hal Erickson; Ben Brody on npr.com; military.com; worldwidewords.org; The Wall Street Journal; Smithsonian magazine; Los Angeles Times; The Philadelphia Inquirer.

Women at War Ibis Reproductive Health; pewsocialtrends.org; Tribune archives and news services.

World War II "Chanel: A Woman of Her Own" by Axel Madsen; "The Greatest War Stories Never Told" by Rick Beyer; "God's Samurai" by Gordon W. Prange with Donald M. Goldstein and Katherine V. Dillon; "Warlord: A Life of Winston Churchill at War, 1874-1945" by Carlo D'Este; "General Patton: A Soldier's Life" by Stanley P. Hirshson; "199 Days: The Battle for Stalingrad" by Edwin P. Hoyt; "Whistling in the Dark: Memory and Culture in Wartime London" by Jean R. Freedman; "1942" by Winston Groom; "The U.S. Home Front, 1941-45" by Alejandro de Quesada; "What Every Person Should Know About War" by Chris Hedges; "Eurekas and Euphorias" by Walter Gratzer; Albuquerque Journal; Smithsonian magazine.

D-Day "D-Day: Operation Overlord Day by Day" by Anthony Hall; "Bodyguard of Lies: The Extraordinary True Story Behind D-Day" by Anthony Cave Brown; "Soldiers Lost at Sea" by James E. Wise and Scott Baron; "Slightly Out of Focus" by Robert Capa; "Voices from D-Day" by Jonathan Bastable; "Fortitude: The D-Day Deception Campaign" by Roger Hesketh; "Andrew Jackson Higgins and the Boats That Won World War II" by Jerry E. Strahan; skylighters.org; U.S. Navy; Museum of Science and Industry.

CHAPTER 10: Science & Technology

Drones "Tesla: A Man Out of Time" by Margaret Cheney; "Reconnaissance Is Black" by David Irvin; "Unmanned Aerial Vehicles: Robotic Air Warfare 1917-2007" by Steven J. Zaloga; "Drone Wars" edited by Peter Bergen and Daniel Rothenberg; "The Thistle and the Drone: How America's War on Terror Became a Global War on Tribal Islam" by Akbar Ahmed; "Marilyn Monroe: The Biography" by Donald Spoto; "The Secret Life of Marilyn Monroe" by J. Randy Taraborrelli; "Drone" by Adam Rothstein; Ben Zimmer at wsj.com; The Washington Post; intercepts.defensenews.com; theguardian.com; The New York Times; The Wall Street Journal; Chicago Tribune; The Associated Press, time.com; engadget.com; assemblymag.com.

Geniuses Katie McCabe in The Washingtonian; "A Most Damnable Invention: Dynamite, Nitrates, and the Making of the Modern World" by Stephen R. Bown; "The Genius Factory" by David Plotz; "IQ and Human Intelligence" by

Nicholas Mackintosh; "Inventors and Inventions, Vol. 2"; "From Thistle Burrs to . . . Velcro" by Josh Gregory; "The Discovery of Penicillin" by Guy de la Bedoyere; "Flanagan's Version: A Spectator's Guide to Science on the Eve of the 21st Century" by Dennis Flanagan; "Obsessive Genius: The Inner World of Marie Curie" by Barbara Goldsmith; The Denver Post; The Globe and Mail; The New York Times; Los Angeles Times; the journal Brain; npr.org; invent.org; semmelweis.org; alumni.stanford.edu.

Poison "Vietnamese Anticolonialism, 1885-1925" by David G. Marr; "The Arsenic Century" by James C. Whorton; "Isak Dinesen: The Life of a Storyteller" by Judith Thurman; "Principles of Clinical Toxicology" edited by J. Douglas Bricker; "Is Arsenic an Aphrodisiac?" edited by William R. Cullen; "Greek Fire, Poison Arrows and Scorpion Bombs" by Adrienne Mayor; New Scientist; Chicago Tribune archives; St. Paul Pioneer Press; huffingtonpost.com; snopes.com; petmd.com; aspca.org.

Extreme Weather "The Quote Verifier" by Ralph Keyes; Illinois' State Climatologist Office; "Tornado Alley" by Howard B. Bluestein; "Scanning the Skies: A History of Tornado Forecasting" by Marlene Bradford; "Frogs: A Chorus of Colors" by John L. Behler and Deborah A. Behler; "Storm Watchers" by John D. Cox; NASA; Accuweather; Palm Beach Post; National Geographic; weather.com.

Ice "Encyclopedia of World Geography" edited by Peter Haggett; "Glossary of Marine Navigation" by Nathaniel Bowditch; "Water Science: Active Science with Water" by Edward Shevick; "Chicago's Pride: The Stockyards, Packingtown, and Environs in the Nineteenth Century" by Louise Carroll Wade; "The Galloping Ghost: Red Grange, An American Football Legend" by Gary Andrew Poole; National Oceanic and Atmospheric Administration; thesmokinggun.com; zamboni.com; news.discovery.com; The Wall Street Journal; ESPN; Chicago Tribune.

Zoos "Big Town, Big Time: A New York Epic: 1898-1998" by Jay Maeder; "Sideshow U.S.A.: Freaks and the American Cultural Imagination" by Rachel Adams; "The Book of Animal Ignorance" by John Lloyd and John Mitchinson; "The Ark in the Park" by Wilfrid Blunt; "Zoo and Aquarium History: Ancient Animal Collections to Zoological Gardens" edited by Vernon N. Kisling; Cincinnati Zoo and Botanical Garden; Buffalo Zoo; Chicago Tribune; Los Angeles Times; The San Diego Union-Tribune; The Washington Post; The New York Times; sfgate.com; people.com; boston.com; abcnews.go.com; KARE-TV.

Elephants "Elephants" by Joyce Poole; "Asian Elephant" by Matt Turner; "Our Movie Houses" by Norman O. Keim and David Marc; "Walt's People" by Didier Ghez; "Maria Callas: An Intimate Biography" by Anne Edwards; "Strong on Music: Reverberations, 1850-1856" by Vera Brodsky Lawrence; "The Illustrated Encyclopedia of Elephants" by S.K. Eltringham and Jeheskel Shoshani; "The Moral Lives of Animals" by Dale Peterson; "Critical Regionalism" by Douglas Reichert Powell; "Lords of the Levee" by Lloyd Wendt and Herman Kogan; "The Ark in the Park" by Mark Rosenthal, Carol Tauber and Edward Uhlir; "Elephants: A Cultural and Natural History" by Karl Groning and Martin Saller; "In the Beat of a Heart" by John Whitfield; Tufts University; Tribune archives; blueridgecountry.com.

Epidemics "A Distant Mirror" by Barbara W. Tuchman; "Daily Life During the Black Death" by Joseph Patrick Byrne; "The Great Influenza" by John M. Barry; "The Greatest Killer: Smallpox in History" by Donald R. Hopkins; "Encyclopedia of Plague and Pestilence" edited by George Childs Kohn; "And the Band Played On" by Randy Shilts; "Love for Sale" by Elizabeth Alice Clement; "Creating the Big Easy" by Anthony J. Stanonis; "No Magic Bullet" by

Allan M. Brandt; "Typhoid Mary: Captive to the Public's Health" by Judith Walzer Leavitt; Collins English Dictionary; The New York Times; pbs.org; npr.org; snopes.com.

Hurricanes "Florida's Hurricane History" by Jay Barnes; "Encyclopedia of Hurricanes, Typhoons, and Cyclones" by David Longshore; "Gerald R. Ford" by Douglas Brinkley; Congressional Record; "Hurricane Camille: Monster Storm of the Gulf Coast" by Philip D. Hearn; "Category 5: The Story of Camille" by Ernest Zebrowski and Judith A. Howard; "Roar of the Heavens" by Stefan Bechtel; Atlantic Oceanographic and Meteorological Laboratory; Sun Herald in Biloxi, Miss.; snopes.com; camille.passchristian.net.

Space "Handbook of Space Engineering, Archaeology, and Heritage" by Beth Laura O'Leary; "The Complete Idiot's Guide to Weird Word Origins" by Paul McFedries; "Meteors in the Earth's Atmosphere" by Edmond Murad and Iwan Prys Williams; "The Nobel Prize" by Burton Feldman; "Don't Know Much About the Universe" by Kenneth C. Davis; "Star Clusters and How to Observe Them" by Mark Allison; "The Handy Astronomy Answer Book" by Charles Liu; spaceflightnow.com; The New York Times; snopes.com; chicagomaroon.com; "People of the Century" by CBS News; BBC News; The Globe and Mail; planetfacts.org; science.nasa.gov; dictionary.reference.com; universetoday.com.

Air Travel "Travia: The Ultimate Book of Travel Trivia" by Nadine Godwin; "Amelia: A Life of the Aviation Legend" by Donald M. Goldstein and Katherine V. Dillon; "How to Make a Tornado," a New Scientist book edited by Mick O'Hare; "Working the Skies" by Drew Whitelegg; The Telegraph; The Sacramento Bee; The Denver Post; "Ask the Pilot" by Patrick Smith on salon.com; imdb.com; straightdope.com; newadvent.org; snopes.com; consumerist.com.

CHAPTER 11: Kids & Education

College "The Damndest Radical: The Life and World of Ben Reitman, Chicago's Celebrated Social Reformer, Hobo King, and Whorehouse Physician" by Roger A. Bruns; "The Reckoning" by David Halberstam; "The Black Revolution on Campus" by Martha Biondi; "Indian Civilization and Culture" by Suhas Chatterje; "Libraries in the Early 21st Century, Vol. 2" edited by Ravindra N. Sharma; The Alcalde; UNESCO; Guinness World Records; National Center for Education Statistics; The New York Times; hardballtimes.com; collegeofcomplexes.org; pcmag.com; wsj.com; thedailybeast.com; trends.collegeboard.org; theweek.com; huffingtonpost.com.

Tests "Fade to Black: A Book of Movie Obituaries" by Paul Donnelley; "Jean Harlow: Tarnished Angel" by David Bret; "City of Nets: A Portrait of Hollywood in the 1940s" by Otto Friedrich; "A Better Pencil: Readers, Writers, and the Digital Revolution" by Dennis Baron; "The Perfection of the Paper Clip" by James Ward; "A Woman in Charge" by Carl Bernstein; "Ike's Final Battle: The Road to Little Rock and the Challenge of Equality" by Kasey S. Pipes; "Law School 101" by R. Stephanie Good; "A Cultural History of Civil Examinations in Late Imperial China" by Benjamin A. Elman; "China's Examination Hell: The Civil Service Examinations of Imperial China" by Ichisada Miyazaki; "Now You See It: How Technology and Brain Science Will Transform the Way We Live, Work, and Learn" by Cathy N. Davidson; National Institutes of Health; The Telegraph; mentalfloss.com; lfanet.org; snopes.com; adage.com; ideas.time.com; nydailynews.com.

Toys "Warman's 101 Greatest Baby Boomer Toys" by Mark Rich; Fortune magazine; Tribune archives and news services.

Teachers "The Ultimate Teachers' Handbook" by Hazel Bennett; "John Wesley Hardin: Dark Angel of Texas" by Leon Claire Metz; "Lone Star Rising: Lyndon Johnson and his Times, 1908-1960" by Robert Dallek; " 'Everybody's Paid but the Teacher': The Teaching Profession and the Women's Movement" by Patricia Anne Carter; "The Montessori Method" by Maria Montessori, edited by Gerald Lee Gutek; "Mussolini" by Peter Neville; "Unusually Stupid Americans" by Kathryn Petras and Ross Petras; govtrack.us; U.S. Department of Education; Pew Research Center; The New York Times; Newsday; spinner.com; cbs.com; cnn.com; news.bbc.co.uk.

Twins "Entwined Lives" by Nancy L. Segal; "The Inner Elvis" by Peter O. Whitmer; "Yoruba Customs and Beliefs Pertaining to Twins" in Twin Research (April 2002); salon.com; baseball-reference.com; Tribune archives and news services.

CHAPTER 12: Money & Finance

Money "Where the Money Was" by Willie Sutton with Edward Linn; "Cassell's Dictionary of Slang" by Jonathon Green; "Complete Book of Presidential Trivia, #2" by J. Stephen Lang; "Aztec Archaeology and Ethnohistory" by Frances F. Berdan; "The History of Money" by Jack Weatherford; "Money, Banking and Monetary Policy" by Thomas Bishop; "The Secret Life of Money: How Money Can Be Food for the Soul" by Tad Crawford; "The Shell Money of the Slave Trade" by Jan Hogendorn and Marion Johnson; Bureau of Engraving and Printing; National Bank of Belgium; history.com; oxforddictionaries.com; worldwidewords.org; usmint.gov; snopes.com; ctvnews.ca; telegraph.co.uk; nutmegcollector.blogspot.com; wsj.com; Ottawa Citizen.

The Lottery "Come Along With Me" by Shirley Jackson; "An Imperfect God: George Washington, His Slaves and the Creation of America" by Henry Wiencek; "The Fortune Cookie Chronicles: Adventures in the World of Chinese Food" by Jennifer 8. Lee; "Ella Fitzgerald: A Biography of the First Lady of Jazz" by Stuart Nicholson; "Government and the Transformation of the Gaming Industry" by Richard McGowan; "Lottery Wars: Case Studies in Bible Belt Politics, 1986-2005" by William Randy Bobbitt; "Lotteries in Colonial America" by Neal Millikan; "The Lottery Wars: Long Odds, Fast Money, and the Battle Over an American Institution" by Matthew Sweeney; "History of Education in New Jersey, Issues 1-3" by David Murray; snopes.com; abc7chicago.com; The Associated Press; The New York Times; Los Angeles Times; The Miami Herald; St. Petersburg Times.

Debt "Debt: The First 5,000 Years" by David Graeber; "Debtors and Creditors in America" by Peter J. Coleman; "The Signers: The 56 Stories Behind the Declaration of Independence" by Dennis Brindell Fradin; "Payback" by Margaret Atwood; "America: The Last Best Hope" by William J. Bennett; "Becoming the Second City" by Richard Junger; "Casell's Dictionary of Slang" by Jonathon Green; "Republic of Debtors: Bankruptcy in the Age of American Independence" by Bruce H. Mann; "A History of the English Language" by Elly Van Gelderen; "The Origins and Development of the English Language" by John Algeo and Thomas Pyles; Bureau of the Public Debt; Congressional Budget Office; The New York Times; Scouting magazine; constitutionfacts.com; CIA Factbook; wordspy.com.

Traffic Tickets "The Last Campaign: Robert F. Kennedy and 82 Days That Inspired America" by Thurston Clarke; "Master of the Senate: The Years of Lyndon Johnson" by Robert A. Caro; "The Montgomery Bus Boycott and the Women Who Started It" by Jo Ann Gibson Robinson; "Ted Kennedy: The Dream That Never Died" by Edward Klein; "Cigars, Whiskey and Winning: Leadership Lessons from General Ulysses S. Grant" by Al Kaltman; "The Big Bam: The

Life and Times of Babe Ruth" by Leigh Montville; "Terrorism Information Sharing and the Nationwide Suspicious Activity Initiative" Mark A. Randol of the Congressional Research Service; "The Stranger Beside Me" by Ann Rule; "Criminal Interdiction" by Steven Varnell; deseretnews.com; cnn.com; sfgate.com; snopes.com; Chicago Tribune; The New York Times; ford.com.

Tipping "Titan: The Life of John D. Rockefeller" by Ron Chernow; "Tipping: An American Social History of Gratuities" by Kerry Segrave; "Turning the Tables: Restaurants and the Rise of the American Middle Class, 1880-1920" by Andrew P. Haley; "Gratuity: A Contextual Understanding of Tipping Norms from the Perspective of Tipped Employees" by Richard Seltzer and Holona LeAnne Ochs; Bureau of Labor Statistics; drunkard.com; hospitality-industry.com; msnbc.msn.com; zagat.com; San Francisco Chronicle; Tribune archives.

Taxes "1927: High Tide of the Twenties" by Gerald Leinwand; CIA Factbook; U.S. Supreme Court; Federal Bureau of Investigation; Encyclopedia Britannica; ushistory.org; irs.gov; snopes.com; The Washington Post; Tribune news services.

CHAPTER 13: Arts & Culture

Social Media "The Social Media Bible" by Lon Safko; The Guardian; Chicago Tribune; Spiegel Online International; healthland.time.com; mashable.com; ijreview.com; techcrunch.com; slate.com; socialmediatoday.com.

Racy Movies "Bombshell: The Life and Death of Jean Harlow" by David Stenn; "The Price of the Ticket: Collected Nonfiction, 1948-1985" by James Baldwin; "The World and Its Double: The Life and Work of Otto Preminger" by Chris Fujiwara; "Censoring Hollywood" by Aubrey Malone; "Some Like It Wilder" by Gene Phillips; "The Continental Actress," by Kerry Segrave and Linda Martin; robertloerzel.com; Chicago Motion Picture Commission report, 1920; Motion Picture Association of America, Swedish Media Council (statensmedierad.se); South Florida Sun Sentinel; The New York Times; The Washington Post; Tribune archives.

TV Ads "Encyclopedia of Television" by Horace Newcomb; "Connecting with Consumers: Marketing for New Marketplace Realities" by Allan J. Kimmel; "Television's Strangest Moments" by Quentin Falk and Ben Falk; "Truth and Rumors: The Reality Behind TV's Most Famous Myths" by Bill Brioux; "What Were They Thinking: The 100 Dumbest Events in Television History" by David Hofstede; "Madonna: An Intimate Biography" by J. Randy Taraborrelli; "Fifties Television" by William Boddy; "Invasion of the Mind Snatchers: Television's Conquest of America in the Fifties" by Eric Burns; "The New Icons?: The Art of Television Advertising" by Paul Rutherford; U.S. House; White House; The Arizona Republic; vintageTVcommercials.com; bulova.com; snopes.com; adcouncil.org; tvacres.com; Nielsen Media Research; ORC International.

TV Technology "The Quotable Tycoon" by David Olive; "Eureka! Scientific Breakthroughs That Changed the World" by Leslie Alan Horvitz; "The Box: An Oral History of Television, 1920-1961" by Jeff Kisseloff; "Television Innovations" by Dicky Howett; "Please Stand By: A Prehistory of Television" by Michael Ritchie; "Canned Laughter" by Peter Hay, National Cable & Telecommunications Association; cbsnews.com; The Observer; ikegami.com; Penton Insight; TVNewser; snopes.com; variety.com.

Film Critics "American Movie Critics" edited by Phillip Lopate; "Your Movie Sucks" by Roger Ebert; "Life Itself: A Memoir" by Roger Ebert; " 'The Movies Are': Carl Sandburg's Film Reviews and Essays, 1920-1928" edited by Arnie Bernstein; "A History of X" by Luke Ford; "Carnal Knowledge" by John Baxter; Newsweek; rottentomatoes.com; Los Angeles Times; The New York Times; Chicago Tribune.

Classical Music The Penguin Companion to Classical Music by Paul Griffiths; Blumenfeld's Dictionary of Musical Theater by Robert Blumenfeld; "Eccentric Britain" by Benedict le Vay; Bartlett's Book of Anecdotes by Clifton Fadiman and Andre Bernard; "The House of Wittgenstein: A Family at War" by Alexander Waugh; "Mendelssohn: A Life in Music" by R. Larry Todd; "Puccini: His Life and Works" by Julian Budden; All Music Guide to Classical Music, edited by Chris Woodstra, Gerald Brennan and Allen Schrott; officialcharts.com.

Modern Art "Anecdotes of Modern Art" by Donald Hall and Pat Corrington Wykes; "The Life and Death of Andy Warhol" by Victor Bockris; "Pop Art" by Tilman Osterwold; "Retailing" edited by Anne M. Findlay and Leigh Sparks; "Lives of Great 20th Century Artists" by Edward Lucie-Smith; "Shock of the New" by Robert Hughes; Art in America magazine; Grove Art Online; artforum.com; artinfo.com; Tribune archives and news services.

Music Festivals "Music of the Gilded Age" by John Ogasapian and N. Lee Orr; "Woodstock: Three Days That Rocked the World" by Mike Evans and Paul Kingsbury; "Alternative Rock" by Dave Thompson; "Back to the Garden: The Story of Woodstock and How It Changed a Generation" by Pete Fornatale; "Hollywood Songsters, Volume 2" by James Robert Parish and Michael R. Pitts; "Chicago Neighborhoods and Suburbs" by Ann Durkin Keating; The New York Times; Milwaukee Journal Sentinel; Sunday Mirror; The Globe and Mail; newportfolkfest.net.

CHAPTER 14: Sports

Football Coaches "Dr. Eddie Anderson, Hall of Fame College Football Coach" by Kevin Carroll; "Johnny U: The Life and Times of John Unitas" by Tom Callahan; "When All the World was Browns Town" by Terry Pluto; "Green Bay Packers: The Complete Illustrated History" by Don Gulbrandsen; "Race and Sport: The Struggle for Equality On and Off the Field" edited by Charles K. Ross; "Fritz Pollard: Pioneer in Racial Advancement" by John M. Carroll; "We Are the Bears!: The Oral History of the Chicago Bears" by Richard Whittingham; "Sports Illustrated: Great Football Writing" by Editors of Sports Illustrated; The Associated Press; Cody Coil of KBTX-TV; Houston Chronicle; Tribune archives.

College Football "Rites of Autumn" by Richard Whittingham; Sarasota Herald-Tribune; Marin Independent Journal; Evansville Courier & Press; Detroit Free Press; The Columbus Dispatch; Auburn University.

Bicycles "Bicycle: The History" by David V. Herlihy; "Bicycling Science" by David Gordon Wilson; "The Secret History of Balls" by Josh Chetwynd; "The Selected Papers of Elizabeth Cady Stanton and Susan B. Anthony, Volume 6" edited by Ann Gordon; Chicago Tribune; The Guardian; VeloNews; Outside; forbes.com; imdb.com; hovding.com; openstreetsproject.org.

Wrigley Field "Wrigley Field: The Unauthorized Biography" by Stuart Shea with George Castle; "Mr. Wrigley's Ball Club: Chicago and the Cubs During the Jazz Age" by Roberts Ehrgott; Society of American Baseball Research; baseball-reference.com; baseball-almanac.com; laist.com; Tribune archives.

Sports Gambling Las Vegas Sun; Tribune news services; "Winning Is the Only Thing" by Randy Roberts and James Olson; "The Man With the $100,000 Breasts and Other Gambling Stories" by Michael Konik; American Heritage Dictionary; The Times of London.

The Olympics "Historical Dictionary of the Modern Olympic Movement" edited by John E. Findling and Kimberly D. Pelle; "The Complete Book of the Olympics" by David Wallechinsky; "General Patton: A Soldier's Life" by Stanley Hirshson; "Johnny Weissmuller: Twice the Hero" by David Fury; "Jesse Owens: An American Life" by William J. Baker; The Wall Street Journal; Tribune news services.

Olympians "The Complete Book of the Olympics" by David Wallechinsky; "Napoleon's Hemorrhoids: And Other Small Events That Changed History" by Phil Mason; "Olympic Gold" by Robin Poke; "Duty, Honor, Victory: America's Athletes in World War II" by Gary Bloomfield; "By the Sword: A History of Gladiators, Musketeers, Samurai, Swashbucklers and Olympic Champions" by Richard Cohen; "Women and Sport: Interdisciplinary Perspectives" edited by D. Margaret Costa and Sharon Ruth Guthrie; "The Olympics' Most Wanted" by Floyd Conner; "Historical Dictionary of the Olympic Movement" by Bill Mallon and Jeroen Heijmans; "Celebrity in the 21st Century: A Reference Handbook" by Larry Z. Leslie; The Atlantic magazine; Tribune archives.

The Olympic Torch "Hitler's Olympics" by Christopher Hilton; bbc.com; olympic.org; National Geographic; "My Olympic Journey" by James Worrall; wired.com; Tribune news services.

Running "Cassell's Dictionary of Slang" by Jonathon Green; "Running Through the Ages" by Edward Seldon Sears; "The Olympic Odyssey" by Phil Cousineau; "The Complete Book of the Summer Olympics" by David Wallechinsky; "The Dickson Baseball Dictionary" by Paul Dickson; "African-American Sports Greats" by David L. Porter; "Only in Oregon" by Christine Barnes; Oxford English Dictionary; baseball-reference.com; espn.go.com; nike.com; npr.org; The Oregonian; The New York Times; The Christian Science Monitor.

ACKNOWLEDGMENTS

The authors wish to thank their many Chicago Tribune editors over the years, especially Marcia Lythcott. The Tribune's photo desk also has been a key resource, particularly Robin Daughtridge and Marianne Mather. Graphic artist Mike Miner provided years of solid support bringing "10 Things" to life in the pages of the newspaper. Finally, our gratitude to John McCormick for contributing amazing facts about Iowa.

ABOUT THE AUTHORS

MARK JACOB is the associate managing editor for metropolitan news at the Chicago Tribune and the coauthor of six books. He lives with his wife in Evanston, Illinois.

STEPHAN BENZKOFER worked for the Chicago Tribune for nearly 20 years and coedited, with Mark Jacob, the paper's popular feature column 10 Things You Might Not Know. He is now the owner of Benzkofer Communications and lives in Oak Park, Illinois, with his family.